The Used Car Book 2002-2003

by Jack Gillis

and Dabney Edwards Nicole Klein

with design by Amy Curran

HarperResource

An Imprint of HarperCollins *Publishers*

The Used Car Book 2002–2003 contains thousands of pieces of information designed to help consumers save money and make a smart choice. Leading the compilation of this data was Dabney Edwards and Nicole Klein, whose tireless and effective work and great spirit made the book possible. As always, steady and calm, Amy Curran kept the project on track and the data in place.

Clarence Ditlow and the staff of the Center for Auto Safety also made major contributions to the book. And as always, keeping everything on track, was my friend and agent, Stuart Krichevsky.

The most important factor in being able to bring this information to the American car buyer for 23 years is the encouragement, support, and love from my brilliant and beautiful wife, Marilyn Mohrman-Gillis.

J.G.

Dedicated to a great staff:
Amy, Carole, Dabney, Nicole and Stephanie
The Best!

THE USED CAR BOOK (2002-2003 edition). Copyright © 2002, 2001, 2000, 1999, 1998, 1997, 1996, 1995, 1994, 1993, 1992, 1991, 1990, 1989, 1988, 1987 by Jack Gillis. All rights reserved. Printed in the United States of America. No part of this book may be used or reproduced in any manner whatsoever without written permission except in the case of brief quotations embodied in critical articles and reviews. For information, address HarperCollins Publishers, Inc., 10 East 53rd Street, New York, NY 10022.

HarperCollins books may be purchased for educational, business, or sales promotional use. For information, please write: Special Markets Department, HarperCollins Publishers, Inc., 10 East 53rd Street, New York, NY 10022.

ISSN: 0895-3899
ISBN: 0-06-273715-5
02 03 RRD 5 4 3 2 1

Table of Contents

Introduction/4

Part One: Finding Them and Checking Them Out/5

Understanding the Classifieds/8
Checking Them Out/9
Questions for the Owner/10
Inside Checklist/11
Outside Checklist/14
Under the Hood/18

The Test Drive/20
Avoiding Odometer Fraud/24
Mechanic's Checklist/26
Safety Checklist/27
Crash Tests/28
Safety Defects and Recalls/29

Part Two: Getting the Best Price and Selling Your Car/31

The "Blue Book" Value/34
Warranties/34

Selling Your Car/36

Part Three: Keeping Them Going/41

Reducing Insurance Costs/41
Tips for Dealing with a
   Mechanic/43
Repair Protection by Credit
   Card/44

Secret Warranties/45
Center for Auto Safety/46

Part Four: How They Rate/47

Best Bets by Price/48
Cars to Stay Away From/50
Ratings Explanation/51

Quick Cross Reference Guide/53
The Ratings/54

Introduction

If you are using this book, you are among the three out of four car buyers who are purchasing a used, instead of new, car. No longer is buying a used car "buying someone else's troubles." In fact, more and more consumers consider it a smart choice. In addition, because year to year model changes are almost imperceptible, it is hard to tell a brand new car from a two- to three-year-old model. The simple bottom line is that used cars cost less to buy and operate. There's also an emotional benefit to driving a used car—that strange rumble or new scrape doesn't cause the same sinking feeling in your stomach as it does when it happens to a shiny, new model.

While used cars are less expensive, rising prices have turned them into major purchases. As the average price has gone up—right now it's around $13,000—so has the average age. Today's cars typically last more than eight years, so you'll be keeping this purchase longer than in the past. That's why it's more important to make a smart decision.

Even the process of buying a used car is getting better. Since the recent introduction of used car superstores, traditional dealers have been scrambling to change the way they treat consumers. And, of course, the Internet has become a powerful tool for car buyers.

Thanks to better reliability and the millions of previously leased vehicles hitting the used car market, there are more used cars available then ever before. *The Used Car Book* will get you started in the right direction by helping you separate the "peaches" from the "lemons."

To make the task as easy as possible, the book is divided into four parts:

◄ Finding Them and Checking Them Out
◄ Getting the Best Price and Selling Your Car
◄ Keeping Them Going
◄ How They Rate

Good luck in your search and safe driving!

Part One: Finding Them and Checking Them Out

Understanding the
    Classifieds/8
Checking Them Out/9
Questions for the Owner/10
Inside Checklist/11
Outside Checklist/14
Under the Hood/18

The Test Drive/20
Avoiding Odometer Fraud/24
Mechanic's Checklist/26
Safety Checklist/27
Crash Tests/28
Safety Defects
    and Recalls/29

The key to finding a good used car is being able to predict its future performance—and the best way to do that is to know how the car was treated and what problems it had in the past. That's why a trusted friend can be the best source for a used car. Among other things, you'll get an honest answer to the question, "Why are you selling it?"

Your chances of finding a good used car depend on where you look. There are five main sources: new car dealers, used car dealers, rental car companies, private sellers, and used car superstores.

New Car Dealers: Buying a used car from a new car dealer means that you will probably pay more for it. However, many dealers keep only the best cars for resale and generally have a wide selection, especially of the higher priced models. In addition, most new car dealers will give you a written warranty. But beware: These warranties are usually full of loopholes in the dealer's favor.

Another benefit of buying from new car dealers is that most have service facilities. This increases the chance that the car was inspected and repaired before being offered for sale. If you trust the dealership and know that it has serviced the car regularly, then a new car dealer can be a good source for a reliable car.

Tip: Used cars of the same brand as the new cars that the dealer sells are your best bets. Dealers can't get parts as easily and as inexpensively for cars from other manufacturers, and they are less likely to make repairs before reselling the car.

Used Car Dealers: You can usually get lower prices on an independent used car lot than from a new car dealer. However, the majority of cars are sold in "as is" condition. Even if a used car dealer offers a warranty, it's often extremely difficult to get repair costs covered.

Another problem with buying from used car dealers is that they often get cast-offs, either from new car dealers or at auctions. In fact, they rarely know the history of the cars they're selling. Also, most used car dealerships do not have service facilities, so they have done little, if any, work on the cars. Many times used car dealers sell cars from lease fleets, taxi companies, or police departments—cars that have excessive wear.

Tip: The longer a dealer has been in the same location, the better your chances are of getting help should a problem arise. Because used car dealerships tend to be transient, it's best to find one that has been in business for at least five years at the same location.

Rental Car Companies: During the past few years, rental car companies have been reselling vehicles from their rental fleets to consumers. Contrary to popular belief, cars sold by the rental car companies haven't necessarily been "driven into the ground" by careless renters. For the most part, these cars are used by business people who simply drive from the airport to a meeting and then back again or by renters who use the cars on longer trips.

Many rental companies have facilities that resemble new car dealerships. They generally offer late models (12 to 18 months old) that have high mileage (an average of 23,000 miles). There are advantages to buying from a rental car company:
◄ You have access to the maintenance history of the car.
◄ Problem cars tend not to be sold through the rental dealerships.
◄ The cars have had regular maintenance work.
◄ There is generally a good selection.
◄ You don't negotiate the price.

On the other hand, buying from a rental car company means buying a late model car with high mileage. Also, these cars tend to be loaded with options, which adds to the overall price. (In general, prices at rental car companies tend to be slightly higher than a private seller's prices.)

Private Sales: One of the best and most common ways to buy a used car is from a private owner. The owner will often accept less than the car's retail value, because he or she doesn't have the overhead and expenses of a dealer. Also, buying from someone you know is the best way to get honest information about how well that car was cared for. On the other hand, buying a car from a private source usually requires a lot of running around in order to compare cars.

On a private sale, you should always call the seller before going to see the car. Asking the right questions over the phone can avoid some wasted trips. (See "Questions for the Owner" on page 10.)

One problem with buying through private sellers is determining whether the seller is truly an independent individual selling a single car or is actually a pro masquerading as a private seller. Don't be afraid to use your intuition, and, if you're in doubt, ask to see the title of the car. If the name on the title doesn't match the name of the seller, ask questions.

Tip: If you know someone who regularly trades in a car that they've taken good care of, contact them and ask if they'd be willing to sell it to you rather than trade it in. They can almost always get more by selling it to you than the wholesale price offered on the trade-in. And you will often pay less than the retail price that the dealer would charge.

Superstores: A relatively new way of buying a used car that avoids the hassles of negotiating the price with traditional dealers and private sellers. What is their appeal? They offer "no-haggle" pricing, an enormous selection, and salespeople who aren't on commission. At a superstore, your first stop will generally be a computer terminal where a salesperson will guide you through selecting a car based on your price range and desired features. The computer will identify the vehicles on the lot that meet your needs and tell you where they are located.

⚠ AUTOMOBILE AUCTIONS

Most newspapers carry ads for used car auctions. In general, cars sold at automobile auctions tend to be vehicles that would be difficult to sell in the regular marketplace. They've often been in accidents, have very high mileage, or have obvious wear and tear problems. Because auto mobile auctions can be intimidating for the average buyer and because there are better sources of used cars, we don't recommend them. However, as a source of entertainment, you might enjoy spending a few dollars to see what happens at one of these.

Understanding the Classifieds

The easiest place to find privately sold cars is through the classified ads. While understanding classified ad "shorthand" won't guarantee that the cars you go to see are all that they claim to be, it will help you weed out the cars that you're interested in from those that won't meet your needs. For example, take the following ad:

> '97 Frd Taur: orig owr, 4 dr, lo mi,
> pw, air, cruise, am/fm, tlt str, snrf,
> mint, dk red, best offer.

Here's what it says: The original owner is selling a dark red, four-door 1997 Ford Taurus with low mileage, power windows, air conditioning, cruise control, am/fm radio, tilt steering wheel, sunroof, in like-new condition. Here is a list of frequently used abbreviations:

ABS = anti-lock brake system
a/c, air = air conditioning
a/t, at, auto = automatic trans.
am/fm = radio, no tape player
cass = cassette tape player
cd = compact disc player
cond = condition
conv = convertible
cpe = 2-door sporty coupe
cruise = cruise control
cu in = cubic inches
cyl = cylinders (3,4,5,6, or 8)
dk = dark (color)
dlr = dealer
dr = doors (2,4, or 5)
exc = excellent
full pwr = all power options
h/back, h/b = hatchback
hdtp = hardtop
hd = heavy duty
lk nw = like new
lo mi = low mileage

lt = light
man trans, mt = manual trans.
mint = superb, like-new
  condition
mpg = miles per gallon
orig owr = original owner
pb = power brakes
ps = power steering
pow seats = power seats
pw = power windows
rear dfg = rear defogger
rf = roof
sac = sacrifice
sed = sedan
spd = speed (3,4, or 5)
snrf = sunroof
t/d, tape = tape player
tlt str = tilt steering wheel
vnyl = vinyl top
wrnty = warranty
wgn = station wagon

Checking Them Out

There are literally millions of used cars in the marketplace. The key to finding a peach is to inspect the car very carefully before you buy. This section is designed to help you separate the peaches from the lemons. By following these guidelines, you'll find that checking out a used car is not as difficult as you may have imagined. In fact, you don't have to be a mechanical genius if you know what to look for.

Our checklist has seven sections. The first six will guide you through the inspection process—looking at the car from the inside, outside, and under the hood, as well as handling the test drive and safety checks. We've also included a special list of items you'll want a mechanic to check for you.

Before you hit the streets, you may want to take a few moments to read through the checklists. You'll get a general sense of the types of things that you should keep your eyes open for when you're looking for a good used car.

It's very important to take notes on the cars that you're considering. Not only is it easy to mix up the various features after you've looked at two or three cars, but it shows the seller that you're serious and will be looking very carefully for potential problems.

While these checklists will help prevent you from buying a lemon, the final step before signing on the dotted line is to have the car inspected by an independent mechanic. Don't forget that the car you are considering must meet certain safety and emissions requirements set forth by your state's Department of Motor Vehicles. Contact your DMV ahead of time to find out what the standards are. Some states require that the car be inspected before it can be registered. If that's a requirement in your state, make sure it has been inspected and that the seller has the documentation to prove it. If it is your responsibility to have the car inspected and/or the emission system checked, write into any contract the fact that the seller will pay for necessary repairs in the event that the car fails to pass inspection.

Shop in good weather, so you'll take the time to really look at the car. Get the names of the previous owners and give them a call. Ask the same questions (see next page) that you would ask the current owner.

Check all documentation carefully for words like "reassumed," which means the vehicle has been returned to the dealer because of recurring mechanical problems. Examine the title carefully; some states clearly identify on the title that the car has been reassumed and why. Most recycled lemons are cars that are one to three years old and have low mileage; they are often described as an "executive car" or a "demo."

If service history documents are available, check them carefully to see that it was well maintained. Service dates and locations will give you a clue as to whether the car was in normal use and who the owner was.

Finally, be sure to check on crash test performance, parts cost, insurance cost, fuel economy, theft rating, bumper performance, and recalls in the car listings in the back of this book.

Questions for the Owner

When responding to an ad for a used car, you should always make a call to the seller first to learn a little more about the car and find out who is selling it. If the seller sounds knowledgeable and forthcoming, that may be an indication that the car has received good care.

Curbstoners and used car dealers often place classified ads. To avoid them, tell the person who answers the phone that you're calling about the car for sale—but don't identify the car. If the person replies "Which one?" they are a professional used car dealer or a curbstoner. Also beware if there are a number of cars listed in the classified ads with the same telephone number.

Contact a previous owner if you're buying a car through a used car dealer. If the dealer can't or won't help you get in contact with the previous owner, the car may have come from an auction or another undesirable source.

If possible, ask the owner these questions:

◄ How long have you owned the car?
◄ Did you buy the car new?
◄ Has the car been in any accidents? What repairs were needed?
◄ What is the mileage?

- Generally, has the car been driven mainly around town or on long trips?
- Was this the only car in your family?
- What do you like best about the car?
- What major repair work has been done on the car? (If you assume that major repair work has been done on the car, the owner may be less defensive and possibly more truthful.)
- Have you ever had any problems with rust? Has the car ever been repainted?
- Why are you selling the car?
- Did you follow the manufacturer's maintenance schedule (found in the owner's manual)?
- Where did you generally get your service performed?
- What would I need to do to put the car into top shape?
- Are there any liens on the car? (If so, the owner owes money on the car.)

Inside Checklist

It's important to check the inside of the car carefully for several reasons. First, the interior of the car can give you a number of clues as to how well that car has been treated. If the car has been neglected on the inside, it is likely that it was neglected mechanically as well. A well-cared-for car is going to be a better buy than one that has not been maintained. A diligent inspection of the interior can help you tell the difference. Second, the cosmetic factor: If you're spending a lot of money on a car, you'll want it to look good. You'll also want to inspect it thoroughly to make sure that it has all of the features that are important to you.

The following ten spot checks will help you to evaluate the condition of the car's interior.

1 Study the seats. The upholstery and carpeting provide important clues as to the kind of care the previous owner gave the car. Check the car's seat cushions carefully. If they are weak, have broken springs, or are full of lumps, that's a sign that the car has had some pretty heavy use. If the rear seats show excessive wear, the car may have been used as a taxi. If they look clean and unused, that's an indication that the car was a one- or two-person car.

2 Look under the mats and try the pedals. If the car has floor mats or seat covers, check underneath them to find what kind of wear occurred before they were installed. Press on the gas, brake, and clutch pedals. They should all operate freely without any excessive play or binding.

3 Examine the doors. Look for heavy wear or discoloration on the upper part of the door panel where the driver's arm would rest. Also, check the inside handles to see if they are loose or worn. If there is a lot of wear and the odometer is relatively low, that's a sign that the odometer could have been turned back.

4 Use your nose. If the car smells musty or heavily deodorized, it probably leaks or, worse, was once underwater. Pull back the carpeting and check for rusted flooring. Also check under the seats for rust.

5 Check the odometer. The average car is driven about 12,000 miles per year. So compare the car's age with its total number of miles. For example, it's not unreasonable to expect a five-year-old car to have 60,000 miles on it. If the mileage is a lot less than the average (12,000 per year times the age of the car), you could have either a cream puff or a car with a rolled-back odometer. If the car has considerably more miles on it than the 12,000-mile average, don't give up on the car until you find out how those miles were put on. For example, 18,000 miles per year of highway driving can do less damage to a car than 6,000 miles per year of stop-and-go city traffic.

6 Review the dash. Take a minute to familiarize yourself with the dashboard layout and try every feature on the dashboard. Make sure everything works with the key turned on but without the engine running. Check the radio, windshield wipers, heater, air conditioner, cigarette lighter, clock, horn, parking brake, rear window defogger, fan, and all the air vents.

7 Turn the ignition on. With the key on but the engine off, make sure the alternator and oil pressure lights go on. If they don't, either the bulbs are burned out or the seller has disconnected

INSPECTING THE CAR: TOOLS OF THE TRADE

Be sure you wear some old clothes so you can peek underneath the car or open the hood and poke around a little bit. Here are some useful items to take along when you go out to inspect a used car:

Flashlight: for inspecting the wheel wells for signs of rust and for looking under the hood.

Rags: for checking the oil and other fluids and cleaning off your hands when you're done.

Magnet: for telling the difference between solid metal fender panels and those that have been filled with plastic body filler.

Screwdriver: for poking around the engine compartment.

Friend: for giving you practical and psychological support. Your friend can help you check the lights, exhaust, and back seat comfort while you're driving, as well as serve as a reminder to the seller that you're considering other cars by making comments like "The other car had more power."

Notebook and Pen: for taking notes. It's easy to forget the good and bad points of the cars you've looked at. Taking notes will prevent you from confusing details of one car with details of another. Using a notebook is also an effective negotiating technique. It shows the seller that you are serious about buying, that you've done your homework, and that you have other options.

the lights to ensure that they won't come on later while you're driving. This is something to put on your checklist for your mechanic to go over. When you turn the engine on, both of the lights should go off. If the oil pressure light stays on, turn the engine off and check the oil level. It may just be that the oil is low. However, if the oil level is okay, this light signals that the car could have major problems. If the alternator light stays on, it means the battery isn't charging, which could be a problem as simple as a loose fan belt or as serious as a bad alternator.

8 **Try all the windows.** Check to see that they slide smoothly and don't bind. Also, make sure that the front seats slide easily.

9 **Look in the glove compartment.** Look for the owner's manual and original warranty papers. If they are present (or if they are still available), and you're buying the car from a third party, you will have the opportunity to contact the previous owner to find out more about the condition of the car. If the warranty papers indicate that the original owner was from a distant area or another state, that's an indication that the car might have become available through an auction or an otherwise less desirable source for used cars. Also examine the original warranty and other papers to determine whether the serial numbers on these papers match the serial numbers on the car. If they don't match, either the car has been stolen or it is the product of two cars that have been welded together.

10 **Inspect convertible tops carefully.** To check a convertible, park the car in bright sunlight and carefully examine the roof from the inside for any holes or cracks in the fabric. Look for stains from leaks. Check the back window for clarity and test the top at least twice to make sure it goes up and down properly. If you have the opportunity, hose down the top or run it through a car wash to test for leaks.

Outside Checklist

There are three reasons to inspect the outside of the car carefully. First, it's one of your best clues as to whether the car has been in an accident. Second, it will help you avoid one of the most insidious of car repair problems—rust. Third, if the exterior shows signs of neglect, the owner may have also neglected the mechanical maintenance of the car.

Tip: Always shop in the daytime. Shopping at night or under the glare of lights in a used car lot can hide problems with the body work.

1 **Examine the glass and test the lights.** Front and back windows are expensive to replace, and problems with them can mean a safety hazard. Test the headlights, taillights, flashers, back-

14

up lights, brake lights, turn signals, and parking lights. (Bring a friend and this task will go a lot faster.)

2 Look carefully for rust. Repairing rust is far more expensive than most mechanical repairs, and rust does more to depreciate the value of a car than any other single item. Take special note of the following areas: wheel wells, rain gutters, window moldings, door frames (especially around the bottom), and the joints where the roof supports connect with the body. If the car has a vinyl top, look for bubbles and push on them with your finger. A crinkly, crunchy sound means there's rust under the vinyl that can be almost impossible to stop. Also check for bubbles or blisters around the trim, which indicate the beginning of rust under the paint.

Rust is a good reason to avoid a particular car, because there is no inexpensive way to repair rust problems.

3 Examine the paint and body. Beware of new paint jobs. A newly painted car may have had a severe rust problem or may have been in a major accident. Unless you know the person selling the car and know why it was repainted, stay away from cars with new paint jobs.

To determine whether a car has been repainted, check for telltale signs: the trim on the inside of the doors doesn't quite match the exterior trim; the color inside the hood and the trunk doesn't match the exterior; or little bits of paint on the rubber molding around the windows and doors or on the chrome.

A magnet can tell you if a fender is the original metal or filled with plastic body filler. Or you can check by tapping on suspect body areas with your knuckles. If the fender sounds hollow, it's probably okay. If it sounds solid, it may have been filled with body filler.

Tip: If the car is a sedan with a large engine, check the roof for holes that have been patched where lights or other equipment could have been mounted. Such a car may have been a cab or police car.

4 Try all the doors, the hood, and the trunk. Make sure the doors, trunk, and hood all open and close easily and tightly. Open the driver's side door and try to move it up and down. If it seems loose, then the car has probably had some heavy use. Also, if the door drops or falls out of place when you open it, again beware of heavy use. When the door is closed, check the gap between the door and the body. If it is uneven, the car may have been in an accident. The bumper can also provide a clue to a car's accident history. Both sides of the bumper should be evenly spaced from the car. If not, an accident could have knocked the bumper out of line.

5 **Look inside the trunk.** If it smells musty, it might leak. Check under the mat or carpeting for rust or other problems. Make sure you have all the jack equipment. Check the spare tire. If it's worn unevenly, it may have been changed with a front tire to hide a front-end problem.

6 **Check for leaks under the car.** A leaking black liquid may be oil from the engine or manual transmission; reddish fluid may be from an automatic transmission; greenish, watery liquid may be antifreeze. Clear water, usually from the air conditioner, is okay. Oily, odorous fluid may be brake fluid. You can recognize gasoline by its smell.

7 **Examine the tail pipe.** Make sure it's cool; then rub your finger inside the tail pipe. You should see a white or grey powder. If your finger is black and sooty, the car may simply need a tune-up. However, if it's black and gummy, the car probably has a problem with its rings or valves and is burning oil.

8 **Check the tires.** New tires may indicate that a serious alignment problem exists. Don't be afraid of old tires. They tell an important story about the car. Inspect them carefully for wear and scuffing. If they are worn irregularly (the middle seems balder than the sides or one side or the other seems to have less tread than the middle), the car has either bad shock absorbers, poor wheel alignment, or poor wheel balance. Don't forget to check the inside of the tires, the side of the tires facing the car. Sometimes, owners of tires that are badly scuffed will merely turn them around so that the good side faces out.

Tip: Check the inner side of the tires for evidence of leaking brake fluid.

9 **Test the shock absorbers.** Push up and down on each corner of the car until it starts bouncing. When you let go, the car should not bounce more than one time. If it does, you'll need to repair or replace the shock absorbers.

10 **Examine the car's overall alignment.** Park on a level surface and look at the car from a squatting position about 20 feet behind it. Are the front tires perfectly aligned with the rear tires? If not, the car has a severe frame problem and should be avoided. Also, you should check to see that the car is level. If one side dips lower than the other or if the front dips lower than the back, the car could have serious suspension or frame problems, and again you should avoid it.

11 **Remove the gas cap.** If a sign on the dash says to use only unleaded gasoline, look down the filler tube to the gas tank to see if the opening is small enough to prevent the larger, leaded gas fuel pump nozzles from fitting in it. If it looks like anything has been punched out, then the owner was probably using leaded gas, which can destroy the catalytic converter and will result in expensive repairs.

TIP **VEHICLE IDENTIFICATION NUMBER (VIN)**

While you are inspecting the vehicle, write down the Vehicle Identification Number (VIN). You'll find it printed on a small strip of metal, either in the edge of the door or on the dashboard right beneath the windshield (look on the driver's side). Then, call the state's Department of Motor Vehicles (DMV) and ask them to look up the VIN in their records. They can tell you if the vehicle has been salvaged, totaled, or stolen.

Under the Hood

While many of us find the engine compartment to be a rather intimidating place, these simple checks can help you steer clear of lemons. Items 1 through 8 should be done before starting the car. Items 9 and 10, checking the oil and automatic transmission fluid, should be done after starting the engine.

Before you start the car:

1 **Check the radiator.** While the engine is cool, open the radiator cap to see if there is a shiny oil film on the top of the fluid in the radiator. If so, engine oil is probably leaking into your cooling system through a cracked head, cylinder block, or a leaky head gasket. All are expensive repairs. If the coolant mixture is rusty, you may need to replace the radiator. Stick your finger inside the filler neck and check for sludge. This usually means that somebody added a "stop leak" product to plug up holes in a leaky radiator.
   Caution: Always make sure the radiator is cool before making these checks.

2 **Examine the engine compartment.** Check the overall cleanliness of the engine, but beware of perfectly clean engines. That's a possible indication that the engine has just been steam cleaned in order to prevent you from seeing various leaks. Inspect the engine carefully and look for leaking around the various components.

3 **Look for maintenance stickers.** Look around the engine compartment, air filter, underside of the hood, and door frames for any maintenance stickers put on by a service station. This may provide a clue to how frequently the car has been serviced. A key factor is frequent oil changes. If the owner regularly changed the oil, the chances of getting a well-running car increase dramatically.

4 **Examine the belts.** Check the fan belts for cracks or shredding and make sure that they are not too loose. When you push down on them, they should give only about half an inch. It's okay for the belts on a four- to five-year-old car to look as though they need to be replaced—they probably do. While you check the belts, wiggle the fan blade and other pulleys connected to the belts. If any are loose, the bearings may be gone, and they will have to be replaced.

5 **Check the wiring.** Check any wires for frayed or worn spots and cracks. If the car is more than two years old and the wiring looks new, the owner could have had a major problem. This isn't necessarily bad, but it's something that you should inquire about. The wires going to the spark plugs (known as the ignition wires) should have no cracks, burn marks, or wear. If so, they most likely will have to be replaced. This isn't a major repair. It's more an indication that the car has received poor preventive maintenance.

6 **Check all the fluids.** Inspect the brake fluid, power steering fluid, and windshield washer fluid. Low power steering or brake fluid could indicate a leak in either of those systems. If the windshield washer fluid is low, put some water in and test the system to see if it works. Low fluids may indicate that the car has been neglected overall.

7 **Look at the battery.** A brand new battery on a car that's less than two or three years old could mean electrical problems. If the car is four or five years old and you're convinced that it has the original battery (it bears a date), you can assume that the electrical system works fine.

8 **Check the air filter.** If it looks particularly dirty, then the owner probably did not do much preventive maintenance, because changing the air filter is one of the easiest things that can be done to keep a car in good shape.

After you start the car:
9 **Check the oil.** After the engine has been running, find the dipstick to check the oil level. If it's low, then the car is either an oil burner, has some kind of oil leak, or the owner has not replaced what was naturally lost. If the oil is fresh, it will be a clear, amber color; if it is dark, it usually indicates that the oil has been in the engine for some time. In older engines the oil will rapidly turn dark which is not necessarily a problem. Gritty or gummy oil is a sign of infrequent oil change, which could signal that the engine has not been very well maintained. If the oil is milky brown or grey or has

small bubbles in it, then water is present, and the car could have a cracked block. Very thin oil that smells like gasoline also indicates severe engine problems. Very thick oil could indicate that the owner is trying to quiet the noise from a failing valve lifter.

10 **Check the automatic transmission fluid.** The automatic transmission has a dipstick, which is usually located at the rear of the engine. Put the emergency brake on and, with the transmission in park, start the car and check the color of the fluid on the transmission dipstick. It should be reddish. If it's dark brown and sludgy, the transmission has been poorly maintained. If it has a burned smell, it means that the transmission has excessive wear and could quite possibly fail shortly. If you notice any metal flecks, actual parts of the gears are being ground up. If the fluid level is low, then the transmission leaks. (Note: This is a very important check. If you can't find the dipstick, put it on your mechanic's checklist.)

Plan on taking every car you're considering for a good long test drive. You should map out two or three types of road ahead of time to include a highway, normal roads for around-town driving, and a bumpy road that will allow you to slow down and check for creaks and groans. If the owner does not allow you to test drive the car, then you have a simple solution: Don't buy it.

The Test Drive

1 **Check the steering.** With the front wheels pointed straight ahead (and the engine on with the car in park for power steering), stick your head out the window and watch the front tire as you slowly turn the steering wheel. The tire should begin to move as you begin to turn the wheel. If the steering wheel has to turn more than two inches before the wheels start moving, the car's steering system could need some expensive repairs.

You can check the power steering when parked by turning the wheel all the way to the left and then all the way to the right. If the car screeches loudly or surges and bounces as you turn the wheel, the car might need a new power steering pump, or it may need repairs to the power steering system.

2 Check the exhaust. While you drive, check your rear-view mirror and note whether any exhaust smoke is coming from the tail pipe. Blue smoke indicates that the engine may need an expensive overhaul. If it's black, the car may simply need a tune-up or carburetor adjustment. If it's white as you start up but stops after a while, it could be water vapor that had built up in the engine and is nothing to worry about. If the white smoke continues throughout the drive, water from the radiator may be leaking into the engine.

3 Check the brakes. After the engine warms up, stop the car and push the brake pedal down as far as you can. It should go no more than an inch and a half to the floor. Keep the pedal down for at least a minute. If, during that period, the pedal seems to sink lower, the car could have serious brake problems.

When it's safe to do so, step on the brakes hard enough to slow down quickly without skidding. If the car dips forward excessively or pulls to one side, it probably needs brake or suspension work.

TIP

ENGINE STRESS TEST

Follow these steps to conduct an engine "stress" test for cars with automatic transmission and power steering: With the engine idling, air conditioner turned on high, lights on with high beams, radio on, and foot on the brake, put the engine in gear—automatic transmission only—and turn the wheel (if equipped with power steering) all the way to the left and right. Everything should continue running smoothly. Listen for screeches or howls in the power steering and feel for smoothness as you turn the wheel. There should be no surges or bouncing.

4 Check the alignment. When it's safe to do so, let go of the steering wheel on a level, straight road to see if the car pulls to either side. This pulling could mean something as simple as improper tire pressure or as serious as steering linkage out of alignment. Caution: Be careful in conducting this test, because if the car is severely out of alignment, the wheels could turn sharply.

5 Listen to the engine. When you're on the highway at cruising speed, listen for unusual sounds of stress and strain. Even if the weather is very cold or very hot, drive with the window rolled all the way down in order to hear any clanks, groans, or other sounds that could signal expensive repairs down the road. As you accelerate, the engine should not feel as if it is laboring. Listen for a pinging or tapping from the engine. This sound may disappear by simply using a higher octane gas, or it may signal the need for a major engine overhaul. Have your mechanic check it out. Even if you can't identify the sounds, report anything unusual to the mechanic who inspects the car for you.

6 **Listen to the engine idle.** Pull over and let the engine idle while the transmission is in park. It should run smoothly. If you notice any acceleration, hesitation, or uneven performance, the problem could be something as simple as an idle adjustment or as serious as a carburetor overhaul. You shouldn't hear any loud tapping noises coming from the engine. If you do, the car may need expensive valve work. If you hear some light ticking or tapping noises, the car may simply need an adjustment. In either case, be sure to put these noises on your mechanic's checklist.

After you've listened to the engine for a while, turn off the key. The engine should stop immediately; if it continues to run for a few seconds, the car might need a carburetor overhaul or a tune-up.

7 **Listen to the transmission.** With your foot on the brake, move the shift lever from drive to reverse several times. If you hear a soft thump or no noise at all, the transmission is operating properly. However, if you hear a loud clank, that's a sign that the car may have a major transmission problem.

In general, the automatic transmission should shift smoothly from gear to gear. Any whining of the transmission, jumping, or irregular performance could indicate big transmission problems down the line. If it seems that the car drops temporarily into neutral while shifting from one gear to the next, your transmission is probably slipping and in need of repair. Don't forget to check the transmission while the car is in reverse. You should drive the car for at least fifty yards in reverse to make sure it runs smoothly and doesn't jump.

If the car has a manual transmission and the engine revs up when you step on the gas with your foot off the clutch and the car in gear, the clutch is slipping. You may have to replace it. If you hear a knocking sound from the transmission, press the clutch in. If the noise disappears, it's probably in the transmission; if it doesn't, there could be problems with the clutch. **Note:** Any clanking sounds you hear when you're testing out your transmission could also indicate problems with the universal joint. For example, if you hear a clank each time you go down a hill, the car may have a worn universal joint.

8 **Listen for clunks.** Take the car out on a very bumpy road, roll down the windows, and drive slowly (five to ten miles per hour) to see if you can hear any unusual clanks or other sounds that may indicate you'll need to have some serious suspension work.

9 **Check the heater and air conditioner.** If it's winter, first check the heater by warming up the car. Then check the air conditioning system. To check the air conditioner, run it through all of its cycles. The air compressor should thump slightly as it kicks on and off. However, if you hear loud banging or rumbling, that's an indication that the air compressor may need replacing. Put your hands over the vents to check the pressure and temperature of the air coming out.

TIP

PURCHASE AGREEMENTS

Draft a purchase agreement to get in writing some of the things that may result in a legal dispute further down the line. Although this may seem to imply a distrust of the other person involved in the transaction, this document ensures that important points, such as when and how payment will occur, how any deposit that may be transferred will be handled, or how the lending of the car for inspection will be arranged, are clear to both parties. If these points are not clear, problems could result, and one of the involved parties could lose out in the end.

Be congenial when bringing up the subject of a purchase agreement. Be sure to point out that the purpose of such an agreement is to protect both parties and to avoid confusion.

10 **Check for inside leaks.** If it's handy on the test drive, try running the car through a car wash. For a few dollars, you'll find out whether the car has any obvious leaks. Otherwise, take the car to a place where you can hose it down vigorously. Directly spray the hose around the windows, vents, and trunk.

Each year, odometers get rolled back an average of 32,000 miles on three million used cars, and an estimated 50 percent of the leased cars on the used car market have odometers that have been rolled back.

Avoiding Odometer Fraud

Federal law makes it illegal to change a car's odometer. No one, not even the owner, is permitted to turn back or disconnect the odometer (except to perform necessary repairs). A new law also requires that the odometer reading be written on the vehicle title when the car is sold. All states require that the seller, or anyone transferring ownership of the vehicle, provide the buyer with a signed statement indicating the mileage on the odometer at the time of the transfer. Unfortunately, odometer fraud is so common that many buyers automatically assume that the mileage on a car's odometer is incorrect.

Be sure to make these checks before purchasing a used car to determine whether the odometer reading is correct:

1 Look for maintenance stickers on the door post or air filter cover, which may give the mileage at the date when last serviced.

2 Check the wear on the foot pedals and the ignition lock. If the odometer reads less than 20,000 miles, the pedals shouldn't show any excessive wear, and the lock shouldn't be heavily scratched.

3 Carefully check the dashboard for scratch marks or missing screws, which indicate that the odometer was tampered with.

4 See if all of the numbers on the odometer line up. Rolled-back odometers often have misaligned numbers.

5 Study the title carefully. All of the numbers should be clear and easy to read. Disreputable sellers may obscure the numbers with an official looking stamp or staple or fold the title right through the middle of the odometer reading, vehicle number, or other important information.

6 If there is an odometer disclosure statement, check the number against the odometer, it should be close.

ODOMETER FRAUD

If you believe that you've been the victim of odometer fraud and that the car you purchased has a rolled-back odometer, the first thing to do is to contact the National Highway Traffic Safety Administration, Odometer Fraud Staff, 400 7th Street, SW, Washington, D.C. 20590, or call the Auto Safety Hotline at 800-424-9393 (202-366-0123 in Washington, D.C.). The agency will send you an odometer complaint form and a letter telling you what evidence you will need to get and what steps you'll need to take. The agency will not help you resolve your complaint; however, if you register the complaint with them, they can gather evidence on widespread problems and collect complaints from the same area or the same dealer.

If you are a victim of odometer fraud, you have the right to recover triple the difference between what you paid for the car and what it was actually worth or $1,500, whichever is greater.

In order to get action, you will have to file suit in your state or federal court. For the court to hear your case, you will need evidence indicating that the odometer has been rolled back. It can include such information as a previous owner's statement on the mileage of the car when it was sold or repair records from the dealer or service station that worked on the car that include the car's odometer reading.

Many states have an odometer enforcement unit within their state attorney general's office. Contact the office, in care of your state capitol, for suggestions on how to proceed with an investigation. In some cases, your state attorney general may bring suit against the seller on your behalf. If not, and you hire a private attorney, the fees are recoverable if you win.

7 Check the name on the title. It should be either the seller's or, if you're buying from a used car dealer, the previous owner's or dealer's name. Be suspicious of titles with out-of-state addresses, post office box addresses, or auction company names.

8 Remember, half of all the leased cars for sale have rolled-back odometers. Compare the driver's seat and door with the passenger's seat and door for wear and tear. If the driver's side looks as though it received far heavier usage, it's a good indication that this was a company car with a single driver.

9 Have your mechanic check the engine compression and look for worn struts or ball joints and transmission problems—all signs of high use.

Mechanic's Checklist

The best "warranty" you can get with a used car is a $45 to $60 independent mechanic's inspection. One of the best places to get an inspection is your local office of the American Automobile Association (AAA). Because AAA inspection centers are not affiliated with repair facilities, they have no incentive to recommend unnecessary repairs. These diagnostic inspections are available to both members and non-members. If the seller will not allow you to take the car for a mechanic's inspection, don't buy it.

While AAA and most mechanics follow standard procedure when inspecting cars, make sure the following areas are included:

1 **Engine Compression:** This check will give you a good idea of the internal condition of the engine, including the valves and piston rings.

2 **Brakes:** The mechanic should take off at least one front and one rear wheel to inspect the condition of the brake disk or drum and brake pads. All the brake lines should be checked for rust or damage.

3 **Front Wheel Bearings and Suspension System:** The ball joint seals should be intact, the structural parts solid and straight, and the springs and shocks properly connected. Check shock absorbers for leakage and loose mountings.

4 **Frame:** Check the frame for rust, breaks, and signs of welding. If the frame or under-body has been welded, the car has either been in an accident or, worse, is actually two different cars welded together.

5 **Exhaust:** Inspect the muffler system and look for loose or missing brackets, rust, and holes.

6 Cooling System: Pressure test the radiator.

7 Electrical: Test the battery and charging system.

8 Transmission: Check the entire drive train.

9 Road Test: Ask if the mechanic will road test the car for you.

10 Repair Estimate: Have the mechanic give you an estimate for the cost of any repairs deemed necessary. This will be a big help when it's time to negotiate.

Safety Checklist

How do you buy for safety? While even a trained engineer would find it difficult to compare the safety of cars just by looking at them, here are some features to check in the used cars you consider.

1 Recessed Knobs and Controls: Are the items on the dashboard recessed below the surface of the dash?

2 Steering Wheel: Does the steering wheel have a large padded hub?

3 Padding: Are the dashboard, sun visors, and roof supports well padded?

4 Doors: Are the doors free of sharp and protruding objects?

5 Headrests: If adjustable, can they be set so the center of the headrest is just above the center of your head? If they are not adjustable, make sure they are high enough. Non-adjustable headrests will not slip out of place.

6 **Fuel Tank:** Is the fuel tank located forward or above the rear axle to prevent leakage in a rear-end collision?

7 **Visibility:** Is your vision free from obstructions or blind spots when you turn your head in either direction? Is there a right side rear-view mirror for better visibility?

8 **Brake Lights:** Does the car have a centrally mounted rear brake light? (These lights can cut rear-end collisions by 50 percent and are required in all models manufactured in 1986 or later. If you are buying an earlier model, they can be installed at a relatively low price.)

9 **Safety Belts:** Are the belts convenient and easy to use? If not, chances are you won't use them. Also check to see that they pull out and retract correctly and are not frayed.

10 **Special Features:** Some late model used cars have special safety features, such as anti-lacerative windshields, better seat belts, anti-lock brakes, and childproof locks. These can increase protection against injury.

Crash Tests

Most of the cars we rate have government crash test results. These crash tests show significant differences in the ability of various automobiles to protect belted occupants during frontal crashes. Our publication of the test results over the years has put pressure on manufacturers to improve the performance of their cars. For example, when the program began, Japanese cars were among the worst performers; now they are among the best.

An occupant's safety depends on the car's ability to absorb any force caused by impact. This is a function of the car's size, weight, and, most importantly, design. In the crash tests, engineers measure how much of the crash force is transferred to the head, chest, and thighs of the occupants.

The test consists of crashing an automobile into a concrete barrier at 35 mph. The effect is similar to that of two identical cars crashing head-on at 35 mph. In the test, each automobile contains electronically monitored dummies in the driver and passenger seats.

This electronic data can then be analyzed in terms of the impact of such a collision on a human being.

We have analyzed the data and presented the results in the back of the book using a Very Good, Good, Average, Poor, or Very Poor performance rating. These ratings provide a means of comparing the overall results of one car with those of another. It is best to compare the test results of cars within the same weight class, such as compacts with compacts; the results should not be used to compare cars with vastly different weights. For example, you should not conclude that a subcompact that is rated "Good" is as safe as a minivan or large car with the same rating.

The results evaluate performance in frontal crashes, which cause about 50 percent of auto deaths and serious injuries. Remember that the results only measure protection for belted occupants. Buying a car equipped with airbags and using safety belts are the most effective means of protecting yourself in an accident.

Note: Not all cars are crash tested, and there is no absolute guarantee that a car that passed the government test will adequately protect you in an accident.

Safety Defects and Recalls

Over 17 million cars and trucks are recalled each year for inspection and safety-related defects. Safety recalls are an effort to reduce injuries and fatalities. When a safety recall occurs, manufacturers are required to notify individual car owners of the defect and to correct the defect quickly and at no cost to the consumer.

The effectiveness of a safety recall campaign is partly the responsibility of the car owner. The owner must bring the car to a dealer for inspection and repair.

If your car has been recalled, take it in for repair as soon as possible. A recalled automobile can be returned to any authorized dealer. The manufacturer, through the dealer, is responsible for fixing the defect, no matter how long ago the recall occurred.

The tables at the end of the book are a quick reference guide for determining whether your car, or the used car you are considering, has ever been recalled. In order to determine whether the defect has already been corrected, you need to find the vehicle identification number, which is located on the dashboard and can be seen by looking in through the windshield. The second step is to call the dealer. If the dealer can't tell you if your particular car has been fixed, then contact the manufacturer. If you still cannot get help, call the U.S. Department of Transportation's toll-free Auto Safety Hotline (800-424-9393; in Washington, D.C. call 202-366-0123) and register a complaint.

Contact the Federal Trade Commission or the Environmental Protection Agency for information on defects and recalls that are not safety-related.

PHONY INSPECTIONS

Beware of dealers who push you toward certain diagnostic centers or mechanics for your inspection. Sometimes mechanics and privately operated diagnostic centers have arrangements with certain used car dealers to ensure that the dealer's car checks out "just fine" in exchange for referrals to the mechanic or diagnostic center.

MECHANICAL PROBLEMS

Don't automatically reject a car with a mechanical problem. The cost of repairing the problem may not be that great (have a mechanic give you an estimate), and you can use the problem and repair estimate to negotiate a lower price on the car.

Part Two: Getting the Best Price and Selling Your Car

The "Blue Book" Value/34
Warranties/34
Selling Your Car/36

The most difficult and intimidating part of buying a used car is negotiating the price. Most of us rarely bargain for the things we buy. So, it's no surprise that we feel uncomfortable negotiating, especially for an item whose value is so difficult to evaluate. This section will acquaint you with the process of negotiating and provide some tips for success. We will also provide some advice on warranties and service contracts.

First of all, the single most important thing you can do to negotiate a good price is to prepare yourself psychologically to get up and walk out. Always remember that you carry the highest trump card:

TIP NEGOTIATING SHORTCUT

Some people get a thrill out of negotiating and will carry the process out to four, five, or even six counteroffers. Most of us, however, could do without the process altogether. One technique that you can try, especially if you've found three or four cars that you really like, involves no bargaining at all. It goes like this: After you have carefully determined a fair value for each of the cars that you are interested in, go to the seller(s) and state up front that you are only going to make one offer for the car. Be honest; simply say that you don't like negotiating and that you have determined what you believe is a very fair price for the car. Make your offer and be prepared to walk away and not listen to a counteroffer. If you have second thoughts later on, you can always call back with another offer. However, if your price is fair and your approach is reasonable, there's a good chance that the seller will respect your seriousness and sell you the car at the price you offered.

the 180-degree turn. If you are always prepared to walk out, you'll always maintain the upper hand in your negotiation.

Another important factor in successful negotiating is the attitude you bring to the process. Try to remain unemotional, detached, and deal in a straightforward manner. You should never exhibit a strong desire for the car. On the other hand, you should not be belligerent and exhibit an attitude that indicates you don't think the car is worth very much.

If you are bargaining with a professional, there will be times when you are waiting for him or her to respond. Professional salespeople often use silence to intimidate a buyer. Don't be intimidated. And don't let long periods of time in which the salesman is "talking with the sales manager" about your deal make you uncomfortable. That is simply a tactic to wear you down, make you nervous, and make you feel like you just want to "get this thing over with." Try not to be nervous. Instead, do something that indicates you are serious about looking other places. Bring the classified section of the newspaper with you and begin circling other cars that you want to check out. Or review your notes on the other cars that you've seen. Also, you should always give the salesperson a time limit. By sending the message that you have other options, you'll increase your bargaining power.

Here are some additional negotiating tips to help you to get the best price on a used car:

Find out how much the car is worth. You really can't begin to negotiate until you've determined the car's actual value. Like any other commodity, a used car will have a wholesale and a retail value; you need to determine both. The value of a car can be found in two basic ways. First, consult the *N.A.D.A. Official Used Car Guide* for the value of the car and the options that come with it. The range between the wholesale and retail value of the car is your bargaining range. And second, review the classified section in a large newspaper and see what people are asking for their cars. Prices in the classified section should be somewhere between the wholesale and retail values printed in the N.A.D.A. book.

Road test first. Never begin negotiating until you have road tested the car and checked it out mechanically.

Determine your maximum price. Before you begin negotiating, determine the most you would pay for the car. For most cars, this should be below the asking price.

Use a notebook. Keep a notebook with you and take notes. Don't hesitate to refer to notes on other cars while the seller is telling you about the current car under consideration. These notes will help you refresh your memory and indicate to the seller that you have other options.

Touch and comment. Use the same technique that new car dealers do when they inspect your trade-in. While you review the car, visibly point out, either to yourself or to a partner, the various problems that you note. An exaggerated touch of some loose part, or running your hand along body damage, can put the seller in a defensive position. In addition to noting the problems audibly, write them down.

Start low. When you've determined that you like the car, your first offer should be 20 percent below the most you would pay for the car.

Prepare to counter. Most of the time (and nearly every time if you're dealing with a used car dealer), your first offer will not be accepted, and the seller will make a counteroffer. Your response, as a rule of thumb, should split the difference between your first offer and the most you're willing to pay for the car (not the counteroffer) unless, of course, the counteroffer is lower.

Take a second look. If the negotiation gets bogged down and you are not getting much movement toward your price, ask to take another look at the car. This indicates to the seller that you may have some second thoughts, and the seller may fear that you might see a problem you hadn't noticed the first time around.

The final offer. If the seller's second counteroffer is below the most you're willing to pay for the car, consider accepting the offer. If it is not, your third offer (which should be your final offer) should be close to what you would be willing to pay for the car. At this point, you should make it very clear that you honestly believe you're offering a fair price and that your last offer is final.

Be ready to walk. You must be prepared to walk away if your third and final offer is not accepted. You'll be surprised at how many times you are called back. Remember, if you've determined the fair value of the car and it's not offered, you can probably find a better deal elsewhere.

Don't forget that there are items other than price to negotiate. The car may need repairs, or you may want more time on the warranty. Remember, if the seller agrees to any of these extras, make sure you get them in writing.

The "Blue Book" Value

The *N.A.D.A. Official Used Car Guide* is published monthly by the National Automobile Dealers Association and is generally recognized as one of the best sources of used car prices. (It is often called the "blue book," but it is actually orange.) The book is a compilation of average used car prices based on reports of actual transactions by dealers and wholesale auctions. Because car prices vary slightly by region, there are nine separate regional editions. Each guide includes the average trade-in or wholesale price, the average loan price, and the average retail price for nearly every car sold within the last seven years. Also included are mileage tables used to adjust the price of the car depending on how many miles it has been driven. The book is available in the reference section of many libraries.

There are other used car pricing guides available that tend to be more regional—for example, *Kelley Blue Book* is used quite frequently in the California area. While anyone can subscribe to these guides, they are generally not available in retail stores. What you will find in a bookstore is a publication called *Edmund's Used Car Prices*, which is published quarterly. Like the *N.A.D.A. Official Used Car Guide*, it includes the current average retail and wholesale prices. However, *Kelley Blue Book* is available online at www.kbb.com.

An important factor to remember when using these "blue books" is that local market conditions may not be reflected in the listed prices. That's why it's important to compare the book prices with those in used car ads and at local used car dealerships. Nevertheless, these books are probably the best source of general information in terms of determining the value of a used car.

Warranties

Most used cars are sold "as is." This means you buy the car with any problems it may have, and the seller guarantees nothing at all, even if the seller will "guarantee the car as is."

With a few exceptions, a warranty that comes with a used car should be of little consequence to you. When used cars are sold in "as is" condition, warranties are difficult to enforce. There are, of course, some exceptions. Warranties from the major rental car companies are generally okay, although they may be rather limited. Also, the warranties that come with used cars that are sold by new car dealers (also limited) are usually backed by the dealer.

Federal law requires posting a buyer's guide on used cars. Anyone who sells six or more used cars in a period of less than 12 months is considered a used car dealer and must post this guide on every car for sale. The buyer's guide spells out what kind of warranty comes with the car, indicates the types of problems that could be present, and lists the name and phone number of the person to contact, should problems arise. If no warranty is applicable, the buyer's guide should read, "As is—no warranty." Information on the buyer's guide is incorporated into the final contract for sale.

If there is a warranty for the car, make sure you take the time to read and understand it. No two used car warranties are alike, so read them carefully. A dealer selling a used car will probably offer a 30-day or 1,000-mile warranty. Some dealers will want to split the cost of repairs with you, while others will cover 100 percent of the cost of repairs under warranty. Remember, you have the right to inspect the warranty before you buy the car. It's the law.

Claims made by the salesperson are considered expressed warranties, and you should have them put in writing if you consider them important. Do not confuse your warranty with a service contract. A service contract is purchased separately; the warranty is

TRANSFERRING WARRANTIES

TIP

The original warranties of many cars can be transferred to the next owner. Unlike extended service contracts, which belong to the purchaser, the car's original warranty stays with the car. So, if the warranty is still in effect, then it is automatically transferred to the new owner. Be sure you get all the warranty documentation from the seller. Most warranties only last throo yoars. Howovor, be sure to also check the mileage limits on the warranty. Most limits only go up to 36,000 miles, so compare the mileage limit to the mileage on the car. If the car's mileage is under the mileage limit and the time limit has not expired, the warranty will transfer—but, both must still be valid.

yours at no extra cost when you buy the car. If you find that the warranty is ambiguous or doesn't offer much coverage, you can use it to negotiate.

Known Defects Disclosure: If a dealer knows about a major defect prior to selling you a used car, the dealer is obligated, by law, to disclose it. If the dealer does not tell you about a defect prior to sale, you may be able to break the contract. You can find out the specific rules that apply in your state by contacting your state attorney general's office.

TIP

TRANSFERRING SERVICE CONTRACTS

If you buy a used car from a private individual who offers you the balance of the car's service contract along with the car, be sure to check it out carefully before you buy the car. Some contracts automatically cancel when the car is resold, and other companies require a hefty transfer fee before extending privileges to the new owner.

Selling Your Car

For most of us, buying a used car carries with it another task—selling our old one. There are three options: You can keep your car, trade it in on the newer car, or sell it yourself. If you decide not to keep your old car, you'll do better by selling it yourself, rather than trading it in. Why? Because even if you get a fair deal, the most a dealer will give you is the wholesale price of that car. If you sell it yourself, you can charge the full retail price.

To decide whether it's worth the effort to sell the car yourself, you need to know the difference between the retail price and the wholesale price. This difference is the money you make by selling the car yourself. For more information on determining the value of your car, see the first part of this section.

Determine the car's value. Pricing your car correctly is very important. In addition to checking the *N.A.D.A. Official Used Car Guide*, take a look through your local newspaper for the prices of cars similar to yours. You may also want to take your car to a couple of used car lots and see how much they'll offer you.

Prepare the car for sale. Even if you decide not to sell it yourself and choose to trade it in, getting the car into the right condition can add more to its value than it will cost, and you'll come out ahead. Clean it thoroughly inside and out. You may want to have the engine steam cleaned to remove accumulated oil and dirt, and you should clean any corrosion from the battery.

Tip: When you clean the car, make sure you tighten anything that might be loose or rattling, such as the license plate or glove box door. Even a minor rattle may discourage a potential buyer.

Don't make major repairs. Any major mechanical repairs or body work will almost always cost more than the increase in price you'll get for the car. Instead of spending a lot of money, simply be honest and straightforward in your ad for the car. For example, if the right fender is crushed and rusted, say so in the ad:

FOR SALE: 95 Ford Escort, runs like a dream, looks like an ugly duckling—Call...

Advertise. Once your car is ready for sale, it's time to advertise it. First, check neighborhood bulletin boards, community newspapers, and employee publications. There are generally many free or low cost places where you can place an ad. If you park in large lots, make a sign for the window and provide your telephone number. (Note: This may be illegal in some areas.) Check with your credit union or church and get your friends to spread the word.

When writing your ad, be honest. Skip the flowery phrases and stick to words that buyers will respond to, such as clean, low mileage, original owner, excellent fuel economy, regular service records available. Your ad should list the year, model, and body style, and you might want to include the number of miles, engine size, or color. If your car has any special features, let people know about them in your ad. The clearer and more honest your ad, the less hassle you'll have in selling.

Generally your ad should not include your address, only your telephone number and times when people may reach you. It's important to list when you'll be available, because if you're not home, a frustrated caller may not call back.

If the free advertising sources aren't generating any buyers, then you should place an ad in your daily newspaper. Before you write your ad, look at how similar cars are written up. Try to make yours sound a little bit different and a little more special. Putting your asking price in the ad will save a lot of phone calls from people who aren't really interested or who can't afford the car.

Respond to the callers. Once prospective buyers start calling, be ready to answer questions. Prepare callers for what to expect when they see the car. If, at first glance, the car looks worse than they expected, the sale will be more difficult.

Make an appointment with each caller for a specific time, rather than allowing them to come "sometime this afternoon." This appointment will increase your chances of the buyers showing up, and, if they're late, you don't have to feel obligated to wait for them. But don't be surprised if some of these folks don't show.

Be honest and helpful. When prospective buyers come, make sure you go along with them on the test drive. This is not only for security but also to help the driver understand all the car's features and to answer any questions. If the buyers continue to show interest, help them arrange a mutually convenient time for a mechanic's appraisal, if they want one.

If possible, park the car in an inconspicuous place, especially if it has some dings and dents. By doing this, you will keep people who stop by from taking a quick look and moving on, rather than knocking on your door and giving you a chance to explain the car's good points.

It's important to prepare yourself psychologically for the sale. First of all, communicate honestly about the car. You'll obtain far more credibility and reduce buyer resistance much more effectively if you're honest about the car's problems. Most people realize that buying a used car means buying something less than perfect. By trying to hide some of the defects, you place the buyers in the position of being far more disappointed when they discover them.

It's equally important to be optimistic about the car. Don't hesitate to tell the buyer how much you enjoy driving the car and point out the special features that you particularly like.

Watch out for the pros! You may get calls from professionals trying to buy cars for resale. Often these people will put tremendous pressure on you to sell the car far below your asking price. A disreputable person may even squirt oil on parts of the car and tell you that it leaks, or they may fiddle with the engine while they're looking under the hood. If the car doesn't run properly during the test drive, they'll try to get you to lower the price. Fortunately, unscrupulous people like this are rare.

Price it right. As long as you've priced the car fairly, stay firm. Most buyers will have checked around and will realize that the car is fairly priced. If you really want to move the car, you may consider under-pricing it by a few hundred dollars. However, if you choose to do this, make sure that you stay firm on the final price. In a normal situation, you should add 10 to 15 percent to your rock bottom price to get the price you're advertising. That way, you have room to negotiate.

Be ready to negotiate. One technique for negotiating, when a buyer's offer is below your actual price, is to state cordially but firmly that you've already turned down an offer for "x" and can't possibly accept something lower. That will let the buyer know your rock bottom price, and the buyer will either have to match it or beat it in order to get the car. In all cases, get the name and telephone number of people that look at your car, and as a last resort you can call them back with a counteroffer.

Get cash. Make sure you always get either cash or a certified check.

Indicate that you are selling "as is," in writing. Remember when selling a car, you are selling it in "as is" condition. In order to prevent problems from coming back to haunt you, make sure you write on the buyer's receipt that the car is being sold in "as is" condition.

Check title transfer procedures. Consult your state Department of Motor Vehicles to determine what requirements you must follow to transfer the title to the new owner. This process usually consists of your signing and dating the title before you pass it on to the buyer and notifying the DMV of the transaction. Making sure that the title is correctly transferred and the DMV properly notified will prevent you from being liable for any accidents or tickets once the transfer is complete.

Finally, unless you live in a state where the license plates stay with the vehicle, keep them.

⚠ CURBSTONERS

Used car sellers who operate out of their homes are often called "curbstoners." These "semi-pros" avoid many of the state and local licensing requirements by representing themselves as private sellers when, in fact, they make a great deal of money selling used cars in their back yards.

There are some legitimate curbstoners. These are people who buy used cars at low prices and take the time to repair them for resale at a profit. A legitimate curbstoner can actually be a good source for a used car. Unfortunately, it's difficult to determine who is legitimate and who is not.

Tip: Ask to see the garage where repairs are done and always have an independent mechanic check the car out.

Many times, curbstoners are selling cars that they've picked up at auctions, stolen cars, or cars with rolled-back odometers. Curbstoners will claim they are simply selling their own cars. Most of them aren't. And if you question why the name on the title doesn't match theirs, they'll probably tell you they're selling the car for a friend or relative. Be cautious, because if it turns out that you purchased a stolen car, you can lose the car and have little or no recourse against the seller.

Following are warning signals which may indicate that you are dealing with an illegal curbstoner:

▸ The seller has several vehicles for sale.
▸ The same phone number appears in more than one ad.
▸ The seller evades questions about the vehicle's history.
▸ The vehicle has no license plates.
▸ The name on the title isn't the seller's name.
▸ The seller meets you at a location that's different from the the address on the title (such as a repair shop, gas station, or vacant lot).

Part Three: Keeping Them Going

Reducing Insurance Costs/41

Tips for Dealing with a Mechanic/43

Repair Protection by Credit Card/44

Secret Warranties/45

Center for Auto Safety/46

The reason why most of us buy a used car in the first place is because it is less expensive than a new car.

In order to make sure that your purchase is, in fact, one that will end up saving you money in the long run, this chapter includes important tips on keeping that car going both economically and safely. In this section, we will provide cost-saving tips on insurance, offer some important safety information that will make the operation of your car safe, give you some maintenance tips that will reduce your operating costs, explain how to get the best deal on tires, and give you some insight on how to resolve those inevitable problems down the road.

Reducing Insurance Costs

Insurance is a big part of ownership expenses, yet it's often forgotten in the showroom. As you shop, remember that the car's design and accident history may affect your insurance rates. Some cars cost less to insure because experience has shown that they are damaged less, less expensive to fix after a collision, or stolen less.

More and more consumers are saving hundreds of dollars by shopping around for insurance. In order to be a good comparison shopper, you need to know a few things about automobile insurance.

A number of factors determine what these coverages will cost you. A car's design can affect both the chances and severity of an accident. A car with a well-designed bumper may escape damage altogether in a low-speed crash. Some cars are easier to repair than others or may have less expensive parts. Cars with four doors tend to be damaged less than cars with two doors.

The reason one car may get a discount on insurance while another receives a surcharge also depends upon the way it is traditionally driven. Sports cars, for example, are usually surcharged due, in part, to the typical driving habits of their owners. Four-door sedans, minivans, and station wagons generally merit discounts. Insurance companies use this and other information to determine whether to offer a discount on insurance premiums for a particular car or whether to levy a surcharge.

Not all companies offer discounts or surcharges, and many cars receive neither. Some companies offer a discount or impose a surcharge on collision premiums only. Others apply discounts and surcharges on both collision and comprehensive coverage. Discounts and surcharges usually range from 10 to 30 percent. Allstate offers discounts of up to 35 percent on certain cars. Remember that one company may offer a discount on a particular vehicle while another may not.

Check with your insurance company to find out whether your company has a rating program.

Here are some of the most common insurance discounts:

Driver Education/Defensive Driving Courses: Many insurance companies offer (and in some cases mandate) discounts to young people who have successfully completed a state-approved driver education course. Typically, this can mean a $40 reduction in the cost of coverage. Also, a discount of 5 to 15 percent is available in some states to those who complete a defensive driving course.

Good Student Discounts: Many insurance companies offer discounts of up to 25 percent on insurance to full-time high school or college students who are in the upper 20 percent of their class, on the dean's list, or have a B or better average.

Mature Driver Credit: Drivers ages 50 and older may qualify for up to a 10 percent discount or a lower price bracket.

Sole Female Driver: Some companies offer discounts of 10 percent for females, ages 30 to 64, who are the only driver in a household, citing favorable claims experience.

Car Pooling: Commuters sharing driving may qualify for discounts of 5 to 25 percent or a lower price bracket.

Anti-Theft Device Credits: Discounts of 5 to 15 percent are offered in some states for cars equipped with a hood lock and an alarm or a disabling device (active or passive) that prevents the car from being started.

First Accident Allowance: Some insurers offer a "first accident allowance," which guarantees that if a customer achieves five accident-free years, his or her rates won't go up after the first at-fault accident.

Deductibles: Opting for the largest reasonable deductible is the obvious first step in reducing premiums. Increasing your deductible to $500 from $200 could cut your collision premium about 20 percent. Raising the deductible to $1,000 from $200 could lower your premium about 45 percent. The discounts may vary by company.

Collision Coverage: The older the car, the less the need for collision insurance. Consider dropping collision insurance entirely on an older car. Regardless of how much coverage you carry, the insurance company will only pay up to the car's "book value." For example, if your car requires $1,000 in repairs but its "book value" is only $500, the insurance company is required to pay only $500.

Tips for Dealing with a Mechanic

Call around. Don't choose a shop simply because it's nearby. Calling a few shops may turn up estimates cheaper by half.

Don't necessarily go for the lowest price. A good rule is to eliminate the highest and lowest estimates; the mechanic with the highest estimate is probably charging too much, and the lowest may be cutting too many corners.

Check the shop's reputation. Call your local consumer affairs agency and the Better Business Bureau. There aren't records on all shops, but unfavorable reports on a shop disqualify it.

Look for certification. Mechanics can be certified by the National Institute for Automotive Service Excellence, an industry-wide yardstick for competence. Certification is offered in eight areas of repair. However, make sure the mechanic working on your car is certified for the repair.

Take a look around. A well-kept shop reflects pride in workmanship. A skilled and efficient mechanic would probably not work in a messy shop.

Don't sign a blank check. The service order you sign should have specific instructions or describe your vehicle's symptoms. Avoid signing a vague work order. Be sure you are called for final approval before the shop does extra work.

Show interest. Ask about the repair but don't act like an expert if you don't really understand what's wrong. Express your satisfaction. If you're happy with the work, compliment the mechanic and ask for him or her the next time you come in. You will get to know each other, and the mechanic will get to know your vehicle.

Develop a "sider." If you know a mechanic, ask about work on the side, evenings or weekends. The labor will be cheaper.

Take a test drive. Before you pay for a major repair, you should take the car for a test drive. If you find that the problem still exists, there will be no question that the repair wasn't properly completed.

Repair Protection by Credit Card

Paying your auto repair bills by credit card can provide a much needed recourse if you are having problems with an auto mechanic. According to federal law, you have the right to withhold payment for sloppy or incorrect repairs. Of course, you may withhold no more than the amount of the repair in dispute.

In order to use this right, you must first try to work out the problem with the mechanic. Also, unless the credit card company owns the repair shop (this might be the case with gasoline credit cards used at gas stations), two other conditions must be met. First, the repair shop must be in your home state (or within 100 miles of your current address), and, second, the cost of repairs must be over $50. Until the problem is settled or resolved in court, the credit card company cannot charge you interest or penalties on the amount in dispute.

If you decide to take action, send a letter to the credit card company and a copy to the repair shop, explaining the details of the problem and what you want as settlement. Send the letter by certified mail with a return receipt requested.

Sometimes the credit card company or repair shop will attempt to put a "bad mark" on your credit record if you use this tactic. Legally, you can't be reported as delinquent if you've given the credit card company notice of your dispute, but a creditor can report that you are disputing your bill, which goes in your record. However, you have the right to challenge any incorrect information and add your side of the story to your file.

For more information, write to the Federal Trade Commission, Credit Practices Division, 601 Pennsylvania Avenue, NW, Washington, D.C. 20580, or visit their website at www.ftc.gov.

Secret Warranties

If dealers report a number of complaints about a certain part and the manufacturer determines that the problem is due to faulty design or assembly, the manufacturer may permit dealers to repair the problem at no charge to the customer even though the warranty has expired. In the past, this practice was often reserved for customers who made a big fuss. The availability of the free repair was never publicized, which is why we call these secret warranties.

Manufacturers deny the existence of secret warranties. They call these free repairs "policy adjustments" or "goodwill service." Whatever they are called, most consumers never hear about them.

Many secret warranties are disclosed in service bulletins that the manufacturers send to dealers. These bulletins outline free repair or reimbursement programs, as well as other problems and their possible causes and solutions.

Service bulletins from many manufacturers also may be on file at the National Highway Traffic Safety Administration. Visit www.nhtsa.dot.gov and look up your vehicle on NHTSA's technical bulletin search.

If you find that a secret warranty is in effect and repairs are being made at no charge after the warranty has expired, contact the Center for Auto Safety, 2001 S Street, NW, Washington, D.C. 20009. They will publish the information so others can benefit.

Disclosure Laws: Spurred by the proliferation of secret warranties and the failure of the FTC to take action, several states, including California, Connecticut, Virginia, and Wisconsin, have passed legislation that requires consumers to be notified of secret warranties on their cars.

Typically, the laws require the following: direct notice to consumers within a specified time after the adoption of a warranty adjustment policy; notice of the disclosure law to new car buyers; reimbursement, within a number of years after payment, to owners who paid for covered repairs before they learned of the extended warranty service; and dealers must inform consumers who complain about a covered defect that it is eligible for repair under warranty.

If you live in a state with a secret warranty law already in effect, write your state attorney general's office (in care of your state capital) for information. To encourage passage of such a bill, contact your state representative (in care of your state capital).

Center for Auto Safety

For over 25 years, the nonprofit Center for Auto Safety (CAS) has told the consumer's story to government agencies, to Congress, and to the courts. Its efforts focus on all consumers rather than only those with individual complaints.

CAS was established in 1970 by Ralph Nader and Consumers Union. As consumer concerns about auto safety issues expanded, so did the work of CAS. It became an independent group in 1972, and the original staff of two has grown to fourteen attorneys and researchers. CAS's activities include:

Representing the Consumer in Washington: CAS follows the activities of federal agencies and Congress to ensure that they carry out their responsibilities to the American taxpayer. CAS brings a consumer's point of view to vehicle safety policies and rule-making. Since 1970, CAS has submitted more than 500 petitions and comments on federal safety standards.

Help CAS Help You: CAS depends on public support. Annual consumer membership is $30 with *The Lemon Book*. All contributions to this nonprofit organization are tax-deductible. Annual membership includes a quarterly newsletter called "Lemon Times." To join, send a check to: Center for Auto Safety, 1825 Connecticut Ave., NW, Suite #330, Washington, D.C. 20009–5708, www.autosafety.org.

Part Four: How They Rate

Best Bets by Price/48   Quick Cross Reference
Cars to Stay Away From/50   Guide/53
Ratings Explanation/51   The Ratings/54

With the huge number of used cars available, your chances of getting a good one are actually better than you may expect. To get you started in the right direction, on the following pages are some cars that we consider to be Best Bets. In developing this list, we sifted through a decade's worth of complaint statistics and safety defect information, as well as crash test results, insurance rates, theft ratings, repair costs, and safety features—all the information you need to make a smart choice. We've called the cars with the best overall ratings Best Bets and, on the next two pages, we've sorted them two ways: by size class and by price. Remember, there is no guarantee that every model of each car on the following lists will be a cream puff, so the mechanic's inspection is crucial before you buy. Nevertheless, if you find one of our Best Bets in good condition—go for it!

Registering Your Complaints: If you have a particular problem with your car, consider filing a complaint with the National Highway Traffic Safety Administration. Call the toll-free Auto Safety Hotline at 800-424-9393 (in Washington, DC, 202-366-0123), and ask for the Vehicle Owners Questionnaire.

Taking the time to complain will do two things—first, it will give the goverment an indication of which cars are causing consumers the most problems. Second, you will be adding your experience to the information we use to prepare the Complaint Index.

Best Bets by Price

<$3,000

Year	Model	Class
1993	Olds Cutlass Cierra	Intermediate

$4-$6,000

Year	Model	Class
1994	Mercury Cougar	Large
1995	Olds Cutlass Cierra	Intermediate

$5-$7,000

Year	Model	Class
1994	Buick LeSabre	Large
1996	Saturn SC/SL/SW	Large

$6-$8,000

Year	Model	Class
1996	Chev. Lumina, Monte Carlo	Large
1996	Chev. Lumina, Olds Silhouette, Pontiac Trans Sport	Minivan
1996	Chrys. Concorde/Dodge Intrepid, Eagle Vision	Intermediate
1994	Oldsmobile 88	Large
1996	Olds Cutlass Cierra	Intermediate
1997	Saturn SC/SL/SW	Large

$7-$9,000

Year	Model	Class
1996	Buick Century	Intermediate
1996	Buick LeSabre	Large
1997	Chev. Lumina, Monte Carlo	Large
1997	Chrys. Concorde/Dodge Intrepid, Eagle Vision	Intermediate
1995	Chrysler New Yorker/LHS	Large
1997	Mercury Sable	Intermediate
1998	Saturn SC/SL/SW	Large

$8-$10,000

Year	Model	Class
1997	Buick Century	Intermediate
1998	Chev. Lumina, Monte Carlo	Large
1996	Chrysler New Yorker/LHS	Large
1999	Ford Contour/Merc. Mystique	Compact
1996	Ford F-Series	Truck
1998	Mazda Truck (B-Series)	Compact Truck
1999	Saturn SC/SL/SW	Large

$9-$11,000

Year	Model	Class
1998	Buick Century	Intermediate
2000	Ford Escort	Subcompact
2000	Saturn SC/SL/SW	Large

$10-$12,000

Year	Model	Class
1999	Buick Century	Intermediate
1999	Chev. Lumina, Monte Carlo	Large
2000	Ford Contour/Merc. Mystique	Compact
2001	Ford Escort	Subcompact
1999	Ford Taurus	Intermediate

$10-$12,000 (cont.)

Year	Model	Class
2002	Hyundai Accent	Subcompact
1999	Mercury Sable	Intermediate
1999	Nissan Frontier	Compact Truck
1999	Oldsmobile 88	Large
2001	Saturn SC/SL/SW	Large

$11-$13,000

Year	Model	Class
1998	Buick LeSabre	Large
1999	Buick Regal	Intermediate
1999	Chevrolet Astro/GMC Safari	Minivan
1999	Chrys. Concorde/Dodge Intrepid, Eagle Vision	Intermediate
1998	Ford Cr. Vic., Merc. Gr. Marquis	Large
2000	Ford Taurus	Intermediate
2001	Hyundai Elantra	Compact

$12-$14,000

Year	Model	Class
1999	Buick LeSabre	Large
2000	Buick Regal	Intermediate
2000	Chevrolet Astro/GMC Safari	Minivan
2000	Oldsmobile Cutlass Cierra	Intermediate
1999	Pontiac Grand Prix	Intermediate
2002	Saturn SC/SL/SW	Large

$13-$15,000

Year	Model	Class
1996	Audi S6	Large
2001	Buick Century	Intermediate
1999	Chev. Caprice, Chev. Impala	Intermediate
2001	Chevrolet Lumina, Monte Carlo	Large
1999	Ford Cr. Vic., Merc. Gr. Marquis	Large
2001	Ford Taurus	Intermediate
1998	Honda Accord	Intermediate
2000	Mazda 626	Compact
2002	Nissan Sentra	Subcompact

$14-$16,000

Year	Model	Class
2000	Buick LeSabre	Large
2001	Buick Regal	Intermediate
2001	Chevrolet Astro/GMC Safari	Minivan
1998	Chrysler New Yorker/LHS	Large
2001	Nissan Frontier	Compact Truck
2000	Pontiac Grand Prix	Intermediate

$15-$17,000

Year	Model	Class
2000	Ford Cr. Vic., Merc. Gr. Marquis	Large
2001	Ford F-Series	Truck
2002	Geo/Chevrolet Prizm	Compact
1999	Honda Accord	Intermediate
2001	Mazda 626	Compact
2001	Pontiac Grand Prix	Intermediate

Best Bets by Price

$16-$18,000

1999	Buick Park Avenue, Cadillac Seville	Large
2001	Chev. Caprice, Chev. Impala	Intermediate
1999	Chrysler Town and Country	Minivan
2000	Dodge Caravan	Minivan
2001	Ford Mustang	Intermediate
2000	Honda Accord	Intermediate
2001	Honda Passport	Sport Utility
2001	Toyota Camry	Intermediate
2001	Volkswagen New Beetle	Subcompact

$17-$19,000

2001	Buick LeSabre	Large
2000	Chevrolet Lumina, Olds Silhouette, Pontiac Trans Sport	Minivan
2001	Ford Cr. Vic., Merc. Gr. Marquis	Large
2000	Ford Windstar	Minivan
2000	Mercury Villager/Nissan Quest	Minivan
2002	Volkswagen New Beetle	Subcompact

$18-$20,000

2001	Ford Windstar	Minivan
2001	Honda Accord	Intermediate
1998	Lincoln Mark VIII	Large
2002	Pontiac Grand Am	Compact
1999	Toyota Avalon	Intermediate

$19-$21,000

2000	Buick Park Ave., Cadillac Seville	Large
2000	Chrysler New Yorker/LHS	Large
2001	Dodge Caravan	Minivan
2002	Ford F-Series	Truck
2002	Ford Taurus	Intermediate
2002	Honda Accord	Intermediate
2001	Mercury Villager/Nissan Quest	Minivan
2001	Subaru Legacy	Compact
2001	Toyota Celica	Compact

$20-$22,000

2000	Audi A4	Intermediate
2000	Chrysler Town and Country	Minivan
2002	Mazda 626	Compact

$21-$23,000

2001	Audi A4	Intermediate
2002	Chev. Caprice, Chev. Impala	Intermediate
2002	Chevrolet Lumina, Monte Carlo	Large
2002	Chrys. Concorde/Dodge Intrepid, Eagle Vision	Intermediate
2002	Ford Windstar	Minivan
2001	Jeep Grand Cherokee	Sport Utility

$22-$24,000

2002	Buick Century	Intermediate
2001	Buick Park Ave., Cadillac Seville	Large
2002	Chevrolet Astro/GMC Safari	Minivan
1998	Lexus ES300	Large
2002	Mercury Villager/Nissan Quest	Minivan
2000	Toyota Avalon	Intermediate

$23-$25,000

2001	Chrysler Town and Country	Minivan
2001	Honda Odyssey	Minivan
2000	Lincoln Town Car	Large
2001	Toyota Sienna	Minivan

$24-$26,000

2002	Ford Cr. Vic., Merc. Gr. Marquis	Large
1999	Lexus ES300	Large
2002	Pontiac Grand Prix	Intermediate

$25-$27,000

2002	Buick Regal	Intermediate
2002	Chrysler Town and Country	Minivan
2002	Honda Odyssey	Minivan
2001	Toyota Avalon	Intermediate
2002	Toyota Sienna	Minivan

$26-$28,000

2001	Acura TL	Large
2001	Lincoln Town Car	Large
2002	Toyota Avalon	Intermediate

$28-$30,000

2000	Lexus ES300	Large
2002	Nissan Pathfinder	Sport Utility
2002	Volvo S80	Intermediate

>30,000

2000	Acura RL	Large
2001	Acura RL	Large
2002	Acura RL	Large
2001	Acura TL	Large
2002	Acura TL	Large
2002	Buick Park Ave., Cadillac Seville	Large
2002	Infiniti QX4	Sport Utility
2001	Lexus ES300	Large
2000	Lincoln Navigator	Sport Utility
2001	Lincoln Navigator	Sport Utility
2002	Lincoln Town Car	Large
2000	Merc.-Bz M-Class	Sport Utility
2001	Merc.-Bz M-Class	Sport Utility
2002	Oldsmobile Aurora	Large

CARS TO STAY AWAY FROM

The following is a list of cars that you may simply want to stay away from. These cars all received a "Very Poor" comparative rating, which is based on many factors, including crash tests, complaints, and repair costs. It is possible you owned one of these cars and had good luck with it. However, in general, we suggest you stay away from buying them because of their "Very Poor" overall rating. Also, avoid used cars with door-mounted belts. If the door pops open in a crash, you lose the protection of the belt.

1994 Acura Vigor
1996 Acura TL
1993-94 BMW 3-Series
1993-1995 Chev. S-
    Series/GMC Sonoma
1993 Chevrolet S10 Blazer,
    Jimmy/Olds Bravada
1994-1996 Chev. Blazer,
    Jimmy/Olds Bravada
1996 Chrysler Sebring, Dodge
    Avenger
1993-97 Dodge Ram Pickup
1993, 1995-96, 1998 Eagle
    Talon, Mitsubishi Eclipse
1999 Ford Explorer
1993 Ford Festiva
1996 Ford Mustang
1993 Ford Probe
1993-94 Geo Metro/Chevrolet
    Metro
1993-1996 Geo Tracker/Chev.
    Tracker
1993-1995 Hyundai Elantra
1998-99 Honda Passport

1993 Hyundai Sonata
1994, 1998-99 Isuzu Amigo
1994-95, 1998-99 Isuzu Rodeo
1993 Isuzu Trooper
1993-94 Jeep Cherokee
1993-94 Jeep Grand Cherokee
1993-94, 1997 Jeep Wranger
1994-95, 1997 Kia Sephia
1995-97, 1999-2002 Land
    Rover Disc., Discovery II
1996 Mazda 626
1994 Mazda MPV
1993-94 Mitsubishi Diamante
1994-95 Mitsubishi Galant
1993-2000 Mitsubishi Montero
1993-96 Nissan Pathfinder
1994-95 Saab 900
1997 Suzuki Grand Vitara
1993-95 Toyota 4Runner
1996 Toyota Tacoma
1994, 1997 Toyota Tercel
1993-96 Volkswagen Golf/Jetta
1993-1996 Volkswagen Passat

Ratings Explanation

The following tables rate hundreds of the most popular used cars. Each table contains information in a number of different categories. Blank spots in the tables mean that information is not available. Here's what you'll find on the tables:

Size Class: The tables begin by giving the car's type: Subcompact, Compact, Intermediate, Large, Minivan, or Sport Utility.

Drive: This category shows whether the car is front-, rear-, or four-wheel drive.

Crash Test: This indicates how well the car performed in the U.S. government's 35-mph frontal crash test program. We have applied the results to those cars that were substantially unchanged from the model that was crash tested.

Airbags: Here we tell you which occupants benefit from this life-saving device and who is left unprotected.

ABS: This safety feature comes in two-wheel and four-wheel versions. Two-wheel ABS is of little value.

Parts Cost: Very High, High, Average, Low, and Very Low ratings are based on nine typical repairs. We compare these costs with all other cars to determine the rating.

Complaints: These ratings are based on the number of complaints on file at the U.S. Department of Transportation. We developed the complaint index to give you a general idea of the experiences other owners have had with their cars.

Insurance: Insurance companies often use rating programs to determine whether or not a car should get a discount or a surcharge on its insurance prices. The ratings are partly based on each car's accident history. If the car is likely to receive neither a discount or surcharge, it is labeled as Regular.

Fuel Economy: This is the EPA-rated fuel economy, in mpg, for city driving. We include the rating we believe represents the most popular engine/transmission combination for that model.

Theft Rating: This rating indicates if the car has a good or bad history of being stolen or broken into, according to statistics compiled by the Highway Loss Data Institute. While based on data collected during the three-year period following each model year, incidence of theft for these cars might vary slightly today.

Bumpers: Manufacturers no longer have to meet a rigid 5 mph crash test standard. Based on tests by the Insurance Institute for Highway Safety, we have categorized the bumpers as Strong, Fair, or Weak. A blank means that no data is available.

Recalls: These numbers indicate how many times each model was recalled for a safety problem. We have only included recalls in which the total number of cars recalled exceeded 500.

Turning Circle: The smaller a car's turning circle, the easier it will be for you to maneuver in and out of tight spaces. Different suspensions or braking systems found on varying models may cause the turning circle to vary.

Weight: This number gives you the weight of the automobile as it is measured by the manufacturer. Different transmissions, options, or trim levels may cause the weight to change.

Wheelbase: This measurement indicates the length from the center of the front wheel to the center of the rear wheel. The wheelbase usually changes when a truly new model is introduced.

Price ($): This column gives you a general idea of cost. This is to help you narrow down your choices within a price category, rather than serve as a predictor of what you should pay for the car. The actual value of the car is based on where you live, the condition of the car, and other unpredictable marketplace conditions.

Overall Rating: This column provides an overall evaluation of each model based on data we've collected since 1980. Each model year is rated Very Poor, Poor, Average, Good, Very Good, or Best Bet, based on crash tests, complaint histories, insurance premiums, theft ratings, repair costs, and safety features. Please note that model years without a crash test have no overall rating.

Note: If the car you are interested in does not appear on these tables, either it is available only in relatively small numbers or we did not have enough useful data to include it.

Note: You will note that there may be several footnotes per vehicle. We have tried to make these footnotes as consistent and concise as possible. Footnotes are placed on the bottom of the left-hand page and continue onto the right-hand page if necessary.

QUICK CROSS REFERENCE GUIDE

We have combined the ratings of nearly identical cars that are sold under different names. To find information on the first car, look up the car written in italics.

Acura RL/*Acura Legend*
Acura TL/*Acura Vigor*
Audi A4/*Audi 80/90*
Audi A6/*Audi 100*
Audi S6/*Audi 100*
Cadillac Seville/*Buick Park Avenue*
Cadillac Seville/*Cadillac Eldorado*
Chevrolet Blazer/*Chevrolet S10 Blazer*
Chevrolet Corsica/*Chevrolet Beretta*
Chevrolet Impala/*Chevrolet Caprice*
Chevrolet Metro/*Geo Metro*
Chev. Monte Carlo/*Chevrolet Lumina*
Chevrolet Prizm/*Geo Prizm*
Chevrolet Tracker/*Geo Tracker*
Chev. Venture/*Chev. Lumina Minivan*
Chrysler LHS/*Chrysler New Yorker*
Chrysler Voyager/*Dodge Caravan*
Dodge Avenger/*Chrysler Sebring*
Dodge Dynasty/*Chrysler New Yorker*
Dodge Intrepid/*Chrysler Concorde*
Dodge Stratus/*Chrysler Cirrus*
Eagle Vision/*Chrysler Concorde*
Ford Aspire/*Ford Festiva*
Ford Expedition/*Ford Bronco*
GMC Jimmy/*Chevrolet S10 Blazer*
GMC Safari/*Chevrolet Astro*
GMC Sierra/*Chevrolet Silverado*
GMC Sonoma/*Chevrolet S-Series*
GMC Suburban/*Chevrolet Suburban*
Infiniti I35/*Infiniti I30*
Isuzu Oasis/*Honda Odyssey*
Land Rover Disc. Series II/*Land Rover Discovery Series*

Lexus LS430/*Lexus LS400*
Lexus SC400/*Lexus SC300*
Lexus SC430/*Lexus SC300*
Mazda B-Series/*Mazda Truck*
Mazda Protégé/*Mazda 323*
Merc. Gr. Marquis/*Ford Crown Victoria*
Mercury Mystique/*Ford Contour*
Mitsubishi Eclipse/*Eagle Talon*
Nissan Quest/*Mercury Villager*
Olds Bravada/*Chevrolet S10 Blazer*
Olds Cutlass/*Olds Cutlass Ciera*
Olds Silhouette/*Chev. Lumina Minivan*
Plymouth Breeze/*Chrysler Cirrus*
Plymouth Laser/*Eagle Talon*
Plymouth Neon/*Dodge Neon*
Plymouth Voyager/*Dodge Caravan*
Pontiac Montana/*Chev. Lumina*
Pontiac Sunfire/*Pontiac Sunbird*
Pontiac Trans Sport/*Chevrolet Lumina*
Saab 9-3/*Saab 900*
Saab 9-5/*Saab 9000*
Saturn SL/*Saturn SC*
Saturn SW/*Saturn SC*
Suzuki Sidekick/*Geo Tracker*
Suzuki Swift/*Geo Metro*
Volkswagen Jetta/*Volkswagen Golf*
Volvo C70/*Volvo 850*
Volvo S70/*Volvo 850*
Volvo C70/*Volvo 850*
Volvo S80/*Volvo 900 Series*
Volvo S90/*Volvo 900 Series*
Volvo V90/*Volvo 900 Series*

Acura CL 1997-2002

The Acura CL offers as standard a more powerful 3.2-liter V6 as the base engine in 2001. A 2.3-liter 4-cylinder engine with the option of a more powerful 3.0-liter V6 was the standard in

1997 Acura CL

past years. The upgraded engine will cause a slight hit in fuel economy, though. Standard safety features include dual airbags, 4-wheel ABS, rear headrests, front side window defoggers, keyless entry, and an anti-theft alarm. If that's not enough, the S version bumps

	1993	1994	1995	1996	1997
Size Class					Large
Drive					Front
Crash Test					N/A
Airbags					Dual
ABS					4-Whl
Parts Cost					Average
Complaints					Average
Insurance					Discount
Fuel Econ.					20
Theft Rating					High
Bumpers					
Recalls					0
Trn. Cir. (ft.)					39
Weight (lbs.)					3004
Whlbase (in.)					106.9
Price					$12-14,000
OVERALL▪					

NO MODEL PRODUCED

▪Cars without crash tests do not receive an overall rating. **Estimate

2002 Acura CL

you up to 260 hp. The options include perforated leather seating, an in-dash navigation system and heated seats. The navigation system comes with a DVD database that covers the entire U.S.

	1998	1999	2000	2001	2002
Size Class	Large	Large	Large	Large	Large
Drive	Front	Front	Front	Front	Front
Crash Test	N/A	N/A	N/A	N/A	N/A
Airbags	Dual	Dual	Dual	Dual/Side	Dl./Sd.(F)
ABS	4-Whl	4-Whl	4-Whl	4-Whl	4-Whl
Parts Cost	Average	Average	Average	Average	Average
Complaints	Good	Very Good	Very Good	Very Good	Average
Insurance	Discount	Discount	Discount	Regular	Regular
Fuel Econ.	20	24	24	19	23
Theft Rating	Average	Average	Average**	Average**	High**
Bumpers		Strong	Strong	Strong	Strong
Recalls	0	0	0	0	0
Trn. Cir. (ft.)	39	39.04	39.04	37.4	37.4
Weight (lbs.)	3004	1365	1365	3470	3470
Whlbase (in.)	106.9	106.9	106.9	106.9	106.9
Price	$14-16,000	$17-19,000	$19-21,000	$20-23,000	$29-31,000
OVERALL■					

Acura Integra 1993-2001

The most affordable of Acura's models, the Integra emphasizes sportiness over luxury. Acura gave it a thorough makeover for 1994 and 1998 models have new front- and rear-

1993 Acura Integra

end styling plus new wheels. The Integra shares its chassis and some other components with the Honda Civic, which was redesigned for 1996. Watch out for 1993 Integras, which are equipped with unsafe, motorized shoulder belts with separate lap belts. Dual airbags became standard with the 1994 redesign, while

	1993	1994	1995	1996	1997
Size Class	Compact	Compact	Compact	Compact	Compact
Drive	Front	Front	Front	Front	Front
Crash Test	N/A	Average	Average	Average	Average
Airbags	None	Dual	Dual	Dual	Dual
ABS	4-Whl*	4-Whl*	4-Whl*	4-Whl*	4-Whl*
Parts Cost	Average	Average	High	High	Very High
Complaints	Good	Average	Good	Very Good	Very Good
Insurance	Surcharge	Surcharge	Surcharge	Surcharge	Surcharge
Fuel Econ.	23	25	25	24	25
Theft Rating	Very High	Very High	Very High	Very High	Very High
Bumpers					
Recalls	0	0	1	0	0
Trn. Cir. (ft.)	33.3	34.8	34.8	34.8	34.8
Weight (lbs.)	2608	2703	2703	2703	2703
Whlbase (in.)	102.4[1]	103.1[1]	103.1[1]	103.1[1]	103.1[1]
Price	$4-6,000	$6-8,000	$8-10,000	$10-12,000	$11-13,000
OVERALL■		Poor	Poor	Average	Average

■Cars without crash tests do not receive an overall rating. [1]Data given for sedan. Wheelbase for coupe for 1993 is 100.4; 1994-2001 is 101.2.
*Optional **Estimate

1999 Acura Integra

ABS comes standard on the 1993 GS and on later LS and GS-R models. The Integra's engines have twin overhead camshafts for maximum performance. Power ranges from 115 hp on early models up to 170 hp on the GS-R's 1.8-liter VTEC engine. Handling ranks equally well among the best small cars, and the ride is firm but certainly tolerable. Front seats, driver's controls, and instruments are fine, but the rear seat is cramped.

	1998	1999	2000	2001	2002
Size Class	Compact	Compact	Compact	Compact	
Drive	Front	Front	Front	Front	
Crash Test	Average	Average	Average	Average	
Airbags	Dual	Dual	Dual	Dual	
ABS	4-Whl*	4-Whl	4-Whl	4-Whl	
Parts Cost	High	High	High	High	
Complaints	Very Good	Very Good	Very Good	Very Good	
Insurance	Surcharge	Surcharge	Surcharge	Surcharge	
Fuel Econ.	25	25	25	25	
Theft Rating	Very High	Very High	Very High	Very High**	
Bumpers		Strong	Strong	Strong	
Recalls	0	0	0	0	
Trn. Cir. (ft.)	34.8	34.8	34.8	34.8	
Weight (lbs.)	2703	2703	2703	2639	
Whlbase (in.)	103.1[1]	103.1[1]	103.1[1]	103.1[1]	
Price	$13-15,000	$15-17,000	$16-18,000	$18-20,000	
OVERALL■	Average	Average	Average	Average	

NO MODEL PRODUCED

Acura Legend 1993-95, RL 1997-2002

The Legend, Acura's luxury flagship, was discontinued in 1996 and replaced by the RL. A larger version of the Legend, the RL has improved upon its predecessor's ride and

1993 Acura Legend

overall comfort. Dual airbags are standard on all models and front side airbags are standard in 1999 and newer models. Standard ABS is also available for every model.

The Legend's V6 grew from 2.5 liters to 3.2 liters by 1994 but

	1993	1994	1995	1996	1997
Size Class	Intermd.	Intermd.	Intermd.		Large
Drive	Front	Front	Front		Front
Crash Test	Average	Average	Average		Good
Airbags	Dual	Dual	Dual		Dual
ABS	4-Whl	4-Whl	4-Whl		4-Whl
Parts Cost	Very High	Very High	Very High		High
Complaints	Good	Very Good	Very Good		Very Good
Insurance	Discount	Discount	Discount		Regular
Fuel Econ.	19	19	18		19
Theft Rating	Very High	Very High	Very High		Very High
Bumpers					
Recalls	0	0	0		1
Trn. Cir. (ft.)	34.8	34.8	34.8		36.1
Weight (lbs.)	3483	3583	3582		3660
Whlbase (in.)	114.6[1]	114.6[1]	114.6[1]		114.6
Price	$9-13,000	$11-13,000	$13-15,000		$17-19,000
OVERALL■	Good	Good	Good		Good

(1996 column: NO MODEL PRODUCED)

■Cars without crash tests do not receive an overall rating. [1]Data given for sedan. Wheelbase for coupe for 1993-95 is 111.4. **Estimate

2002 Acura RL

has since become a 3.5-liter V6; its power is ample. The manual transmission shifts gracefully, while the automatic is rough. Front seats are comfortable, and there's enough room in back for two to travel serenely. Instrument panel and controls are first rate.

	1998	1999	2000	2001	2002
Size Class	Large	Large	Large	Large	Large
Drive	Front	Front	Front	Front	Front
Crash Test	Good	Good	Good	Good	Good
Airbags	Dual	Dual/Side	Dual/Side	Dual/Side	Dl./Sd.(F)
ABS	4-Whl	4-Whl	4-Whl	4-Whl	4-Whl
Parts Cost	Very High	Very High	Very High	Very Low	Very High
Complaints	Very Good	Very Good	Very Good	Very Good	Very Good
Insurance	Regular	Regular	Discount	Discount	Discount
Fuel Econ.	19	18	18	18	20
Theft Rating	Very High	Very High**	Very High**	Very High**	Average**
Bumpers		Strong	Strong	Strong	Strong
Recalls	1	0	0	0	0
Trn. Cir. (ft.)	36.1	36.1	36.1	36.1	36.1
Weight (lbs.)	3660	3840	3840	3840	3898
Whlbase (in.)	114.6	114.6	114.6	114.6	114.6
Price	$22-23,000	$28-30,000	$31-34,000	$34-36,000	$43-$45,000
OVERALL■	Good	Very Good	BEST BET	BEST BET	BEST BET

Acura Vigor 1993-94, TL 1996-2002

The Vigor and the TL are, in many ways, the ultimate Honda Accord, spiced up with impressive but seldom-used extras. On the TL and the Vigor LS, you'll find leather seats and a wood trimmed dash;

1993 Acura Vigor

if you don't mind cloth seats, you can save by getting a base TL or a Vigor GS. All Vigors have a driver's airbag and ABS; the 1994 Vigor comes with standard dual airbags. All TLs come standard with dual airbags and 4-wheel ABS. For 2000, side airbags were added. Vigors have a 2.5-liter engine with a nice 5-speed man-

	1993	1994	1995	1996	1997
Size Class	Intermd.	Intermd.		Large	Large
Drive	Front	Front		Front	Front
Crash Test	Poor	Poor		Good	Good
Airbags	Driver#	Dual		Dual	Dual
ABS	4-Whl	4-Whl	NO MODEL PRODUCED	4-Whl	4-Whl
Parts Cost	Very High	Very High		Very High	Very High
Complaints	Good	Very Poor		Good	Very Poor
Insurance	Regular	Regular		Discount	Regular
Fuel Econ.	20	20		20	20
Theft Rating	Very High	Very High		Very High	Very High
Bumpers					
Recalls	0	0		1	1
Trn. Cir. (ft.)	36.2	36.2		36.1	36.1
Weight (lbs.)	3142	3197		3252	3282
Whlbase (in.)	110.4	110.4		111.8	111.8
Price	$6-8,000	$8-10,000		$12-14,000	$15-17,000
OVERALL■	Poor	Very Poor		Good	Very Poor

■Cars without crash tests do not receive an overall rating. #Passenger side optional **Estimate

2002 Acura TL

ual or a crude shifting automatic overdrive. You have your choice of a 2.5-liter or a 3.2-liter engine on the TL. As with the Vigor, the TL's handling is quite good, but the ride is almost too firm. A shorter wheelbase model was introduced in 1999. Front seat riders have adequate comfort. Two will fit in the back, but three is a definite squeeze. The body doesn't filter out noise too well, which is surprising for such an expensive car. Good crash test results make the Acura TL a better choice than the Vigor.

	1998	1999	2000	2001	2002
Size Class	Large	Large	Large	Large	Large
Drive	Front	Front	Front	Front	Front
Crash Test	Good	Good	Good	Good	Good
Airbags	Dual	Dual	Dual/Side	Dual/Side	Dl./Sd.(F)
ABS	4-Whl	4-Whl	4-Whl	4-Whl	4-Whl
Parts Cost	Very High	High	High	Average	Average
Complaints	Very Good	Good	Good	Very Good	Very Good
Insurance	Regular	Regular	Regular	Discount	Discount
Fuel Econ.	20	19	19	19	23
Theft Rating	Very High	Low	Low	Low**	Low**
Bumpers		Strong	Strong	Strong	Strong
Recalls	1	0	2	1	2
Trn. Cir. (ft.)	36.8	36.8	36.8	36.8	36.8
Weight (lbs.)	3446	3446	3446	3446	3494
Whlbase (in.)	108.1	108.1	108.1	108.1	108.1
Price	$17-19,000	$22-24,000	$24-26,000	$26-28,000	$31-33,000
OVERALL■	Good	Good	Good	BEST BET	BEST BET

Audi 100 1993-94, A6 1995-2002, S6 1995-1998

With a redesign of the 100 in 1995, Audi switched to an alphanumeric naming system, and the A6/S6 was born. This replacement for the 100 offers sleeker lines and a

1993 Audi 100

plusher interior. Other models are variations on the 100—the 200 has a turbocharged engine and plusher trim; the Quattro has full-time 4-wheel drive; the S6 has sport suspension, turbocharger, and four-wheel drive; and wagon versions are available. In 1993, Dual

	1993	1994	1995	1996	1997
Size Class	Large	Large	Large	Large	Large
Drive	Front/All	Front/All	Front/All	Front/All	Front/All
Crash Test	N/A	N/A	Very Good	Very Good	Very Good
Airbags	Dual	Dual	Dual	Dual	Dual
ABS	4-Whl	4-Whl	4-Whl	4-Whl	4-Whl
Parts Cost	Average	Average	Very High	Very High	Very High
Complaints[1]	Very Poor	Poor	Poor	Very Good	Good
Insurance	Discount	Discount	Discount	Discount	Discount
Fuel Econ.	19	18	19	19	19
Theft Rating	Low	Low	Low	Very Low	Low
Bumpers					
Recalls	1	2	2	2	2
Trn. Cir. (ft.)	34.8	34.8	34.8	34.8	34.8
Weight (lbs.)	3329	3363	3363	3582	3428
Whlbase (in.)	105.8	105.8	105.8	105.8	105.8
Price	$7-9,000	$9-11,000	$11-13,000	$13-15,000	$16-18,000
OVERALL■			Good	**BEST BET**	Very Good

■Cars without crash tests do not receive an overall rating. [1]Data for A6. S6 received a Poor in '95, Very Good in '96 for Complaints. *Optional
**Estimate

2002 Audi A6

airbags became standard as well as 4-wheel ABS.

All models offer a V6 (except S6). Audi features the Quattro all-wheel drive system, which improves handling and wet weather traction. Inside, accommodations are fairly good for four. The controls on earlier models are inferior to many cheaper cars, but the gauges are fine. The S6 was phased out 1998 and the redesigned A6 has not been crash tested for the 1998-2002 model years.

	1998	1999	2000	2001	2002
Size Class	Large	Large	Large	Large	Large
Drive	Front/All	Front/All	Front/All	Front/All	Front/All
Crash Test	N/A	N/A	N/A	N/A	N/A
Airbags	Dual/Side	Dual/Side	Dual/Side	Dual/Side	Dl./Sd.*/Hd.
ABS	4-Whl	4-Whl	4-Whl	4-Whl	4-Whl
Parts Cost	Average	Very High	Very High	Very High	Very High
Complaints	Very Poor	Very Poor	Poor	Very Poor	Very Poor
Insurance	Discount	Discount	Discount	Discount	Discount
Fuel Econ.	17	17	17	17	21
Theft Rating	Low	Low**	Low**	Low**	Low**
Bumpers		Strong	Strong	Strong	Strong
Recalls	3	1	1	2	0
Trn. Cir. (ft.)	38.3	38.3	38.3	38.3	38.3
Weight (lbs.)	3473	3473	3473	3473	3759
Whlbase (in.)	108.7	108.7	108.7	108.7	108.7
Price	$21-23,000	$24-27,000	$27-29,000	$29-31,000	$36-38,000
OVERALL■					

Audi 80/90 1993-95, A4 1996-2002

Audi not only redesigned the 90 for 1996 but renamed it too. In 1998, Audi introduced a wagon version of the same: the Avant. The Audi A4 comes standard with more features than ever before and a slick new look. ABS remains standard on all models and a driver's side airbag is standard on the 1993 90. Dual airbags became standard on 1994 models and side airbags were added in 1998. For 2002, standard head airbags were intro-

1993 Audi 90

	1993	1994	1995	1996	1997
Size Class	Intermd.	Intermd.	Intermd.	Intermd.	Intermd.
Drive	Front/All	Front/All	Front/All	Front/All	Front/All
Crash Test	N/A	N/A	N/A	Very Good	Very Good
Airbags	Driver	Dual	Dual	Dual	Dual
ABS	4-Whl	4-Whl	4-Whl	4-Whl	4-Whl
Parts Cost	Very Low	Very Low	Very Low	Very Low	Very Low
Complaints	Very Poor	Very Poor	Very Poor	Very Poor	Poor
Insurance	Discount	Discount	Discount	Regular	Regular
Fuel Econ.	20	20	20	18	20
Theft Rating	Average	Average	Average	Average	Very Low
Bumpers					
Recalls	1	1	2	2	3
Trn. Cir. (ft.)	34	34.1	34.1	36.4	36.4
Weight (lbs.)	3186	3197	3197	2976	2877
Whlbase (in.)[1]	102.81	102.81	102.81	103.01	103.01
Price	$6-8,000	$8-10,000	$10-12,000	$13-15,000	$13-15,000
OVERALL■				Good	Very Good

■Cars without crash tests do not receive an overall rating.[1]Wheelbase for Quattro for 1993-95 is 102.2; 1996-97 is 102.6. *Optional **Estimate

2002 Audi A4

duced. The A4 comes standard with a 1.8-liter four-cylinder and has recently been classified as an Ultra Low Emission Vehicle. The Quattro all-wheel drive system improves handling and traction on slick roads, especially on this surprisingly light car. There is also a sport package for the A4, which lowers the car, tightens the suspension, and adds some sporty wheels.

	1998	1999	2000	2001	2002
Size Class	Intermd.	Intermd.	Intermd.	Intermd.	Intermd.
Drive	Front/All	Front/All	Front/All	Front/All	Front/All
Crash Test	Very Good	Very Good	Very Good	Very Good	N/A
Airbags	Dual/Side	Dual/Side	Dual/Side	Dual/Side	Dl./Sd.*/Hd.
ABS	4-Whl	4-Whl	4-Whl	4-Whl	4-Whl
Parts Cost	Low	Very Low	Very Low	Very Low	Very Low
Complaints	Very Poor	Very Poor	Average	Good	Average
Insurance	Regular	Regular	Regular	Regular	Regular
Fuel Econ.	23	23	23	23	23
Theft Rating	Low	Average	Very Low	Average**	Average**
Bumpers		Strong	Strong	Strong	Strong
Recalls	3	2	0	0	0
Trn. Cir. (ft.)	36.4	36.4	36.4	36.4	36.4
Weight (lbs.)	2877	2877	2877	2998	3362
Whlbase (in.)	103	103	102.6	103	104.3
Price	$16-18,000	$18-20,000	$20-22,000	$21-23,000	$27-29,000
OVERALL■	Good	Very Good	BEST BET	BEST BET	Average

Audi A8 1997-2002

Audi came out with a luxury flagship in 1997 bringing to the market a safe and reliable car. Despite the lightweight aluminum frame, the car performs well in crash tests.

1997 Audi A8

Dual airbags were standard in 1997 and 1998, but both side and head airbags have been added since. 4-wheel ABS is also standard on all models. You can choose between the 3.7-liter V8 engine, front-wheel drive, or the 4.2-liter V8 Quattro. The electronically

	1993	1994	1995	1996	1997
Size Class					Large
Drive					Front/All
Crash Test					Very Good
Airbags					Dual
ABS					4-Whl
Parts Cost					Very High
Complaints					Very Poor
Insurance					Regular
Fuel Econ.					20
Theft Rating					
Bumpers					Strong
Recalls					1
Trn. Cir. (ft.)					40.2
Weight (lbs.)					3682
Whlbase (in.)					113
Price					$22-24,000
OVERALL■					Poor

NO MODEL PRODUCED

■Cars without crash tests do not receive an overall rating.**Estimate

2002 Audi A8

controlled five-speed automatic with dynamic shift program (DSP) and hill detection capability provides for controlled driving, giving the manual feel without the clutch.

The L version has more legroom than the cramped S series. The luxury version from Audi is the company's best hope for competing with the big luxury sedans of Mercedes, BMW, and Lexus.

	1998	1999	2000	2001	2002
Size Class	Large	Large	Large	Large	Large
Drive	Front/All	Front/All	Front/All	Front/All	Front/All
Crash Test	Very Good	Very Good	Very Good	Very Good	Very Good
Airbags	Dual	Dual/Side	Dual/Side	Dual/Side	Dual/Side/Head
ABS	4-Whl	4-Whl	4-Whl	4-Whl	4-Whl
Parts Cost	Very High	Very High	Very High	Very High**	Very High**
Complaints	Average	Very Good	Very Good	Very Good	Poor
Insurance	Regular	Regular	Regular	Regular	Discount
Fuel Econ.	20	20	19	20	20
Theft Rating					
Bumpers	Strong	Strong	Strong	Strong	Strong
Recalls	1	1	1	2	1
Trn. Cir. (ft.)	40.2	40.2	40.2	40.2	40.2
Weight (lbs.)	3682	3682	4068	4068	4068
Whlbase (in.)	113	113	113.4	113.4	113.4
Price	$27-29,000	$30-32,000	$46-48,000	$55-57,000	$62-67,000
OVERALL■	Good	Very Good	Very Good	Very Good	Very Good

BMW 3-Series 1993-2002

For years, the 3-Series has been the cheapest BMW sold in the U.S., and with 8 variations of sedan, coupe and convertible there's a lot to choose from. The 1994 325i convertibles

1993 BMW 3-Series

received new, rounded styling. For 1996, BMW created an inexpensive (low $20,000s) hatchback version that revived the "ti" name from the '70s and should broaden the 3-Series appeal. Starting in 1994, all models have 4-wheel standard ABC, and standard dual airbags, whereas the '93 only had driver airbags.

	1993	1994	1995	1996	1997
Size Class	Compact	Compact	Compact	Compact	Compact
Drive	Rear	Rear	Rear	Rear	Rear
Crash Test	Good	Good	Good	Good	Good
Airbags	Driver	Dual	Dual	Dual	Dual
ABS	4-Whl	4-Whl	4-Whl	4-Whl	4-Whl
Parts Cost	Very High	Very High	High	High	Very High
Complaints	Very Poor	Poor	Average	Good	Good
Insurance	Surcharge	Surcharge	Surcharge	Surcharge	Surcharge
Fuel Econ.	20	26	22	20	23
Theft Rating	Very High	Very High	Very High	Very High	Very High
Bumpers					
Recalls	4	3	3	1	1
Trn. Cir. (ft.)	34.1	34.1	34.1	34.1	34.1
Weight (lbs.)	2860	2866	2866	3086	3086
Whlbase (in.)	106.3	106.3	106.3	106.3	106.3
Price^	$10-12,000	$11-13,000	$12-14,000	$13-15,000	$15-17,000
OVERALL*	Very Poor	Very Poor	Poor	Poor	Poor

*Cars without crash tests do not receive an overall rating. ^Prices based on the sedan 325i for 2001, 323i 4dr for 1995-2000. *Optional
**Estimate

2002 BMW 3-Series

The 318 has a 1.8-liter 4-cylinder engine through 1995; 1996 and later models have a 1.9-liter engine. All-new in 1999, the 318 disappeared after 1999 and the base model is now the much faster 325, which has a 2.5-liter 6-cylinder, and the 328 has a 2.8-liter 6-cylinder. Either engine can be teamed with a 5-speed manual or automatic overdrive. Look for winter weather packages with limited slip differentials and traction control. The controls and gauges are outstanding.

	1998	1999	2000	2001	2002
Size Class	Compact	Compact	Compact	Compact	Compact
Drive	Rear	Rear	Rear	Rear	Rear
Crash Test	Good	N/A	N/A	N/A	N/A
Airbags	Dual/Side*	Dual/Side*	Dual/Side*	Dual/Side*	Dl./Sd./Hd.
ABS	4-Whl	4-Whl	4-Whl	4-Whl	4-Whl
Parts Cost	High	High	High	High	High
Complaints	Average	Good	Good	Poor	Very Good
Insurance	Surcharge	Surcharge	Surcharge	Regular	Regular
Fuel Econ.	23	20	23	21	22
Theft Rating	Very High	High	High	High**	High**
Bumpers		Strong	Weak		
Recalls	0	0	0	2	2
Trn. Cir. (ft.)	34.1	34.4	34.4	34.4	34.4
Weight (lbs.)	3075	3250	3250	3250	3241
Whlbase (in.)	106.3	107.3	107.3	107.3	107.3
Price	$19-21,000	$23-25,000	$26-28,000	$28-30,000	$30-32,000
OVERALL■	Average				

BMW 5-Series 1993-95, 1997-2002

The BMW 5-Series took a break from the long running 89-95 series and came back in 1997 with a more powerful engine, upscale design, and is loaded with safety. Passenger side airbags became standard in '94. In 1995 it came standard with 6 airbags, 2 optional. In '97 the side-impact airbags became standard and rear-seat side-impact airbags are optional. In 2000, the airbags came with a "brain," deploying softer or harder depending on impact. Four-wheel drive ABS and traction control are standard.

1997 BMW 5-Series

	1993	1994	1995	1996	1997
Size Class	Intermd.	Intermd.	Intermd.		Large
Drive	Rear	Rear	Rear		Rear
Crash Test	N/A	N/A	N/A		N/A
Airbags	Dual	Dual	Dual		Dual/Side
ABS	4-Whl	4-Whl	4-Whl		4-Whl
Parts Cost	High	High	High		High
Complaints	Average	Poor	Average		Average
Insurance	Regular	Regular	Regular		Regular
Fuel Econ.	18	20	20		21
Theft Rating	Very High	Very High	Very High		Very High
Bumpers	Weak	Weak	Weak		Weak
Recalls	4	5	3		0
Trn. Cir. (ft.)	36.1	36.1	36.1		37.1
Weight (lbs.)	3560	3560	3560		3505
Whlbase (in.)	108.7	108.7	108.7		111.4
Price	$10-12,000	$13-15,000	$16-17,000		$23-25,000
OVERALL■					

(Column 1996: NO MODEL PRODUCED)

■Cars without crash tests do not receive an overall rating. **Estimate

70

2002 BMW 5-Series

In '93 it had an in-line 6-cylinder, with 189 hp. The newer models have better engines; the '97 models came standard with a 2.8, 24-valve inline 6-cylinder on the 528i, and a 4.4-liter DOHC 32-valve V8 for the upscale versions, available in 6-speed manual or 5-speed automatic. The 5-Series comes as a sedan, wagon or sport wagon (added in '99) in the later years. The 5-Series is fun to drive and it can reach 60 mph in 7 seconds. Overall, the 5-Series is full of safety, but a hefty price to buy and maintain.

	1998	1999	2000	2001	2002
Size Class	Large	Large	Large	Large	Large
Drive	Rear	Rear	Rear	Rear	Rear
Crash Test	N/A	N/A	N/A	N/A	N/A
Airbags	Dual/Side	Dual/Side	Dual/Side	Dual/Side	Dl./Sd./Hd.
ABS	4-Whl	4-Whl	4-Whl	4-Whl	4-Whl
Parts Cost	High	Very High	High	High	Very High
Complaints	Average	Very Good	Good	Good	Very Good
Insurance	Regular	Regular	Regular	Regular	Regular
Fuel Econ.	21	21	21	21	21
Theft Rating	Very High	Very High	Very High	Very High**	Very High**
Bumpers	Weak	Weak	Weak	Weak	Weak
Recalls	2	2	1	1	2
Trn. Cir. (ft.)	37.1	37.1	37.1	37.1	37.1
Weight (lbs.)	3505	3549	3549	3549	3549
Whlbase (in.)	111.4	111.4	107.3	107.3	107.3
Price	$27-29,000	$31-33,000	$34-36,000	$36-38,000	$37-39,000
OVERALL■					

BMW Z3 1998-2002

Ever since its splashy debut in a James Bond film, the Z3 has become a surefire way to turn heads on the road. The Z3 is a convertible based on the 3-Series platform. The original 1.9-

1999 BMW Z3

liter 4-cylinder engine was upgraded to the base 2.5-liter inline 6 engine and an optional 2.8-liter in-line 6 and beefier 3.2-liter in-line 6 are available. Dual and side airbags are standard as well as 4-wheel ABS. The Z3 is an attractive and popular sports car but,

	1993	1994	1995	1996	1997
Size Class					
Drive					
Crash Test					
Airbags					
ABS					
Parts Cost					
Complaints		NO MODEL PRODUCED			
Insurance					
Fuel Econ.					
Theft Rating					
Bumpers					
Recalls					
Trn. Cir. (ft.)					
Weight (lbs.)					
Whlbase (in.)					
Price					
OVERALL■					

■Cars without crash tests do not receive an overall rating.**Estimate

2002 BMW Z3

unfortunately, has yet to be crash tested. This vehicle is extremely (many say too) fast, so be careful!

	1998	1999	2000	2001	2002
Size Class	Compact	Compact	Compact	Compact	Compact
Drive	Rear	Rear	Rear	Rear	Rear
Crash Test	N/A	N/A	N/A	N/A	N/A
Airbags	Dual	Dual/Side	Dual/Side	Dual/Side	Dl./Sd.(F)
ABS	4-Whl	4-Whl	4-Whl	4-Whl	4-Whl
Parts Cost	High	High	Very High	Average	Very High
Complaints	Average	Very Good	Good	Good	Good
Insurance	Discount	Discount	Discount	Discount	Discount
Fuel Econ.	23	19	19	21	24
Theft Rating	High	Average**	Average**	Average**	Average**
Bumpers		Weak	Weak	Weak	Weak
Recalls	0	1	0	1	0
Trn. Cir. (ft.)	32.8	32.8	32.8	32.8	32.8
Weight (lbs.)	2723	2723	2723	2723	2899
Whlbase (in.)	96.3	96.3	96.3	96.3	96.3
Price	$20-21,000	$24-25,000	$25-27,000	$27-29,000	$33-35,000
OVERALL■					

Buick Century 1993-2002

Few changes had taken place for the Buick Century until 1997 when the Century was redesigned, making it much sleeker and safer. All models from 1993 to 1996 have

1993 Buick Century

GM's horrid door-mounted seat belts. Some 1993 models had an optional driver airbag; it became standard for 1994. Dual airbags became standard in 1997 and side airbags were added in 2002. ABS wasn't available until it became standard in 1994. The Century rides well on smooth roads, but it can become unsure over rough roads or

	1993	1994	1995	1996	1997
Size Class	Intermd.	Intermd.	Intermd.	Intermd.	Intermd.
Drive	Front	Front	Front	Front	Front
Crash Test	Average[1]	Good	Good	Good	Good
Airbags	Driver[2]	Driver	Driver	Driver	Dual
ABS	None	4-Whl	4-Whl	4-Whl	4-Whl
Parts Cost	Very Low	Low	Very Low	Very Low	Low
Complaints	Good	Average	Poor	Good	Good
Insurance	Discount	Discount	Discount	Discount	Discount
Fuel Econ.	20	22	25	24	20
Theft Rating	Average	Average	Low	Average	Average
Bumpers	Weak	Weak	Weak	Weak	
Recalls	3	7	2	1	1
Trn. Cir. (ft.)	38.5	38.5	38.5	38.5	36.5
Weight (lbs.)	2949	2974	2986	2950	3348
Whlbase (in.)	104.9	104.9	104.9	104.9	109
Price	$4-6,000	$5-7,000	$6-8,000	$7-9,000	$8-10,000
OVERALL■	Very Good	Good	Very Good	BEST BET	BEST BET

■Cars without crash tests do not receive an overall rating. [1]Data given for sedan. Crash test for coupe is Good. [2]Data given for model without airbags. Crash test for model with driver airbag is Good. *Optional **Estimate

2002 Buick Century

bumps. Wagons with the 4-cylinder engine lack reserve power; get the 3.8-liter V6 found on some Century models instead: it's powerful, but you'll pay for it with lower gas mileage. Room inside and comfort for four are passable; however, this improves for 1997. Controls before 1997 are dated and inefficient. After the 1997 redesign, crash test performance became only average. Traction control, ABS and daytime running lamps are standard.

	1998	1999	2000	2001	2002
Size Class	Intermd.	Intermd.	Intermd.	Intermd.	Intermd.
Drive	Front	Front	Front	Front	Front
Crash Test	Average	Average	Average	Average	Average
Airbags	Dual	Dual	Dual	Dual	Dual/Side
ABS	4-Whl	4-Whl	4-Whl	4-Whl	4-Whl
Parts Cost	Very Low	Low	High	Low	Low
Complaints	Average	Good	Good	Very Good	Good
Insurance	Discount	Discount	Discount	Discount	Discount
Fuel Econ.	20	20	20	20	23
Theft Rating	Very Low	Very Low	Very Low	Very Low[**]	Very Low[**]
Bumpers		Strong	Strong	Strong	Strong
Recalls	1	0	4	2	0
Trn. Cir. (ft.)	37.5	37.5	37.5	37.5	37.5
Weight (lbs.)	3335	3335	3335	3335	3353
Whlbase (in.)	109	109	109	109	109
Price	$9-11,000	$10-12,000	$11-13,000	$13-15,000	$22-24,000
OVERALL[■]	**BEST BET**	**BEST BET**	Good	**BEST BET**	**BEST BET**

Buick LeSabre 1993-2002

The LeSabre and its near-twins, the Olds 88 and the Pontiac Bonneville, have been consistent sellers for GM, and they show no sign of slowing down. The LeSabre's body changed in

1993 Buick LeSabre

1997 and again in 2000. The 1993 model comes with a driver's airbag and conventional, height adjustable belts. Buick added a passenger airbag for 1994. In 1999, side airbags were added to the list of standard safety features. ABS was standard on all LeSabres beginning in 1993. There is only one engine choice, and, unfortu-

	1993	1994	1995	1996	1997
Size Class	Large	Large	Large	Large	Large
Drive	Front	Front	Front	Front	Front
Crash Test	Good	Good	Good	Good	Good
Airbags	Driver	Dual	Dual	Dual	Dual
ABS	4-Whl	4-Whl	4-Whl	4-Whl	4-Whl
Parts Cost	Average	Low	Average	Average	Average
Complaints	Poor	Average	Average	Very Good	Poor
Insurance	Discount	Discount	Discount	Discount	Discount
Fuel Econ.	18	19	19	19	19
Theft Rating	Very Low	Very Low	Very Low	Very Low	Very Low
Bumpers					
Recalls	2	0	1	2	2
Trn. Cir. (ft.)	40.7	40.7	40.7	40.7	40.7
Weight (lbs.)	3433	3449	3442	3430	3441
Whlbase (in.)	110.8	110.8	110.8	110.8	110.8
Price	$4-6,000	$5-7,000	$6-8,000	$7-9,000	$9-11,000
OVERALL■	Good	**BEST BET**	Very Good	**BEST BET**	Good

■Cars without crash tests do not receive an overall rating.**Estimate

76

2002 Buick LeSabre

nately, it's not as powerful as other GMs. With standard suspension, the LeSabre rides well on good roads, but the cornering is mediocre. To improve handling, look for LeSabres with T-Type or Grand Touring packages. Trunk space is generous. The LeSabre shares another unfortunate characteristic with the Olds 88: a flashy, badly designed dashboard. If you want a large GM car, consider a Bonneville.

	1998	1999	2000	2001	2002
Size Class	Large	Large	Large	Large	Large
Drive	Front	Front	Front	Front	Front
Crash Test	Good	Good	Very Good	Very Good	Very Good
Airbags	Dual	Dual	Dual	Dual/Side	Dl./Sd.(F)
ABS	4-Whl	4-Whl	4-Whl	4-Whl	4-Whl
Parts Cost	Low	Low	Low	Average	High
Complaints	Average	Good	Poor	Very Good	Poor
Insurance	Discount	Discount	Discount	Discount	Discount
Fuel Econ.	19	19	19	19	23
Theft Rating	Very Low	Very Low	Very Low	Very Low**	Very Low**
Bumpers		Strong	Strong	Strong	Strong
Recalls	0	0	1	0	1
Trn. Cir. (ft.)	40.7	40.7	39.5	39.5	40.7
Weight (lbs.)	3443	3443	3567	3567	3567
Whlbase (in.)	110.8	110.8	112.2	112.2	112.2
Price	$11-13,000	$12-14,000	$14-16,000	$17-19,000	$25-27,000
OVERALL■	BEST BET	BEST BET	BEST BET	BEST BET	Very Good

Buick Park Avenue 1993-2002, Cadillac Seville 1998-2002

The Buick Park Avenue is very similar to the LeSabre, but considered to be more luxurious. Buick overhauled the Park Avenue 1997, making it roomier. The 1993 models featured

1993 Buick Park Avenue

regular belts with a standard driver airbag; 1994 models added a front passenger airbag. ABS is standard on all models. In all models since 1996, you can drive 100,000 miles before your first tune-up.

Most cars have a 3.8-liter V6 with an optional supercharged ver-

	1993	1994	1995	1996	1997
Size Class	Large	Large	Large	Large	Large
Drive	Front	Front	Front	Front	Front
Crash Test	N/A	N/A	N/A	N/A	Good
Airbags	Driver	Dual	Dual	Dual	Dual
ABS	4-Whl	4-Whl	4-Whl	4-Whl	4-Whl
Parts Cost	Low	Low	Low	Average	Average
Complaints	Average	Good	Poor	Good	Poor
Insurance	Discount	Discount	Discount	Discount	Discount
Fuel Econ.	19	19	19	19	19
Theft Rating	Very Low	Very Low	Very Low	Very Low	Very Low
Bumpers					
Recalls	2	0	1	3	2
Trn. Cir. (ft.)	39.4	40	40	39.4	40
Weight (lbs.)	3536	3533	3532	3536	3879
Whlbase (in.)	110.7	110.8	110.8	110.8	113.8
Price	$4-6,000	$6-8,000	$7-9,000	$9-11,000	$12-14,000
OVERALL▪					Good

▪Cars without crash tests do not receive an overall rating.#Complaint data for Park Ave. Seville received a Very Good in '98, and Good in 2000-2002. **Estimate

2002 Buick Park Avenue

sion on Ultra models. For 2001, a new Ultra Special Edition was added. A high-end audio system and Stabilitrak (all-weather control) are available. The Park Avenue specializes in a soft, smooth ride at the expense of its handling ability. There's plenty of room for five and an ample sized trunk. The dashboard is more stylish than functional but improved after the 1997 makeover.

	1998	1999	2000	2001	2002
Size Class	Large	Large	Large	Large	Large
Drive	Front	Front	Front	Front	Front
Crash Test	Good	Good	Good	Good	Good
Airbags	Dual	Dual	Dual	Dual	Dl./Sd.(F)
ABS	4-Whl	4-Whl	4-Whl	4-Whl	4-Whl
Parts Cost	Low	Low	Low	Low	Average
Complaints#	Poor	Good	Good	Good	Average
Insurance	Discount	Discount	Discount	Discount	Discount
Fuel Econ.	19	19	19	19	23
Theft Rating	Very Low	Very Low	Very Low	Very Low**	Very Low**
Bumpers		Strong	Strong	Strong	Strong
Recalls	0	0	2	0	0
Trn. Cir. (ft.)	39.4	39.4	39.7	39.7	40
Weight (lbs.)	3740	3778	3778	3778	3778
Whlbase (in.)	113.8	113.8	113.8	113.8	113.8
Price	$14-16,000	$16-18,000	$19-21,000	$22-24,000	$34,-36,000
OVERALL■	Very Good	**BEST BET**	**BEST BET**	**BEST BET**	**BEST BET**

Buick Regal 1993-2002

The Regal, unchanged for seven years, was redesigned for 1998. It is closely related to the Olds Cutlass Supreme and Pontiac Grand Prix. Although no airbags are avail-

1993 Buick Regal

able for the 1993 model, 1994 models added a standard driver's airbag and 1995 models came equipped with dual airbags. ABS was optional in 1993 and standard for 1995. The 1996 Regal meets the government's 1997 side impact standard. The Regal's 2.8-liter V6 provides adequate power in this unusually heavy mid-size car.

	1993	1994	1995	1996	1997
Size Class	Intermd.	Intermd.	Intermd.	Intermd.	Intermd.
Drive	Front	Front	Front	Front	Front
Crash Test	Good	Very Poor	Average	Average	Good
Airbags	None	Driver	Dual	Dual	Dual
ABS	4-Whl*	4-Whl*	4-Whl	4-Whl	4-Whl
Parts Cost	Low	Low	Average	Average	Average
Complaints	Average	Poor	Poor	Average	Average
Insurance	Discount	Discount	Discount	Discount	Discount
Fuel Econ.	19	19	19	20	20
Theft Rating	Very Low	Very Low	Very Low	Very Low	Very Low
Bumpers					
Recalls	3	4	8	2	2
Trn. Cir. (ft.)	36.7	36.7	36.7	39	39
Weight (lbs.)	3250	3240	3335	3232	3355
Whlbase (in.)	107.5	107.5	107.5	107.5	107.5
Price	$4-6,000	$5-7,000	$6-8,000	$7-9,000	$9-11,000
OVERALL■	Good	Poor	Average	Good	Very Good

■Cars without crash tests do not receive an overall rating.*Optional **Estimate

2002 Buick Regal

Along with the LS and GS trim levels, a special Olympic version is available for 2001. You'll find more power in later models. Typical of Buicks, the Regal provides a good ride on good roads and low-grade handling; the heavy-duty suspension should help improve cornering ability. The controls and displays are awful, especially the digital instruments on the 1990 sedans; however, this improves for 1997. Interior space is reasonable, but comfort is no better than average. Trunk space is generous.

	1998	1999	2000	2001	2002
Size Class	Intermd.	Intermd.	Intermd.	Intermd.	Intermd.
Drive	Front	Front	Front	Front	Front
Crash Test	Good	Good	Good	Good	Good
Airbags	Dual	Dual	Dual	Dual	Dual
ABS	4-Whl	4-Whl	4-Whl	4-Whl	4-Whl
Parts Cost	Average	Low	Average	Very Low	Low
Complaints	Poor	Good	Very Good	Very Good	Good
Insurance	Discount	Discount	Discount	Discount	Discount
Fuel Econ.	19	18	18	18	23
Theft Rating	Very Low	Low	Very Low	Very Low**	Very Low**
Bumpers		Strong	Strong	Strong	Strong
Recalls	1	0	4	2	0
Trn. Cir. (ft.)	37.5	37.5	37.5	37.5	37.5
Weight (lbs.)	3562	3543	3543	3543	3461
Whlbase (in.)	109	109	109	109	109
Price	$10-12,000	$11-13,000	$12-14,000	$14-16,000	$25-27,000
OVERALL▪	Very Good	BEST BET	BEST BET	BEST BET	BEST BET

Cadillac DeVille 1993-2002

Previously having the same body and chassis as the Buick Park Avenue and the Oldsmobile Aurora, the Cadillac DeVille is now a little more spacious. Changes beginning with

1993 Cadillac DeVille

1997s included a new interior and a restyled exterior along with improved handling. The DeVille was new for 1994 and is now based on the Seville/Eldorado chassis; the coupe model disappeared after 1993. These Cadillacs come with a standard driver's airbag for 1993, and dual airbags are standard from 1995 on. ABS is standard

	1993	1994	1995	1996	1997
Size Class	Large	Large	Large	Large	Large
Drive	Front	Front	Front	Front	Front
Crash Test	N/A	N/A	N/A	N/A	Very Good
Airbags	Driver	Driver	Dual	Dual	Dual/Side
ABS	4-Whl	4-Whl	4-Whl	4-Whl	4-Whl
Parts Cost	Low	Low	High	Very High	Very High
Complaints	Average	Average	Good	Poor	Average
Insurance	Discount	Discount	Discount	Discount	Discount
Fuel Econ.	16	16	16	17	17
Theft Rating	Average	Low	Low	Very Low	Very Low
Bumpers					
Recalls	1	1	1	1	1
Trn. Cir. (ft.)	41	41	41	41.6	40.7
Weight (lbs.)	3605	3757	3758	3981	4009
Whlbase (in.)	113.8	113.8	113.8	113.8	113.8
Price	$5-7,000	$7-9,000	$9-11,000	$11-13,000	$14-16,000
OVERALL▪					Very Good

▪Cars without crash tests do not receive an overall rating.*Optional **Estimate

82

2002 Cadillac DeVille

on all models. The 1996 DeVille has Cadillac's powerful but thirsty NorthStar V8. On later models, the DeVille comes standard with many safety features such as traction control, side airbags, and night vision. The 2002 comes standard with DVD-based navigation and XM radio. There is the added security of good crash test results in models before 2000. For 2000, the DeVille received a major redesign and crash tests became poor.

	1998	1999	2000	2001	2002
Size Class	Large	Large	Large	Large	Large
Drive	Front	Front	Front	Front	Front
Crash Test	Very Good	Very Good	Poor	Poor	Poor
Airbags	Dual/Side	Dual/Side	Dual/Side	Dual/Side	Dual/Side*
ABS	4-Whl	4-Whl	4-Whl	4-Whl	4-Whl
Parts Cost	Very High	Very High	Very High	Very High	Very High
Complaints	Poor	Average	Good	Very Good	Average
Insurance	Discount	Discount	Discount	Discount	Discount
Fuel Econ.	17	17	17	17	21
Theft Rating	Low	Low	High	High**	High**
Bumpers		Weak	Weak	Weak	Strong
Recalls	2	0	1	1	1
Trn. Cir. (ft.)	41	41	40.2	40.2	40.2
Weight (lbs.)	4012	4012	4012	4012	3904
Whlbase (in.)	113.8	113.8	115.3	115.3	115.3
Price	$17-19,000	$19-21,000	$25-27,000	$28-30,000	$42-45,000
OVERALL■	Good	Very Good	Average	Good	Good

Cadillac Eldorado/Seville 1993-2002

The Eldorado has not had many stylistic changes since 1993. All models have dual airbags and side airbags were added in 1998. ABS is also standard on all models. The 1993

1993 Cadillac Seville

models offer Cadillac's sophisticated NorthStar V8; it's powerful but delivers poor gas mileage. For 1994, all models received the more modern rear suspension. Base Eldorados have plenty of features, but avoid the digital gauges. Handling improves on Touring

	1993	1994	1995	1996	1997
Size Class	Large	Large	Large	Large	Large
Drive	Front	Front	Front	Front	Front
Crash Test	Average	Average	Average	Average	Average
Airbags	Dual	Dual	Dual	Dual	Dual
ABS	4-Whl	4-Whl	4-Whl	4-Whl	4-Whl
Parts Cost	Average[1]	Very High	High[1]	Very High	Very High
Complaints[2]	Poor	Poor	Average	Poor	Average
Insurance	Discount	Discount	Discount	Discount	Discount
Fuel Econ.	16	16	16	17	17
Theft Rating[3]	Very High	Average	Low	Very High	Very High
Bumpers					Weak
Recalls	2	2	1	1	1
Trn. Cir. (ft.)	40.2	40.2	40.2	40.4	40.4
Weight (lbs.)[4]	3604	3773	3774	3765	3900
Whlbase (in.)[5]	108	108	108	108	108
Price	$9-11,000	$11-13,000	$12-14,000	$14-16,000	$17-19,000
OVERALL■	Average	Poor	Good	Poor	Poor

■Cars without crash tests do not receive an overall rating. [1]Data given for Eldorado. Parts Cost for Seville for 1993-98 is Very High. [2]Data given for Eldorado. Complaints rating for Seville in 1992 is Good; 1995 is Average. [3]Data given for Eldorado. Theft rating for Seville in 1993, 96-

2002 Cadillac Eldorado

and STS models, but the ride still suffers. Room is okay in front, somewhat tighter in back. The seats are as comfortable and roomy as you'd expect from a car priced this high. An upgraded chassis control system, which greatly improves traction and stability, can be found on the 1997 models. The 2000 and 2001 models come in two trim levels: base and touring coupe. Some later models will have the OnStar GPS System.

	1998	1999	2000	2001	2002
Size Class	Large	Large	Large	Large	Large
Drive	Front	Front	Front	Front	Front
Crash Test	Good	Good	Good	Good	Good
Airbags	Dual/Side	Dual/Side	Dual/Side	Dual/Side	Dl./Sd.(F)
ABS	4-Whl	4-Whl	4-Whl	4-Whl	4-Whl
Parts Cost	Very High	Very High	Very High	Very High	Very High
Complaints[2]	Poor	Good	Very Good	Very Good	Good
Insurance	Discount	Discount	Discount	Discount	Discount
Fuel Econ.	17	17	17	17	21
Theft Rating[3]	High	Very High**	Very High**	Very High**	Very High**
Bumpers	Weak	Weak	Weak	Weak	Strong
Recalls	1	0	0	0	1
Trn. Cir. (ft.)	40.4	40.4	40.4	40.4	40.4
Weight (lbs.)[4]	3843	3070	3876	3876	3814
Whlbase (in.)[5]	108	108	108	108	108
Price	$19-21,000	$23-25,000	$26-28,000	$29-31,000	$38-41,000
OVERALL■	Average	Good	Very Good	Very Good	Very Good

2002 is Average. [4]Data given for Eldorado. Weight for Seville is 3970 from 1999-2002. [5]Data given for Eldorado. Wheelbase for Seville is 111.0 for 1993-97, 112.2 in 1999-2002. **Estimate

Chevrolet Astro/GMC Safari 1993-2002

GM's response to Chrysler's minivans was the Chevy Astro and the GMC Safari. They were poor competitors at first; however, they have done well enough to stick around. The

1993 Chevrolet Astro

addition of extended length models and a 4-wheel drive option were the Astro/Safari's only major changes until 1996, when they received fresh new interior designs, making them more like GM's other minivans. In the 1994 model year, a driver's airbag became standard, but crash test results remained abysmal. They improved a

	1993	1994	1995	1996	1997
Size Class	Minivan	Minivan	Minivan	Minivan	Minivan
Drive	Rear/4	Rear/4	Rear/4	Rear/4	Rear/4
Crash Test	Very Poor	Very Poor	Very Poor	Very Poor	Average
Airbags	None	Driver	Driver	Dual	Dual
ABS	4-Whl	4-Whl	4-Whl	4-Whl	4-Whl
Parts Cost	Very Low	Very Low	Very Low	Low	Low
Complaints[1]	Poor	Very Poor	Very Poor	Very Poor	Very Poor
Insurance	Discount	Discount	Discount	Discount	Discount
Fuel Econ.	16	16	16	16	17
Theft Rating	Very Low	Very Low	Low	Low	Low
Bumpers					Weak
Recalls	2	2	2	1	2
Trn. Cir. (ft.)	39.5	40.5	39.5	39.5	39.5
Weight (lbs.)	4160	3653	3998	3998	4197
Whlbase (in.)	111	111	111	111	111
Price	<$3,000	$3-5,000	$5-7,000	$6-8,000	$8-10,000
OVERALL■	Poor	Poor[2]	Poor	Poor	Average

■Cars without crash tests do not receive an overall rating.[1]Complaint data for Astro given in 1993-95, 1997, and 2001-02. Astro received Poor in 1996, Good in 1999, and Average in 2000. [2]Data given for Astro. Overall rating for Safari based on footnotes in 1994 is Poor. **Estimate

2002 Chevrolet Astro

bit in 1998—they were average from then to now. The 1996 model comes with dual airbags and ABS is standard on all models from 1993 on. The 4.3-liter V6, the standard engine from 1990 on, has enough power for heavy use, but it delivers poor gas mileage. The ride is unsettling, and getting in and out of the front seats is tricky. Beyond just basic towing and hauling, the Astro/Safari lacks the personal touches that make the Chrysler and newer GM minivans so popular.

	1998	1999	2000	2001	2002
Size Class	Minivan	Minivan	Minivan	Minivan	Minivan
Drive	Rear/4	Rear/4	Rear/4	Rear/4	Rear/4
Crash Test	Average	Average	Average	Average	Average
Airbags	Dual	Dual	Dual	Dual	Dual
ABS	4-Whl	4-Whl	4-Whl	4-Whl	4-Whl
Parts Cost	Low	Low	Low	Low	Low
Complaints[1]	Poor	Poor	Average	Very Good	Good
Insurance	Discount	Discount	Discount	Discount	Discount
Fuel Econ.	16	16	16	16	17
Theft Rating	Low	Low	Low**	Low**	Low**
Bumpers	Weak	Strong	Strong	Strong	Strong
Recalls	1	0	0	0	0
Trn. Cir. (ft.)	39.5	38.3	38.3	38.3	43.8
Weight (lbs.)	4197	4186	4186	4100	4187
Whlbase (in.)	111.2	111.2	111.2	111.2	111.2
Price	$9-11,000	$11-13,000	$12-14,000	$14-16,000	$22-24,000
OVERALL■	Good	Very Good	Very Good	BEST BET	BEST BET

Chevrolet Beretta/Corsica 1993-96

1993 Chevrolet Beretta

The Beretta and Corsica share the same chassis and are distant cousins to GM's other compacts. The 93 models have a driver's airbag and conventional front belts; 1994 models regressed to door-mounted belts in front with a driver airbag. Door-mounted belts don't work if the door pops open. ABS became standard in 1992. Unfortunately, the Beretta/Corsica remained one of the few 1996 models with only one airbag. For 1997, the flashier, all-new Malibu replaced the Beretta/Corsica. The early 2-liter 4-cylinder

	1993	1994	1995	1996	1997
Size Class	Compact	Compact	Compact	Compact	NO MODEL PRODUCED
Drive	Front	Front	Front	Front	
Crash Test[1]	Good	Poor	Poor	Poor	
Airbags	Driver	Driver	Driver	Driver	
ABS	4-Whl	4-Whl	4-Whl	4-Whl	
Parts Cost	Low	Low	Low	Low	
Complaints	Average	Average	Average	Average	
Insurance[2]	Surcharge	Surcharge	Surcharge	Surcharge	
Fuel Econ.	21	21	24	25	
Theft Rating	Low	Avg.	Avg.	Very Low	
Bumpers	Weak	Weak	Weak	Weak	
Recalls	0	2	1	1	
Trn. Cir. (ft.)	35.5	35.5	35.5	35.5	
Weight (lbs.)	2665	2715	2756	2756	
Whlbase (in.)	103.4	103.4	103.4	103.4	
Price	<$3,000	<$3,000	<$3,000	<$3,000	
OVERALL■	Average	Very Poor	Poor	Poor	

■Cars without crash tests do not receive an overall rating. [1]Based on Corsica. Beretta received a Very Good. [2]Based on Corsica. Beretta insurance is Regular for 1993-94.

1995 Chevrolet Corsica

engine is a slow-poke; the 2.2-liter 4-cylinder on later models is better. For more power, you can pick from two V6s. The 5-speed isn't much fun to shift, and the unreliable automatic on pre-1994 models has only 3 speeds. The 1994 V6 models have automatic overdrive, which helps acceleration and fuel economy. Look for the Beretta GT or models with F-41 suspension or sport handling package.

	1998	1999	2000	2001	2002
Size Class					
Drive					
Crash Test					
Airbags					
ABS					
Parts Cost					
Complaints					
Insurance					
Fuel Econ.					
Theft Rating			NO MODEL PRODUCED		
Bumpers					
Recalls					
Trn. Cir. (ft.)					
Weight (lbs.)					
Whlbase (in.)					
Price					
OVERALL■					

Chevrolet Camaro 1993-2002

The Camaro and its close cousin, the Pontiac Firebird, went through a major redesign in the early 90's and hasn't changed much for the last 9 years. Both have consistently

1993 Chevrolet Camaro

been good performers in the government's crash test program. Dual airbags have been standard since 1993 as well as 4-wheel ABS. New for 1996 is a more powerful standard 3.8-liter V6 with more horsepower than in years past. The IROC and Z-28 models have a powerful 5.7-liter V8 and the 35th anniversary edition has a 325 hp

	1993	1994	1995	1996	1997
Size Class	Intermd.	Intermd.	Intermd.	Intermd.	Intermd.
Drive	Rear	Rear	Rear	Rear	Rear
Crash Test	Very Good	Very Good	Very Good	Very Good	Very Good
Airbags	Dual	Dual	Dual	Dual	Dual
ABS	4-Whl	4-Whl	4-Whl	4-Whl	4-Whl
Parts Cost	Low	Average	Low	Average	Average
Complaints	Poor	Poor	Poor	Poor	Average
Insurance	Surcharge	Surcharge	Surcharge	Surcharge	Surcharge
Fuel Econ.	19	17	19	19	19
Theft Rating	Low	Average	Average	Average	Average
Bumpers					
Recalls	1	1	1	0	1
Trn. Cir. (ft.)	40.3	39.3	40.7	40.7	40.7
Weight (lbs.)	3241	3324	3342	3306	3307
Whlbase (in.)	101.1	101.1	101.1	101.1	101.1
Price	$3-5,000	$5-7000	$7-9,000	$9-11,000	$10-12,000
OVERALL■	Average	Poor	Average	Average	Average

■Cars without crash tests do not receive an overall rating.**Estimate

2002 Chevrolet Camaro

V8. Automatics have been troublesome, but sports car enthusiasts will prefer the manual transmission anyway. The Camaro delivers a firm ride and good handling with either engine choice. The dashboard has all the needed gauges, though some of the smaller controls are hard to operate. The Camaro is roomy for the driver and front seat passenger, but the rear seat is very small, even for young children—but this is not your typical family car.

	1998	1999	2000	2001	2002
Size Class	Intermd.	Intermd.	Intermd.	Intermd.	Intermd.
Drive	Rear	Rear	Rear	Rear	Rear
Crash Test	Very Good	Very Good	Very Good	Very Good	Very Good
Airbags	Dual	Dual	Dual	Dual	Dual
ABS	4-Whl	4-Whl	4-Whl	4-Whl	4-Whl
Parts Cost	High	High	High	High	Very High
Complaints	Very Poor	Poor	Poor	Good	Poor
Insurance	Surcharge	Surcharge	Surcharge	Surcharge	Surcharge
Fuel Econ.	18	19	19	19	23
Theft Rating	High	Average	High	High**	High**
Bumpers		Strong	Strong	Strong	Strong
Recalls	0	0	0	0	1
Trn. Cir. (ft.)	40.7	40.8	40.8	40.8	40.8
Weight (lbs.)	3331	3306	3306	3306	3323
Whlbase (in.)	101.1	101.1	101.1	101.1	101.1
Price	$13-15,000	$15-17,000	$17-19,000	$18-20,000	$18-22,000
OVERALL■	Poor	Average	Poor	Good	Poor

Chevrolet Caprice 1993-96, Impala 1994-96, 1999-2002

The Caprice is the cheapest of GM's full-size rear-wheel drive cars. For 1991, the Caprice received a new, aerodynamic but unappealing body, which kept buyers away. The Impala

1993 Chevrolet Caprice

reappeared in 1994, after an unsuccessful reincarnation in the mid-1980's, as the Impala SS, a sportier, more powerful Caprice. The Impala was redesigned in 1999 and given a more sporty appeal. The 1991 and later models have a standard driver airbag, joined by a

	1993	1994	1995	1996	1997
Size Class	Large	Large	Large	Large	
Drive	Rear	Rear	Rear	Rear	
Crash Test	Average	Poor	Poor	Poor	
Airbags	Driver	Dual	Dual	Dual	
ABS	4-Whl	4-Whl	4-Whl	4-Whl	
Parts Cost	Very Low	Very Low	Very Low	Very Low	
Complaints	Average	Poor	Good	Average	
Insurance	Discount	Discount	Discount	Discount	
Fuel Econ.	18	17	18	18	
Theft Rating	Very Low	Low	Average	Average	
Bumpers					
Recalls	1	6	9	6	
Trn. Cir. (ft.)	38.9	38.9	39.9	39.9	
Weight (lbs.)	4202	4045	4061	4061	
Whlbase (in.)	115.9	115.9	115.9	115.9	
Price	$3-5,000	$5-7,000	$7-9,000	$11-13,000	
OVERALL■	Very Good	Average	Very Good	Good	

NO MODEL PRODUCED

■Cars without crash tests do not receive an overall rating.*Optional **Estimate

2002 Chevrolet Impala

passenger airbag for 1994 and side airbags for 2001. ABS is standard on all models since 1993. The Impala SS also gets standard traction control, giving it more powerful handling and control. The Caprice's standard V6 performs adequately, but not if you load up with passengers or cargo. The Impala's 3.4-liter V6 is more powerful and the handling and control of the Impala is much better than the Caprice.

	1998	1999	2000	2001	2002
Size Class		Intermd.	Intermd.	Intermd.	Intermd.
Drive		Front	Front	Front	Front
Crash Test		Very Good	Very Good	Very Good	Very Good
Airbags		Dual	Dual	Dl./Sd.(F)	Dl./Sd.(F)
ABS		4-Whl*	4-Whl*	4-Whl	4-Whl
Parts Cost		Low	High	Low	Low
Complaints		Very Good	Poor	Very Good	Poor
Insurance		Regular	Regular	Regular	Discount
Fuel Econ.		24	24	25	25
Theft Rating		Average	Average	Average**	Average**
Bumpers					
Recalls					
Trn. Cir. (ft.)		38	38	38	38
Weight (lbs.)		3308	3308	3308	3308
Whlbase (in.)		110.5	110.5	110.5	110.5
Price		$13-15,000	$14-16,000	$16-18,000	$21-23,000
OVERALL■		BEST BET	Average	BEST BET	BEST BET

NO MODEL PRODUCED

Chevrolet Cavalier 1993-2002

The styling of the Cavalier has remained unchanged since its much-appraised redesign in 1995. Cavaliers come in a coupe, sedan, wagon, or convertible, though a

1993 Chevrolet Cavalier

wagon version has not been offered since 1995. The 1990-94 models have door-mounted seat belts in front. ABS became standard in 1992, but airbags were not offered until the 1995 redesign added two. The 4-cylinder engines in Cavaliers perform adequately. If you want an automatic, you're stuck with a 3-speed and inferior gas

	1993	1994	1995	1996	1997
Size Class	Compact	Compact	Compact	Compact	Compact
Drive	Front	Front	Front	Front	Front
Crash Test	Good	Good	Good	Good	Good
Airbags	None	None	Dual	Dual	Dual
ABS	4-Whl	4-Whl	4-Whl	4-Whl	4-Whl
Parts Cost	Low	Low	Average	Low	High
Complaints	Average	Poor	Average	Poor	Average
Insurance	Regular	Discount	Discount	Surcharge	Surcharge
Fuel Econ.	23	23	25	26	25
Theft Rating	Very Low	Very Low	Very Low	Very Low	Very Low
Bumpers	Weak	Weak	Weak	Weak	Weak
Recalls	2	2	4	6	5
Trn. Cir. (ft.)	34.3	34.3	35.6	35.6	35.6
Weight (lbs.)	2678	2520	2537	2617	2617
Whlbase (in.)	101.3	101.3	104.1	104.1	104.1
Price	<$3,000	$3-5,000	$4-6,000	$5-7,000	$6-8,000
OVERALL■	Average	Good	Very Good	Poor	Poor

■Cars without crash tests do not receive an overall rating.**Estimate

2002 Chevrolet Cavalier

mileage, unless you get a 1996 or 1997 model with the optional 4-speed automatic. The early 5-speed transmission isn't too smooth, but did improve around 1988. A 2.2-liter engine comes standard on the base coupe and sedan models; on the LS and Z24 trim levels, a more powerful 2.4-liter engine is available. A new engine was offered in 2002 including two new trim levels. Accommodations for four in any Cavalier are tight, but the wagon's cargo area is a practical shape.

	1998	1999	2000	2001	2002
Size Class	Compact	Compact	Compact	Compact	Compact
Drive	Front	Front	Front	Front	Front
Crash Test	Good	Good	Good	Good	Good
Airbags	Dual	Dual	Dual	Dual	Dual
ABS	4-Whl	4-Whl	4-Whl	4-Whl	4-Whl
Parts Cost	Average	Low	Low	Low	Low
Complaints	Good	Very Good	Very Good	Very Good	Good
Insurance	Surcharge	Surcharge	Surcharge	Surcharge	Surcharge
Fuel Econ.	25	24	24	24	27
Theft Rating	Low	Average	Average	Average**	Average**
Bumpers	Weak	Strong	Strong	Strong	Strong
Recalls	1	0	0	0	0
Trn. Cir. (ft.)	35.6	35.6	35.6	35.6	35.6
Weight (lbs.)	2630	2617	2617	2617	2676
Whlbase (in.)	104.1	104.1	104.1	104.1	104.1
Price	$8-10,000	$10-12,000	$12-14,000	$13-15,000	$14-16,000
OVERALL■	Good	Very Good	Very Good	Very Good	Very Good

Chevrolet Lumina 1993-2000, Monte Carlo 1995-2002

The Chevrolet Lumina shared its structure with the Buick Regal, Pontiac Grand Prix, and Olds Cutlass Supreme. A new, more luxurious Lumina appeared in the spring of 1994 as a 1995

1993 Chevrolet Lumina

model, and the Monte Carlo name was revived for the new 1995 coupe. ABS is optional after 1992, standard on the Monte Carlo from 1996 on. But, you won't find airbags before 1995, when standard dual airbags were introduced. The original Monte Carlo came with V6 or V8 engines, including a high performance SS model.

	1993	1994	1995	1996	1997
Size Class	Intermd.	Intermd.	Large	Large	Large
Drive	Front	Front	Front	Front	Front
Crash Test	N/A	N/A	Good[1]	Good[1]	Good[1]
Airbags	None	None	Dual	Dual	Dual
ABS	4-Whl*	4-Whl*	4-Whl*	4-Whl*	4-Whl*
Parts Cost	Low	Low	Average	Very Low	Average
Complaints	Poor	Average	Poor	Good	Good
Insurance	Discount	Discount	Discount	Discount	Discount[2]
Fuel Econ.	17	19	19	20	20
Theft Rating	Very Low	Low	Low	Very Low	Very Low
Bumpers	Weak	Weak	Weak	Weak	Weak
Recalls	1	0	6	2	0
Trn. Cir. (ft.)	39	39	36.7	36	36.7
Weight (lbs.)	3187	3333	3330	3330	3243
Whlbase (in.)	107.5	107.5	107.5	107.5	107.5
Price	$3-5,000	$4-6,000	$5-7,000	$6-8,000	$7-9,000
OVERALL■			Average	BEST BET	Very Good

■Cars without crash tests do not receive an overall rating. [1]Data given for Monte Carlo. Crash test for Lumina is Very Good. [2]Data given for Lumina. Insurance rating for Monte Carlo in 1997 is Regular. *Optional **Estimate

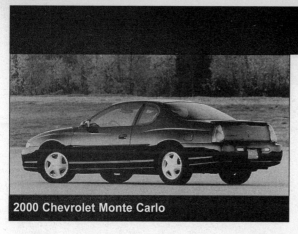

2000 Chevrolet Monte Carlo

The back seat is difficult to access, and the trunk is smaller in exchange for styling. Many 1990-93 Luminas, particularly those sold to rental fleets, have an underpowered 4-cylinder engine with a 3-speed automatic. The hot Z-34 model, on Luminas and 1995 Monte Carlos, has a 4-cam V6 and 5-speed or automatic overdrive. The handling is disappointing on the base models. Room inside is adequate for four. In 2001, the Lumina is only available for fleet sales.

	1998	1999	2000	2001	2002
Size Class	Large	Large	Large	Large	Large
Drive	Front	Front	Front	Front	Front
Crash Test	Good[1]	Good[1]	Very Good	Very Good	Very Good
Airbags	Dual	Dual	Dual	Dual	Dl./Sd.(F)
ABS	4-Whl	4-Whl	4-Whl	4-Whl	4-Whl
Parts Cost	Low	Low	Low	Low	Low
Complaints	Average	Very Good	Very Good	Very Good	Poor
Insurance	Discount	Discount	Regular	Regular	Discount
Fuel Econ.	20	20	20	20	25
Theft Rating	Low	Low	Average	Average[**]	Average[**]
Bumpers	Weak				
Recalls	0	0	4	2	0
Trn. Cir. (ft.)	36.7	36.7	36.7	36.7	36.7
Weight (lbs.)	3330	3330	3330	3330	3330
Whlbase (in.)	107.5	107.5	107.5	107.5	107.5
Price	$8-10,000	$10-12,000	$11-13,000	$13-15,000	$21-23,000
OVERALL[■]	Very Good	**BEST BET**	Very Good	**BEST BET**	**BEST BET**

Chev. Lumina '93-96, Venture '97-'02, Olds Silh. '93-'01, Pont. Tr. Sp. '93-98, Pont. Montana '99-'01

GM's belated response to the front-wheel drive minivans made by Chrysler, these vehicles received significant changes for 1994, mainly new front-end styling that made them look

1993 Chevrolet Lumina Minivan

more earthbound than the previous models. A redesign for 1997 updated the exterior styling and improved the interior, and the Lumina was replaced with the Venture. Four-wheel ABS is standard from 1992 on. The standard 3.1-liter V6 and 3-speed automatic, available through 1995, deliver substandard acceleration and gas

	1993	1994	1995	1996	1997
Size Class	Minivan	Minivan	Minivan	Minivan	Minivan
Drive	Front	Front	Front	Front	Front
Crash Test	Very Good	Good	Good	Good	Good
Airbags	None	Driver	Driver	Driver	Dual
ABS	4-Whl	4-Whl	4-Whl	4-Whl	4-Whl
Parts Cost	Very Low	Very Low	Very Low	Very Low	Low
Complaints	Very Poor	Poor	Very Poor	Good	Very Poor
Insurance	Discount	Discount	Discount	Discount	Regular
Fuel Econ.	18	19	19	19	18
Theft Rating	Average	Average	Average	Average	Average
Bumpers		Weak	Weak	Weak	Weak
Recalls	4	5	4	0	3
Trn. Cir. (ft.)	43.1	43.1	43.1	43.1	37.4
Weight (lbs.)	3370	3554	3516	3593	3702
Whlbase (in.)	109.8	109.8	109.8	109.8	112
Price	<$3,000	$3-5,000	$4-6,000	$6-8,000	$10-12,000
OVERALL■	Average	Good	Average	**BEST BET**	Poor

■Cars without crash tests do not receive an overall rating.**Estimate

2002 Chevrolet Venture

mileage. The 3.8-liter V6 and automatic overdrive, optional from 1992-95, are far better suited to these vehicles. A new, more powerful 3.4-liter V6 from 1996 to 2002 is standard.

Like the Chrysler, the Venture offers sliding doors on both sides. Rear child seats are an excellent optional feature on 1994 and later models. Center and rear seats are easy to remove, but cargo room is small.

	1998	1999	2000	2001	2002
Size Class	Minivan	Minivan	Minivan	Minivan	Minivan
Drive	Front	Front	Front	Front	Front
Crash Test	Good	Good	Good	Good	Good
Airbags	Dual/Side	Dual/Side	Dual/Side	Dual/Side	Dl./Sd.(F)
ABS	4-Whl	4-Whl	4-Whl	4-Whl	4-Whl
Parts Cost	Low	Average	Average	Average	High
Complaints	Very Poor	Poor	Average	Average	Poor
Insurance	Regular	Regular	Discount	Discount	Discount
Fuel Econ.	18	18	18	18	22
Theft Rating	Very Low	Very Low	Very Low	Very Low[**]	Very Low[**]
Bumpers	Weak		Strong	Strong	Strong
Recalls	4	1	1	3	0
Trn. Cir. (ft.)	37.4	37.4	37.4	37.4	37.4
Weight (lbs.)	3699	3699	3699	3699	3699
Whlbase (in.)	112	112	112	112	112
Price	$12-14,000	$14-16,000	$17-19,000	$19-21,000	$23-25,000
OVERALL■	Average	Good	**BEST BET**	Very Good	Very Good

Chevrolet Malibu 1997-2002

1997 Chevrolet Malibu

Introduced in 1997, the Malibu is available in a base and LS. For the 1997-2000 models, the base has a 2.4-liter engine, which delivers 150 hp. Optional on the base and standard on the LS is a 3.1-liter V6 engine. For 1999, leather seats and a power seat for the driver were added to the LS model. A revised grill, which it borrowed from the Impala, was new for 2000.

The 2001 and 2002 Chevrolet Malibus come with a standard 3.1-

	1993	1994	1995	1996	1997
Size Class					Intermd.
Drive					Front
Crash Test					Good
Airbags					Dual
ABS					4-Whl
Parts Cost					High
Complaints					Poor
Insurance					Regular
Fuel Econ.		NO MODEL PRODUCED			20
Theft Rating					Average
Bumpers					
Recalls					1
Trn. Cir. (ft.)					36.1
Weight (lbs.)					3051
Whlbase (in.)					107
Price					$7-8,000
OVERALL■					Poor

■Cars without crash tests do not receive an overall rating.**Estimate

100

2002 Chevrolet Malibu

liter V6 engine but few other changes. You'll find good interior room and fine handling. The Malibu is Chevy's challenge to the best selling Taurus, Camry, and Accord trio. The LS version comes with cruise control, power seats, keyless entry and a rear defogger.

	1998	1999	2000	2001	2002
Size Class	Intermd.	Intermd.	Intermd.	Intermd.	Intermd.
Drive	Front	Front	Front	Front	Front
Crash Test	Good	Good	Good	Good	Good
Airbags	Dual	Dual	Dual	Dual	Dual
ABS	4-Whl	4-Whl	4-Whl	4-Whl	4-Whl
Parts Cost	High	Very High	High	High	Average
Complaints	Very Poor	Poor	Average	Very Good	Poor
Insurance	Regular	Regular	Regular	Regular	Regular
Fuel Econ.	23	22	20	20	23
Theft Rating	Low	Average	Average	Average**	Average**
Bumpers		Strong	Strong	Strong	Strong
Recalls	0	0	1	0	1
Trn. Cir. (ft.)	36.4	36.3	36.3	36.3	36.3
Weight (lbs.)	3051	3051	3051	3051	3051
Whlbase (in.)	107	107	107	107	107
Price	$8-10,000	$9-11,000	$11-13,000	$12-14,000	$18-20,000
OVERALL■	Poor	Average	Average	Very Good	Average

Chev. S10 Blazer 1993-94, Blazer 1995-2002, Jimmy/Olds Bravada 1993-2002, Trail Blazer 2002

What used to be the S10 Blazer is now simply the Blazer. This new Blazer is not to be confused with what used to be the larger Blazer, which is now the Tahoe. And finally, the fully

1993 Chevrolet S10 Blazer

equipped Bravada, introduced in 1991 to compete against deluxe vehicles like the Ford Explorer and Nissan Pathfinder, was discontinued after 1994 but revived for 1996. The 1995 Blazer and Jimmy should be better competitors against their upper level sport utility competitors. All Bravadas before 1996 have conventional lap-shoul-

	1993	1994	1995	1996	1997
Size Class	Sp. Util.	Sp. Util.	Sp. Util.	Sp. Util.	Sp. Util.
Drive	Rear/4	Rear/4	Rear/4	Rear/4	Rear/4
Crash Test	Poor	Poor	Average	Average	Average
Airbags	None	None	None	Driver	Driver
ABS	4-Whl	4-Whl	4-Whl	4-Whl	4-Whl
Parts Cost	Low	Very Low	Very Low	Low	Low
Complaints	Very Poor	Very Poor	Very Poor	Very Poor	Poor
Insurance	Surcharge[1]	Surcharge	Surcharge	Surcharge[1]	Regular
Fuel Econ.	17	17	17	18	18
Theft Rating	Very High	Very High	Average	Very High	Average
Bumpers				Weak	Weak
Recalls	1	2	6	6	4
Trn. Cir. (ft.)	34.6	34.6	35.2	39.5	35.2
Weight (lbs.)	3365	3205	3306	4023	3874
Whlbase (in.)	100.5	100.5	100.5	100.5	100.5
Price	$4-6,000	$5-7,000	$7-9,000	$8-10,000	$9-11,000
OVERALL■	Very Poor	Very Poor	Very Poor	Very Poor	Poor

■Cars without crash tests do not receive an overall rating. [1]Data given for S10 Blazer. Insurance rating for Bravada is Regular. *Optional
**Estimate

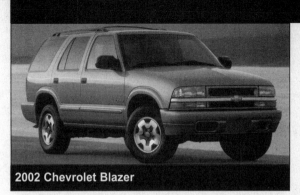

2002 Chevrolet Blazer

der belts but no airbags. Bravadas and 4-door Blazers and Jimmys have 4-wheel ABS from 1990 on; 2-door Blazers and Jimmys have 4-wheel ABS since 1993. The Blazer and Jimmy come with a V6 standard engine offering strength for hauling or trailer towing. You can choose from 5-speed or optional automatic overdrive and 2- or 4-wheel drive. Suspension packages help improve the ride and handling.

	1998	1999	2000	2001	2002
Size Class	Sp. Util.	Sp. Util.	Sp. Util.	Sp. Util.	Sp. Util.
Drive	Rear/4	Rear/4	Rear/4	Rear/4	Rear/4
Crash Test	Average	Average	Poor	Poor	
Airbags	Dual	Dual	Dual	Dual	Dual
ABS	4-Whl	4-Whl	4-Whl	4-Whl	4-Whl
Parts Cost	Low	Average	Average	Average	Average
Complaints	Poor	Good	Good	Good	Poor
Insurance	Regular	Discount	Surcharge	Surcharge	Surcharge
Fuel Econ.	17	16	16	15	19
Theft Rating	Average	Average	Average	Average**	Average**
Bumpers	Weak				
Recalls	4	1	3	3	0
Trn. Cir. (ft.)	35.2	35.2	34.8	34.8	35.2
Weight (lbs.)	4046	3848	3518	3518	3518
Whlbase (in.)	100.5	100.5	100.5	100.5	100.5
Price	$11-13,000	$13-15,000	$15-17,000	$18-20,000	$20-22,000
OVERALL■	Poor	Very Good	Poor	Poor	

Chevrolet S-Series, GMC Sonoma 1994-2002

The long running Chevy S-Series began a new series in 1995, adding a 4.3-liter, 6-cylinder option to the 2.3-liter, 4-cylinder engine. Both the S-Series and Sonoma come in

1994 GMC Sonoma

2- or 4-wheel drive and have many options, such as a crew cab or an Xtreme Appearance Package. Airbags were not available until 1996, when a driver's airbag became standard. Passenger airbags were added in 1998. 4-wheel ABS is standard on all models. The

	1993	1994	1995	1996	1997
Size Class	Cmpt Pkup	Cmpt Pkup	Cmpt Pkup	Cmpt Pkup	Cmpt Pkup
Drive	Rear/4	Rear/4	Rear/4	Rear/4	Rear/4
Crash Test	Poor	Poor	Poor	Poor	Poor
Airbags	None	None	Driver	Driver	Dual
ABS	4-Whl*	4-Whl*	4-Whl*	4-Whl	4-Whl
Parts Cost	Very Low	Very Low	Low	Very Low	Very Low
Complaints[1]	Poor	Very Poor	Very Poor	Very Poor	Poor
Insurance	Regular	Regular	Regular	Regular	Regular
Fuel Econ.[#]	22	20	20	21	19
Theft Rating	Average	Average	Average	Low	Low
Bumpers					
Recalls	3	5	5	6	5
Trn. Cir. (ft.)	36.9	36.9	36.9	36.9	36.9
Weight (lbs.)	2874	2874	2874	2874	2874
Whlbase (in.)	108.3	108.3	108.3	108.3	108.3
Price	$3-5,000	$4-6,000	$5-7,000	$6-8,000	$7-9,000
OVERALL**	Very Poor	Very Poor	Very Poor	Poor	Poor

*Cars without crash tests do not receive an overall rating. [1]Based on GMC Sonoma. [#]Fuel Economy based on 2-WD version, 6 cyl. *Optional
**Estimate

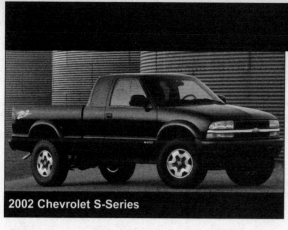
2002 Chevrolet S-Series

1993-94 models faired poorly on the crash tests with a slight improvement between 1995 and '99. Slight stylistic changes in 2000, however, caused the S-Series to do poorly in crash tests once again.

	1998	1999	2000	2001	2002
Size Class	Cmpt Pkup	Cmpt Pkup	Cmpt Pkup	Cmpt Pkup	Cmpt Pkup
Drive	Rear/4	Rear/4	Rear/4	Rear/4	Rear/4
Crash Test	Poor	Poor	Poor	Poor	Poor
Airbags	Dual	Dual	Dual	Dual	Dual
ABS	4-Whl	4-Whl	4-Whl	4-Whl	4-Whl
Parts Cost	Very Low	Low	Low	Average	Average
Complaints[1]	Average	Very Good	Average	Good	Very Good
Insurance	Regular	Surcharge	Surcharge	Surcharge	Surcharge
Fuel Econ.#	19	18	19	19	19
Theft Rating	Very Low	Very Low	Very Low	Very Low**	Very Low**
Bumpers					
Recalls	5	1	3	1	0
Trn. Cir. (ft.)	36.9	36.9	36.9	36.9	36.9
Weight (lbs.)	2874	2874	2874	2874	2874
Whlbase (in.)	108.3	108.3	108.3	108.3	108.3
Price	$8-10,000	$10-12,000	$11-13,000	$12-14,000	$14-16,000
OVERALL■	Average	Good	Poor	Poor	Average

Chevrolet/GMC Suburban 1993-2002

The Suburban is a 4-door station wagon version of a Chevrolet C/K pickup. The Suburban is extremely large, over 5,000 pounds, and about as long as a Cadillac Fleetwood. The Suburban

1993 Chevrolet Suburban

ban stayed the same for nearly 20 years, with GM waiting until 1992 before it changed the Suburban over, using the newer C/K chassis and sheet metal. For 2000, the Suburban was only a Chevy model. Four-wheel ABS has been standard since 1992, and a driver's side airbag was added in 1995. Dual airbags became standard in

	1993	1994	1995	1996	1997
Size Class	Sp. Util.	Sp. Util.	Sp. Util.	Sp. Util.	Sp. Util.
Drive	Rear/4	Rear/4	Rear/4	Rear/4	Rear/4
Crash Test	Very Good	Very Good	Very Good	Very Good	Good
Airbags	None	None	Driver	Driver	Dual
ABS	4-Whl	4-Whl	4-Whl	4-Whl	4-Whl
Parts Cost	Very Low	Low	Very Low	Very Low	Low
Complaints	Very Poor	Very Poor	Very Poor	Very Poor	Very Poor
Insurance	Regular	Regular	Discount	Discount	Discount
Fuel Econ.	12	13	13	13	13
Theft Rating	High	High	Very High	Very High	Very High
Bumpers					
Recalls		2	7	3	1
Trn. Cir. (ft.)	47.8	47.8	47.5	43.7	43.7
Weight (lbs.)	4657	4672	4691	4634	4802
Whlbase (in.)	131.5	131.5	131.5	131.5	131.5
Price	$9-11,000	$11-13,000	$13-15,000	$15-17,000	$16-18,000
OVERALL■	Poor	Poor	Average	Good	Average

■Cars without crash tests do not receive an overall rating.**Estimate

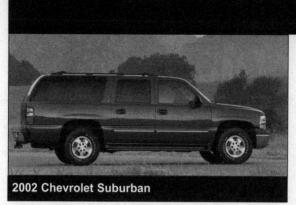

2002 Chevrolet Suburban

1998 and in 2000, side airbags were added.

Given the Suburban's weight, even without any load, the standard 5.3-liter V8 has a lot of work to do. However, you can get a 6.0 liter V8 or 7.4-liter V8 option. Both engines come with automatic overdrive. You can also find a 6.2-liter diesel that improves gas mileage somewhat, but its reliability on early models is questionable. Four-wheel drive is available. The cargo space is large and functional in shape.

	1998	1999	2000	2001	2002
Size Class	Sp. Util.	Sp. Util.	Sp. Util.	Sp. Util.	Sp. Util.
Drive	Rear/4	Rear/4	Rear/4	Rear/4	Rear/4
Crash Test	Good	Good	Good	Good	Good
Airbags	Dual	Dual	Dual	Dual	Dl./Sd.(F)
ABS	4-Whl	4-Whl	4-Whl	4-Whl	4-Whl
Parts Cost	Low	Low	Low	Low	Average
Complaints	Average	Very Poor	Good	Good	Average
Insurance	Discount	Discount	Discount	Discount	Discount
Fuel Econ.	13	14	14	14	16
Theft Rating	High	High	High	High**	High**
Bumpers					
Recalls	1	0	2	2	0
Trn. Cir. (ft.)	43.7	43.7	43.7	43.7	42.3
Weight (lbs.)	4825	4820	4820	4820	5219
Whlbase (in.)	131.5	131.5	131.5	131.5	130
Price	$19-21,000	$21-23,000	$23-25,000	$26-28,000	$36-38,000
OVERALL■	Very Good	Good	Very Good	Very Good	Very Good

Chevy Silverado 1999-2002, GMC Sierra 1993-2002

Created in 1999 to replace the Chevy C/K Series, the Chevrolet Silverado and GMC Sierra have both been relatively successful in their attempt to compete with the Ford

1994 GMC Sierra

F-150. Dual airbags have come standard since the debut of the Silverado/Sierra and 4-wheel ABS is standard as well.

A variety of engines power the Silverado/Sierra, including 6.6-liter diesel and an 8.1-liter V8, in addition to the 4.3-liter V6, 4.8-

	1993	1994	1995	1996	1997
Size Class	Truck	Truck	Truck	Truck	Truck
Drive	Rear/4	Rear/4	Rear/4	Rear/4	Rear/4
Crash Test	Very Good	Very Good	Very Good	Very Good	Very Good
Airbags	None	None	Driver*	Driver	Dual
ABS	4-Whl*	4-Whl*	4-Whl	4-Whl	4-Whl
Parts Cost	Very Low	Very Low	Very Low	Very Low	Very Low
Complaints	Very Good	Good	Average	Average	Average
Insurance	Regular	Regular	Regular	Regular	Regular
Fuel Econ.	16	16	18	17	16
Theft Rating	Very High	Very High	Average	Average	Average
Bumpers					
Recalls	2	2	5	2	0
Trn. Cir. (ft.)	39.8	39.8	39.8	39.8	39.8
Weight (lbs.)	4035	4035	4035	4035	4035
Whlbase (in.)	117.5	117.5	117.5	117.5	117.5
Price	$3-5.000	$4-6,000	$5-7,000	$6-8,000	$7-9,000
OVERALL*	Very Good	Good	Good	Very Good	Very Good

*Cars without crash tests do not receive an overall rating.*Optional **Estimate

108

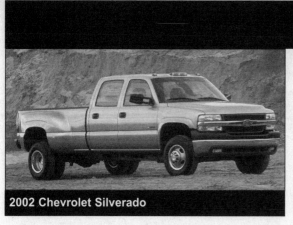
2002 Chevrolet Silverado

liter V8, 5.3-liter V8, 6.0-liter V8 and a 6.5-liter turbo-diesel V8. With so many engine choices to choose from, the Silverado/Sierra is great for towing, but average crash tests scores make it less desirable than the Ford F-150. For the same amount of money and more safety, you should consider the F-150.

	1998	1999	2000	2001	2002
Size Class	Truck	Truck	Truck	Truck	Truck
Drive	Rear/4	Rear/4	Rear/4	Rear/4	Rear/4
Crash Test	Very Gd.	Average	Average	Average	Average
Airbags	Dual	Dual	Dual	Dual	Dual
ABS	4-Whl	4-Whl	4-Whl	4-Whl	4-Whl
Parts Cost	Low	Very Low	Low	Average	Average
Complaints	Good	Average	Good	Very Good	Average
Insurance	Regular	Regular	Regular	Discount	Discount
Fuel Econ.	17	16	16	16	16
Theft Rating	Average	Average	Average	Average**	Average**
Bumpers					
Recalls	0	2	2	0	0
Trn. Cir. (ft.)	39.8	40.1	40.1	40.1	40.1
Weight (lbs.)	4035	3956	3956	3956	3956
Whlbase (in.)	117.5	119	119	119	119
Price	$9-12,000	$13-15,000	$14-16,000	$16-18,000	$19-21,000
OVERALL■	Very Good	Good	Good	Very Good	Good

Chrysler 300M 1998-2002

Chrysler introduced their flagship in 1999 naming it after the 300 series from decades ago. The 300M comes with standard front airbags, and side-impact airbags for the front seat, 4-wheel ABS, and traction control standard. Head airbags are also standard for 2002 models. The roomy interior makes for a nice passenger ride. The 3.5-liter V6 gives the car a fast kick. Luxurious standard features include heated leather seats, a four-disc stereo sys-

1999 Chrysler 300M

	1993	1994	1995	1996	1997
Size Class					
Drive					
Crash Test					
Airbags					
ABS					
Parts Cost					
Complaints					
Insurance					
Fuel Econ.					
Theft Rating					
Bumpers					
Recalls					
Trn. Cir. (ft.)					
Weight (lbs.)					
Whlbase (in.)					
Price					
OVERALL■					

NO MODEL PRODUCED

■Cars without crash tests do not receive an overall rating.**Estimate

2002 Chrysler 300M

tem, and the Autostick manual/automatic transmission. A leather interior, anti-theft system, fog lamps, heated rearview mirrors, dual airbags, 4-wheel ABS all come standard.

	1998	1999	2000	2001	2002
Size Class		Large	Large	Large	Large
Drive		Front	Front	Front/Side	Front/Side
Crash Test		Average	Average	Average	Average
Airbags		Front	Front	Front/Side	Fr./Side/Head
ABS		4-Whl	4-Whl	4-Whl	4-Whl
Parts Cost		Low	Low	Low	Low
Complaints		Poor	Good	Very Good	Average
Insurance		Regular	Regular	Regular	Discount
Fuel Econ.		21	21	21	21
Theft Rating		Very High	Very High	Very High**	Very High**
Bumpers		Weak	Weak	Weak	Weak
Recalls		1	5	2	0
Trn. Cir. (ft.)		37.6	37.6	37.6	37.6
Weight (lbs.)		3591	3591	3591	3591
Whlbase (in.)		113	113	113	113
Price		$17-19,000	$20-22,000	$22-24,000	$28-30,000
OVERALL■		Average	Average	Very Good	Very Good

Chrysler Cirrus 1995-2000, Dodge Stratus 1995-2002, Plymouth Breeze 1996-2000

In 1995, Chrysler replaced the LeBaron sedan and Dodge Spirit with the JA cars, the Chrysler Cirrus and Dodge Stratus. The JA cars looked similar to a Honda or Toyota in profile;

1995 Chrysler Cirrus

however, the front fascias were designed more aggressively. Plymouth rounded out the trio with the Breeze in 1996. Dual airbags and ABS were standard from their '95 introduction on. Like their LH cousins, their cab-forward design increases interior room. Three engine choices were available originally: 2.0-liter, 2.4-liter, and a

	1993	1994	1995	1996	1997
Size Class			Intermd.	Intermd.	Intermd.
Drive			Front	Front	Front
Crash Test			Average	Average	Average
Airbags			Dual	Dual	Dual
ABS			4-Whl*	4-Whl*	4-Whl*
Parts Cost			High	High	Low
Complaints			Very Poor	Very Poor	Average
Insurance			Discount	Discount	Regular
Fuel Econ.	NO MODEL PRODUCED		20	20	20
Theft Rating			Very Low	Very Low	Very Low
Bumpers			Weak	Weak	Weak
Recalls			6	6	3
Trn. Cir. (ft.)			37	37	37
Weight (lbs.)			2931	2931	2920
Whlbase (in.)			108	108	108
Price			$4-6,000	$5-7,000	$6-8,000
OVERALL■			Poor	Poor	Average

■Cars without crash tests do not receive an overall rating.*Optional **Estimate

112

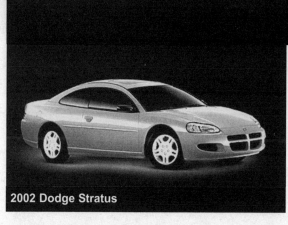
2002 Dodge Stratus

powerful 2.5-liter. However, for '97, the 2.5-liter was replaced by a 2.4-liter V6. Consider the 2.4-liter, optional on the Stratus and standard on the upscale Cirrus. The Breeze is limited in options. The cars received an average rating in the government's crash tests. The Autostick, a combination stick and automatic, is an option on the Stratus. The Breeze and Cirrus were discontinued after 2000 but a new Stratus coupe was introduced for 2001 to take their place in the lineup.

	1998	1999	2000	2001	2002
Size Class	Intermd.	Intermd.	Intermd.	Intermd.	Intermd.
Drive	Front	Front	Front	Front	Front
Crash Test	Average	Average	Average	Very Good	Very Good
Airbags	Dual	Dual	Dual	Dual	Dl./Sd. (F)*
ABS	4-Whl*	4-Whl*	4-Whl*	4-Whl*	4-Whl*
Parts Cost	Very Low	Low	Low	Very Low	Low
Complaints	Average	Average	Good		Average
Insurance	Regular	Regular	Regular	Regular	Regular
Fuel Econ.	19	19	19	20	23
Theft Rating	Average	High	Average**	Average**	Average**
Bumpers	Weak	Weak	Weak	Weak	Weak
Recalls	1	0	4	7	0
Trn. Cir. (ft.)	37	37	37	36.8	36.8
Weight (lbs.)	3181	3146	3146	3226	3200
Whlbase (in.)	108	108	108	108	108
Price	$7-9,000	$9-11,000	$11-13,000	$14-16,000	$18-21,000
OVERALL■	Good	Average	Average	Average	Very Good

Chrysler Concorde/Dodge Intrepid 1993-2002, Eagle Vision 1993-98

These three cars, dubbed "LH" cars, are Chrysler's successful first foray into cab-forward design. This design pushes the wheels farther toward the corners of the car,

1995 Chrysler Concorde

increasing interior room and improving the ride and handling while not changing the overall size of the car. The Concorde and Intrepid have similar styling, though the Concorde is much more plush. Dual airbags have always been standard, while front side airbags are optional. ABS has been standard on the Concorde, optional on the

	1993	1994	1995	1996	1997
Size Class	Intermd.	Intermd.	Intermd.	Intermd.	Intermd.
Drive	Front	Front	Front	Front	Front
Crash Test	Very Good	Very Good	Very Good	Very Good	Very Good
Airbags	Dual	Dual	Dual	Dual	Dual
ABS	4-Whl*	4-Whl*	4-Whl*	4-Whl*	4-Whl*
Parts Cost	Very Low	Very Low	Very Low	Very Low	Very Low
Complaints#	Very Poor	Very Poor	Very Poor	Poor	Very Poor
Insurance	Discount	Discount	Discount	Discount	Discount
Fuel Econ.	20	20	20	19	19
Theft Rating	Low	Low	Low	Very Low	Very Low
Bumpers					
Recalls	3	2	1	1	1
Trn. Cir. (ft.)	37.7	37.7	37.7	37.7	37.7
Weight (lbs.)	3320	3310	3310	3318	3411
Whlbase (in.)	113	113	113	113	113
Price	>$3,000	$4-6,000	$5-7,000	$6-8,000	$7-9,000
OVERALL"	Very Good	Very Good	Very Good	BEST BET	BEST BET

"Cars without crash tests do not receive an overall rating. #Based on Chrysler Concorde. Intrepid and Eagle received an Avg. in '97. *Optional
**Estimate

114

2002 Dodge Intrepid

Intrepid and Vision.

The base 2.7-liter V6 is both powerful and efficient enough; the 3.2-liter V6 or 3.5-liter V6 is slightly more powerful and just as efficient, though you may have to use more expensive fuel. For a good balance between ride and handling, look for the "touring" suspension, optional in 1993 and standard thereafter; for a firmer ride, try to find an LH with the "performance" suspension. The interior comfort is excellent, and the cars performed well on the crash tests.

	1998	1999	2000	2001	2002
Size Class	Intermd.	Intermd.	Intermd.	Intermd.	Intermd.
Drive	Front	Front	Front	Front	Front
Crash Test	Good	Good	Good	Good	Good
Airbags	Dual	Dual	Dual	Dual	Dl./Sd.(F)*
ABS	4-Whl*	4-Whl*	4-Whl*	4-Whl*	4-Whl*
Parts Cost	Low	Low	Low	Low	Low
Complaints	Average	Average	Good	Very Good	Good
Insurance	Discount	Discount	Regular	Regular	Discount
Fuel Econ.	19	19	19	19	23
Theft Rating	Low	Average	Average	Average**	Average**
Bumpers		Strong	Strong	Strong	Strong
Recalls	1	0	6	2	0
Trn. Cir. (ft.)	37.5	37.6	37.6	37.6	37.6
Weight (lbs.)	3463	3556	3556	3556	3469
Whlbase (in.)	113	113	113	113	113
Price	$9-11,000	$11-13,000	$14-16,000	$16-18,000	$21-23,000
OVERALL▪	Very Good	**BEST BET**	Good	Very Good	**BEST BET**

Chrysler New Yorker 1993-97, LHS 1994-2001, Dodge Dynasty 1993

The older New Yorker and Dynasty share almost nothing with the handsome LHS/New Yorker that was new for 1994. The early New Yorker shared its "square" styling

1995 Chrysler New Yorker

with the new Dodge Dynasty, catering to people who want the elegance of a Cadillac in a cheaper package. The Dynasty's base engine is a weak 2.5-liter 4-cylinder, while the New Yorker comes with a stronger V6 that's optional on the Dynasty and standard on the Dynasty LE. After 1994, a 3.5 V6 is plenty powerful and deliv-

	1993	1994	1995	1996	1997
Size Class	Intermd.	Large	Large	Large	Large
Drive	Front	Front	Front	Front	Front
Crash Test	Good	Good	Good	Good	Good
Airbags	Driver	Dual	Dual	Dual	Dual
ABS	4-Whl*	4-Whl	4-Whl	4-Whl	4-Whl
Parts Cost	Very Low	Very Low	Low	Low	Very Low
Complaints#	Poor	Very Poor	Good	Very Good	Poor
Insurance	Discount	Discount	Discount	Discount	Discount
Fuel Econ.	20	18	18	18	17
Theft Rating	Very Low	Average	Average	Average	Average
Bumpers	Weak				
Recalls	1	2	0	1	1
Trn. Cir. (ft.)	40	37.7	37.7	37.7	37.7
Weight (lbs.)	3273	3483	3592	3596	3619
Whlbase (in.)	104.3	113	113	113	113
Price	$3-5,000	$5-7,000	$7-9,000	$8-10,000	$10-12,000
OVERALL"	Very Good	Very Good	**BEST BET**	**BEST BET**	Very Good

"Cars without crash tests do not receive an overall rating. #Complaints based on New Yorker '93-97, LHS '98-01. Dynasty scored Very Poor in '93. *Optional **Estimate

2001 Chrysler LHS

ers average mileage.

The interior is comfortable for four with generous trunk space. The gauges look misaligned; it's hard to tell which one is which. On later models, an array of luxury features comes standard with your only options being a sunroof and CD player, and the front controls improve greatly. The LHS is the only survivor for 2001 and it was completely redesigned in 1999. It's 2.7-liter V6 and numerous luxury and safety features herald it as Chrysler's flagship sedan.

	1998	1999	2000	2001	2002
Size Class	Large	Large	Large	Large	
Drive	Front	Front	Front	Front	
Crash Test	Good	Average	Average	Average	
Airbags	Dual	Dual	Dual	Dual	
ABS	4-Whl	4-Whl	4-Whl	4-Whl	
Parts Cost	Low	Low	Low	Low	
Complaints	Very Good	Poor	Very Good	Very Good	
Insurance	Discount	Discount	Discount	Discount	
Fuel Econ.	17	18	18	18	
Theft Rating	Average	Average**	Average**	Average**	
Bumpers					
Recalls	1	0	2	2	
Trn. Cir. (ft.)	37.7	37.6	37.6	37.6	
Weight (lbs.)	3619	3579	3579	3579	
Whlbase (in.)	113	113	113	113	
Price	$14-16,000	$17-19,000	$19-21,000	$20-22,000	
OVERALL■	BEST BET	Very Good	BEST BET	BEST BET	

NO MODEL PRODUCED

Chrysler Sebring 1995-2002, Dodge Avenger 1995-2001

In 1995, the Chrysler Sebring and Dodge Avenger quickly became attractive alternatives to Celica, Prelude, and Integra buyers. The interior and exterior were redesigned in

1995 Chrysler Sebring

1997, giving the Sebring/Avenger a minor facelift. Dual airbags have been standard since their introduction, and side and head airbags became standard in 2002. Four-wheel ABS was optional in 1995, standard since 1996. Excellent crash test performers, the Sebring and Avenger also come with 5-mph bumpers from '96 on.

	1993	1994	1995	1996	1997
Size Class			Compact	Compact	Compact
Drive			Front	Front	Front
Crash Test			Very Good	Very Good	Very Good
Airbags			Dual	Dual	Dual
ABS			4-Whl*	4-Whl*	4-Whl*
Parts Cost			High	High	Very Low
Complaints[1]			Very Poor	Very Poor	Very Poor
Insurance			Surcharge	Surcharge	Surcharge
Fuel Econ.			22	22	20
Theft Rating			Average	Average	Average
Bumpers					
Recalls			1	4	4
Trn. Cir. (ft.)			39.4	39.4	39.4
Weight (lbs.)			2908	2908	2959
Whlbase (in.)			103.7	103.7	103.7
Price			$6-8,000	$8-10,000	$10-12,000
OVERALL■			Poor	Very Poor	Poor

NO MODEL PRODUCED

■Cars without crash tests do not receive an overall rating. [1]Based on Sebring. Avenger received Poor in '97, Average in "98, and Poor in 2000.
*Optional **Estimate

2002 Chrysler Sebring

The standard 2.0-liter 4-cylinder engine will probably not satisfy the sports car buyers Chrysler is hoping to reach. The peppier 2.5-liter V6 is a better choice. You'll find ample head- and legroom, even for rear passengers. Some negatives include a skimpy trunk, and repair bills tend to be high. Please note that the Chrysler Sebring JT convertible, introduced in '96, is not the same as the coupe hardtop Sebring; it is based on the Cirrus. For 2001, the Sebring was all-new and Chrysler added a sedan to the lineup.

	1998	1999	2000	2001	2002
Size Class	Compact	Compact	Compact	Compact	Compact
Drive	Front	Front	Front	Front	Front
Crash Test	Very Good	Very Good	Very Good	Very Good	Very Good
Airbags	Dual	Dual	Dual	Dual	Dl./Sd./Hd.
ABS	4-Whl*	4-Whl*	4-Whl*	4-Whl*	4-Whl*
Parts Cost	Average	Average	Average	High	Average
Complaints[1]	Very Poor	Average	Very Poor	Average	Average
Insurance	Surcharge	Surcharge	Surcharge	Surcharge	Regular
Fuel Econ.	20	21	19	20	23
Theft Rating	High	High	High	High**	Very High**
Bumpers		Strong	Strong	Strong	Weak
Recalls	3	0	0	6	0
Trn. Cir. (ft.)	39.4	39.4	39.4	36.1	36.1
Weight (lbs.)	2595	2967	2967	3100	3118
Whlbase (in.)	103.7	103.7	103.7	103.7	103.7
Price	$12-14,000	$13-15,000	$14-16,000	$18-20,000	$18-21,000
OVERALL■	Poor	Good	Poor	Poor	Very Good

Chrysler Town and Country 1993-2002

The Chrysler Town and Country, redesigned in 1996, has an extended wheelbase, giving it much more interior room. At a cost of about 20-40% more than its Dodge/Plymouth

1995 Chrysler Town and Country

siblings, you'll get lots of power equipment and the option of leather upholstery, along with, on more recent models, a plethora of cup holders, captain's chairs, and other nice luxuries. In 1992, a driver airbag became standard, and in 1994, standard dual airbags were added. Optional ABS is available on 1993-95 models and

	1993	1994	1995	1996	1997
Size Class	Minivan	Minivan	Minivan	Minivan	Minivan
Drive	Front/All	Front/All	Front/All	Front/All	Front/All
Crash Test	Very Good	Good	Good	Good	Good
Airbags	Driver	Dual	Dual	Dual	Dual
ABS	4-Whl*	4-Whl*	4-Whl*	4-Whl*	4-Whl*
Parts Cost	Low	Low	Very Low	Low	Low
Complaints	Very Poor	Very Poor	Average	Very Poor	Very Poor
Insurance	Discount	Discount	Discount	Discount	Discount
Fuel Econ.	19	18	20	20	17
Theft Rating	Very High	Very High	High	Very High	Very High
Bumpers		Weak	Weak		Weak
Recalls	7	4	3	6	4
Trn. Cir. (ft.)	40.5	41	41	37.6	37.6
Weight (lbs.)	3059	3135	3305	3528	3877
Whlbase (in.)	119.3	119.3	119.3	119.3	119.3
Price	$4-6,000	$6-8,000	$8-10,000	$9-11,000	$12-14,000
OVERALL■	Average	Average	Very Good	Average	Average

■Cars without crash tests do not receive an overall rating.*Optional **Estimate

2002 Chrysler Town and Country

became standard in 1996.

The Town and Country comes with a good 3.8-liter V6 with a standard automatic overdrive. Handling is decent, but you can't get the sport handling package found on the Dodge and Plymouth Grand models. Inside there is plenty of room front and back. The controls and displays improve with time, and the optional child safety seats are worth looking for. The Town and Country, along with the rest of the Chrysler minivan line, was redesigned for 2001.

	1998	1999	2000	2001	2002
Size Class	Minivan	Minivan	Minivan	Minivan	Minivan
Drive	Front/All	Front/All	Front/All	Front/All	Front/All
Crash Test	Good	Good	Good	Good	Good
Airbags	Dual	Dual	Dual	Dual	Dl./Sd./Hd.
ABS	4-Whl*	4-Whl*	4-Whl	4-Whl	4-Whl
Parts Cost	Very Low	Very Low	Very Low	Very Low	Very Low
Complaints	Poor	Average	Good	Very Good	Average
Insurance	Discount	Discount	Discount	Discount	Discount
Fuel Econ.	17	17	18	18	20
Theft Rating	Low	Average	Average	Average**	Average**
Bumpers	Weak		Strong	Strong	
Recalls	2	1	0	2	1
Trn. Cir. (ft.)	39.5	39.5	39.4	39.4	39.4
Weight (lbs.)	4082	4082	4045	4045	4107
Whlbase (in.)	119.3	119.3	119.3	119.3	119.3
Price	$14-16,000	$16-18,000	$20-22,000	$23-25,000	$25-27,000
OVERALL■	Very Good	**BEST BET**	**BEST BET**	**BEST BET**	**BEST BET**

Dodge Caravan/Plymouth Voyager 1993-2000, Chrysler Voyager 2001-2002

These pioneering minivans, new for 1996, have become the standard against which all other minivans are judged. The longer versions are called "Grand" and are

1993 Dodge Caravan

the most popular. The longer wheelbase translates into more space behind the third seats. In 1992, a driver's airbag became standard and rear child safety seats joined the option list. ABS is optional on 1993-95 models, standard for '96, and dual airbags became standard in 1994. The base 4-cylinder engine is suitable only if you don't

	1993	1994	1995	1996	1997
Size Class	Minivan	Minivan	Minivan	Minivan	Minivan
Drive	Front/All	Front/All	Front/All	Front/All	Front/All
Crash Test	Very Good	Good	Good	Good	Good
Airbags	Driver	Dual	Dual	Dual	Dual
ABS	4-Whl*	4-Whl*	4-Whl*	4-Whl*	4-Whl*
Parts Cost	Low	Low	Very Low	Low	Low
Complaints[1]	Very Poor	Very Poor	Poor	Very Poor	Poor
Insurance	Discount	Discount	Discount	Discount	Discount
Fuel Econ.	19	18	20	20	20
Theft Rating	Low	Average	Average	Very Low	Average
Bumpers		Weak	Weak		Weak
Recalls	7	3	3	8	6
Trn. Cir. (ft.)	40.5	41	41	37.6	37.6
Weight (lbs.)	3059	3135	3305	3528	3533
Whlbase (in.)	112.3	112.3	112.3	113.3	113.3
Price	$3-5,000	$4-6,000	$5-7,000	$8-10,000	$10-12,000
OVERALL▪	Good	Average	Good	Good	Good

▪Cars without crash tests do not receive an overall rating. [1]Based on Caravan results. *Optional **Estimate

2002 Dodge Caravan

load the vehicle much; otherwise, look for the bigger 2.6-liter 4-cylinder or one of the V6 engines. Buy the latest model you can afford and you can't go wrong.

Controls and displays improved as time went on and the optional built-in child restraints are definitely worth looking for. The Plymouth line was dropped in 2001 and Plymouth's shorter wheelbase version became the Chrysler Voyager.

	1998	1999	2000	2001	2002
Size Class	Minivan	Minivan	Minivan	Minivan	Minivan
Drive	Front/All	Front/All	Front/All	Front/All	Front/All
Crash Test	Good	Good	Good	Good	Good
Airbags	Dual	Dual	Dual	Dual	Dl./Sd.(F)*
ABS	4-Whl*	4-Whl*	4-Whl*	4-Whl*	4-Whl*
Parts Cost	Low	Low	Very Low	Low	Average
Complaints[1]	Very Poor	Poor	Very Good	Very Good	Average
Insurance	Discount	Discount	Discount	Discount	Discount
Fuel Econ.	20	20	19	19	20
Theft Rating	Low	Low	Average	Average**	Average**
Bumpers	Weak	Strong	Strong	Strong	Strong
Recalls	2	1	0	2	1
Trn. Cir. (ft.)	37.6	37.6	37.6	37.6	37.6
Weight (lbs.)	3517	3517	3517	3517	3869
Whlbase (in.)	113.3	113.3	113.3	113.3	113.3
Price	$12-14,000	$13-16,000	$16-18,000	$19-21,000	$21-23,000
OVERALL■	Good	Very Good	**BEST BET**	**BEST BET**	Very Good

Dodge Dakota 1993-2002

The Dodge Dakota is a compact pickup that was made to compete with Chevy's S-Series and the Ford Ranger. It has remained virtually the same since 1993 with only minor cosmetic changes.

1993 Dodge Dakota

Driver airbags were standard from 1993 to 1996; in 1997 a passenger airbag was added. Four-wheel ABS has remained optional over the last decade.

There are many options from which to choose on the Dodge Dakota. A standard 2.5-liter 4-cylinder engine is standard, but more

	1993	1994	1995	1996	1997
Size Class	Pickup	Pickup	Pickup	Pickup	Pickup
Drive	2WD/4WD	2WD/4WD	2WD/4WD	2WD/4WD	2WD/4WD
Crash Test	Good	Good	Good	Good	Good
Airbags	Driver	Driver	Driver	Driver	Dual
ABS	4-Whl*	4-Whl*	4-Whl*	4-Whl*	4-Whl*
Parts Cost	Very Low	Very Low	Very Low	Very Low	Very Low
Complaints	Poor	Poor	Poor	Poor	Poor
Insurance	Regular	Regular	Regular	Regular	Regular
Fuel Econ.	16	16	17	16	16
Theft Rating	Low	Low	Very Low	Very Low	Average
Bumpers					
Recalls	1	3	0	1	5
Trn. Cir. (ft.)	35.8	35.8	35.8	35.8	35.8
Weight (lbs.)	3831	3831	3831	3831	3831
Whlbase (in.)	111.9	111.9	111.9	111.9	111.9
Price	<$3,000	$2-4,000	$4-6,000	$6-8,000	$9-11,000
OVERALL■	Good	Average	Good	Good	Average

■Cars without crash tests do not receive an overall rating.*Optional **Estimate

2002 Dodge Dakota

powerful V6's and V8's are offered. You'll also have to choose between a short or long bed, two- or four-wheel drive, manual or automatic transmission, regular or club cab, and several different packages.

The Dakota has fared well in crash tests and its smooth ride and superior handling makes it equal to or better than its Ford and Chevy counterparts.

	1998	1999	2000	2001	2002
Size Class	Pickup	Pickup	Pickup	Pickup	Pickup
Drive	2WD/4WD	2WD/4WD	2WD/4WD	2WD/4WD	2WD/4WD
Crash Test	Good	Good	Good	Good	Good
Airbags	Dual	Dual	Dual	Dual	Dual
ABS	4-Whl*	4-Whl*	4-Whl*	4-Whl*	4-Whl*
Parts Cost	Low	Low	Very Low	Low	Low
Complaints	Poor	Poor	Poor	Good	Poor
Insurance	Surcharge	Surcharge	Surcharge	Surcharge	Surcharge
Fuel Econ.	16	16	16	16	16
Theft Rating	Average	Average	Average	Average**	Average**
Bumpers					
Recalls	6	4	4	2	0
Trn. Cir. (ft.)	35.8	35.8	35.8	35.8	35.8
Weight (lbs.)	3831	3831	3831	3831	3831
Whlbase (in.)	111.9	111.9	111.9	111.9	111.9
Price	$10-12,000	$11-13,000	$13-15,000	$14-16,000	$16-18,000
OVERALL■	Poor	Poor	Poor	Average	Average

Dodge Durango 1998-2002

Based on the Dakota pickup, the Durango accommodates more passengers and has a more heavy-duty appeal. It was first built in 1999 to compete with the Ford Explorer—a

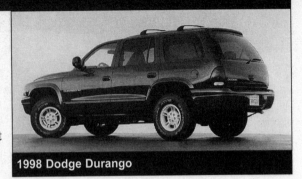

1998 Dodge Durango

tough competitor. The Durango comes standard with both dual and front side airbags and standard 2-wheel ABS (4-wheel ABS is optional).

The Durango comes with three different engine choices: a base

	1993	1994	1995	1996	1997
Size Class					
Drive					
Crash Test					
Airbags					
ABS					
Parts Cost		NO MODEL PRODUCED			
Complaints					
Insurance					
Fuel Econ.					
Theft Rating					
Bumpers					
Recalls					
Trn. Cir. (ft.)					
Weight (lbs.)					
Whlbase (in.)					
Price					
OVERALL■					

■Cars without crash tests do not receive an overall rating.*Optional **Estimate

2002 Dodge Durango

3.9-liter V6, a 5.2-liter V8 and a 5.9-liter V8. The V6 is adequate for everyday driving, but if you're towing heavy loads, it is better to go with one of the V8's. Because of the large engines, the fuel economy is very poor and the driving distance is short, but that is typical of large sport utility vehicles. The Durango did well in crash tests.

	1998	1999	2000	2001	2002
Size Class	Sp. Util.	Sp. Util.	Sp. Util.	Sp. Util.	Sp. Util.
Drive	2WD/4WD	2WD/4WD	2WD/4WD	2WD/4WD	2WD/4WD
Crash Test	Good	Good	Good	Good	Good
Airbags	Dual	Dual	Dual	Dual	Dl./Sd.(F)*
ABS	4-Whl*	4-Whl*	4-Whl*	4-Whl*	4-Whl*
Parts Cost	Low	Very Low	Low	Very Low	Average
Complaints	Poor	Poor	Average	Very Good	Poor
Insurance	Regular	Regular	Regular	Regular	Surcharge
Fuel Econ.	14	17	17	15	16
Theft Rating	Very High	Very High	Very High	Very High**	Very High**
Bumpers					
Recalls	4	3	1	2	0
Trn. Cir. (ft.)	38.9	38.9	38.9	38.9	38.9
Weight (lbs.)	3831	3831	3831	3831	3831
Whlbase (in.)	115.9	115.9	115.9	115.9	115.9
Price	$17-19,000	$18-20,000	$20-22,000	$21-23,000	$24-26,000
OVERALL■	Poor	Average	Good	Very Good	Poor

Dodge Ram Pickup 1993-2002

Probably the most distinct and stylish of the heavy-duty trucks, the Dodge Ram remains one of Dodge's best sellers. Its fashionable front end and old-fashioned power make it a

1994 Dodge Ram

very popular choice in the full-size pickup market. No airbags were offered until 1995, when a driver airbag became standard, and it wasn't until 1998 that dual airbags became standard. In 1999, the Ram offered dual and optional front side airbags—a rarity in the pickup market. Optional 4-wheel ABS has been offered since its

	1993	1994	1995	1996	1997
Size Class	Pickup	Pickup	Pickup	Pickup	Pickup
Drive	Rear/4	Rear/4	Rear/4	Rear/4	Rear/4
Crash Test	N/A	N/A	N/A	N/A	N/A
Airbags	None	None	Driver	Driver	Driver
ABS	4-Whl*	4-Whl*	4-Whl*	4-Whl*	4-Whl*
Parts Cost	Very Low	Very Low	Very Low	Very Low	Very Low
Complaints	Average	Very Poor	Very Poor	Very Poor	Poor
Insurance	Regular	Regular	Regular	Regular	Regular
Fuel Econ.	13	13	13	13	14
Theft Rating	Low	Low	Low	Low	Average
Bumpers					
Recalls	1	18	12	10	6
Trn. Cir. (ft.)	40.9	40.9	40.9	40.9	40.9
Weight (lbs.)	4,900	4,900	4,900	4,900	4,900
Whlbase (in.)	118.7	118.7	118.7	118.7	118.7
Price	$4-6,000	$6-8,000	$8-10,000	$10-12,000	$12-14,000
OVERALL▪	Very Poor	Very Poor	Very Poor	Very Poor	Very Poor

▪Cars without crash tests do not receive an overall rating.*Optional **Estimate

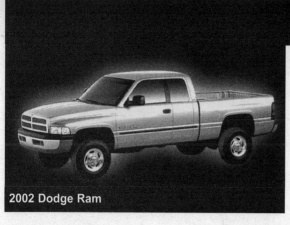
2002 Dodge Ram

creation.

In 2002 the Ram was slightly restyled and with the restyling came two new engines. The 1500 now comes with a standard 3.7-liter "magnum" V6, which outperforms and replaces the 3.9-liter V6. A 4.7-liter "magnum" V8 is also offered and replaces the 5.2-liter V8. Other engines are also offered for the larger trucks. Good crash tests and safety options make this truck a great pick in the standard truck market, but check out why other consumers complained.

	1998	1999	2000	2001	2002
Size Class	Pickup	Pickup	Pickup	Pickup	Pickup
Drive	Rear/4	Rear/4	Rear/4	Rear/4	Rear/4
Crash Test	Good	Good	Good	Good	Good
Airbags	Dual	Dual/Side	Dual/Side	Dual/Side	Dual/Side (F)*
ABS	4-Whl*	4-Whl*	4-Whl*	4-Whl*	4-Whl*
Parts Cost	Low	Average	Low	Very Low	Very High
Complaints	Poor	Average	Very Good	Average	Average
Insurance	Regular	Regular	Regular	Regular	Regular
Fuel Econ.	14	14	14	14	14
Theft Rating	Very High	Very High	High	High**	High**
Bumpers					
Recalls	11	8	5	8	0
Trn. Cir. (ft.)	40.9	40.9	40.9	40.9	40.9
Weight (lbs.)	4,900	4,900	4,900	4,900	4,900
Whlbase (in.)	118.7	118.7	118.7	118.7	118.7
Price	$13-15,000	$14-17,000	$17-19,000	$18-20,000	$22-24,000
OVERALL■	Poor	Average	Very Good	Good	Poor

Dodge/Plymouth Neon 1995-2002

1995 Dodge Neon

The Neon is Chrysler's first small car to take advantage of the cab-forward design that has attracted so many customers to Chrysler's larger cars. Because of its design, the Neon has surprising room for such a small car. Sales have been quite high, though complaints have taken their toll. You can find the Neon in either a two- or four-door version with three trim levels. Dual airbags have been standard since its inception and front side airbags became optional for 2002. Also, 1995 and 1996 models

	1993	1994	1995	1996	1997
Size Class	NO MODEL PRODUCED		Subcomp.	Subcomp.	Subcomp.
Drive			Front	Front	Front
Crash Test			Average	Average	Average
Airbags			Dual	Dual	Dual
ABS			4-Whl*	4-Whl*	4-Whl*
Parts Cost			Low	Low	Very Low
Complaints			Very Poor	Poor	Very Poor
Insurance			Surcharge	Surcharge	Surcharge
Fuel Econ.			28	28	29
Theft Rating			Very Low	Very Low	Very Low
Bumpers			Weak	Weak	Weak
Recalls			7	2	1
Trn. Cir. (ft.)			35.4	35.4	35.4
Weight (lbs.)			2385	2385	2385
Whlbase (in.)			104	104	104
Price			$3-5,000	$4-6,000	$5-7,000
OVERALL■			Poor	Poor	Average

■Cars without crash tests do not receive an overall rating. *Optional **Estimate

2002 Dodge Neon

meet the 1997 government standards for side impact protection. For 2000, the Neon was redesigned. The single-cam version of the 2-liter engine that is found in the base sedan provides adequate power. The cab-forward design leads to a wider and longer car that produces more interior room. Your best bet may be to find a coupe or sedan with the dual-cam engine. Also, look for the built in child restraints, as they are an excellent feature.

	1998	1999	2000	2001	2002
Size Class	Subcomp.	Subcomp.	Subcomp.	Subcomp.	Subcomp.
Drive	Front	Front	Front	Front	Front
Crash Test	Good	Good	Good	Average	Average
Airbags	Dual	Dual	Dual	Dual	Dl./Sd.(F)*
ABS	4-Whl*	4-Whl*	4-Whl*	4-Whl*	4-Whl*
Parts Cost	Very Low	Very Low	Very Low	Very Low	Very Low
Complaints	Very Poor	Very Good	Poor	Good	Poor
Insurance	Surcharge	Surcharge	Surcharge	Surcharge	Surcharge
Fuel Econ.	29	27	27	27	27
Theft Rating	Very Low	Low	Average	Average**	Average**
Bumpers	Weak		Strong	Strong	Strong
Recalls	0	1	3	1	0
Trn. Cir. (ft.)	35.4	35.4	35.5	35.5	35.5
Weight (lbs.)	2470	2470	2564	2564	2590
Whlbase (in.)	104	104	105	105	105
Price	$6-8,000	$7-8,000	$9-10,000	$10-12,000	$13-15,000
OVERALL■	Average	Very Good	Good	Very Good	Good

Eagle Talon 1993-98, Mitsubishi Eclipse 1991-2002, Plymouth Laser 1991-94

The Talon came out in the fall of 1989 as a 1990 model, and several months after the Talon, the identical Mitsubishi Eclipse and Plymouth Laser made their debuts. The Talon

1993 Eagle Talon

and Eclipse were redesigned for 1995, while the Laser was dropped after 1994. The Eclipse was completely redesigned for 2000. Like the Eclipse, the Talon is available in a 4-wheel drive model called the TSi AWD. ABS was optional starting in 1991 and became standard in 2000. Side front airbags also became standard in 2002.

	1993	1994	1995	1996	1997
Size Class	Compact	Compact	Compact	Compact	Compact
Drive	Front/All	Front/All	Front/All	Front/All	Front/All
Crash Test	Very Good	Very Good	Good	Good	Good
Airbags	None	None	Dual	Dual	Dual
ABS	4-Whl*	4-Whl*	4-Whl*	4-Whl*	4-Whl*
Parts Cost	Very High	Very High	High[1]	Average	Low
Complaints	Poor	Good	Very Poor	Very Poor	Poor
Insurance	Surcharge	Surcharge	Surcharge	Surcharge	Surcharge
Fuel Econ.	21	20	22	23	23
Theft Rating	Very Low	Low	Average	Low	Average
Bumpers	Strong	Strong			
Recalls	2	2	6	4	4
Trn. Cir. (ft.)	35.4	35.4	38.1	38.1	38.1
Weight (lbs.)	2542	2542	2822	2767	2729
Whlbase (in.)	97.2	97.2	98.8	98.8	98.8
Price	$3-5,000	$5-7,000	$7-9,000	$8-10,000	$10-12,000
OVERALL■	Very Poor	Poor	Very Poor	Very Poor	Poor

■Cars without crash tests do not receive an overall rating.[1]Data given for Talon. Parts cost for Eclipse/Laser in 1995 is Average. Laser in 1995 is average, in 1998 is low. *Optional **Estimate

2002 Mitsubishi Eclipse

The base models of these coupes are well equipped, though some options such as a rear wiper and power locks are only available on the upper level Laser RS, Talon ES and TSI, and Eclipse GS. The upper level models' 2-liter twin-cam engine outperforms the base models' 1.8-liter, yet its gas mileage isn't much worse. Handling on the upper level models is superior to the DL's. Ride is firm in all versions, exactly what you'd expect from a high caliber sports car.

	1998	1999	2000	2001	2002
Size Class	Compact	Compact	Compact	Compact	Compact
Drive	Front	Front	Front	Front	Front
Crash Test	Good	N/A	N/A	N/A	N/A
Airbags	Dual	Dual	Dual	Dual	Dl./Sd.(F)
ABS	4-Whl*	4-Whl*	4-Whl	4-Whl	4-Whl
Parts Cost	Average[1]	Low	Low	Low	Very Low
Complaints	Very Poor	Average	Poor	Poor	Very Poor
Insurance	Surcharge	Surcharge	Surcharge	Surcharge	Surcharge
Fuel Econ.	23	23	23	23	23
Theft Rating	Very High	Very High	Average	Average**	Average**
Bumpers		Strong	Strong	Strong	Strong
Recalls	5	0	4	4	0
Trn. Cir. (ft.)	38.1	38.1	36.5	36.5	35.4
Weight (lbs.)	2729	3858	2822	2822	2922
Whlbase (in.)	98.8	98.8	100.8	100.8	100.8
Price	$12-14,000	$13-15,000	$14-16,000	$18-20,000	$19-22,000
OVERALL■	Very Poor				

Ford Aerostar 1993-97

A lackluster competitor through the years while up against Chrysler's mini-vans, Ford had hoped to change its luck in the minivan market with the new Windstar, which was added to the lineup in 1995. The Windstar was originally supposed to replace the Aerostar, but the Aerostar sold surprisingly well, despite all its deficiencies, prompting Ford to keep it around until 1997. The Aerostar pressed on without major exterior changes since its debut in the early 80s until 1997.

1993 Ford Aerostar

	1993	1994	1995	1996	1997
Size Class	Minivan	Minivan	Minivan	Minivan	Minivan
Drive	Rear/4	Rear/4	Rear/4	Rear/4	Rear/4
Crash Test	Average	Average	Average	Average	Average
Airbags	Driver	Driver	Driver	Driver	Driver
ABS	2-Whl	2-Whl	2-Whl	2-Whl	2-Whl
Parts Cost	Low	Average	Average	Low	Average
Complaints	Very Poor	Poor	Poor	Average	Average
Insurance	Discount	Discount	Discount	Discount	Discount
Fuel Econ.	18	16	17	18	17
Theft Rating	Low	Average	Very Low	Very Low	Very Low
Bumpers					
Recalls	3	4	6	5	4
Trn. Cir. (ft.)	42.4	42.4	42.4	42.4	42.4
Weight (lbs.)	3296	3296	3400	3646	3646
Whlbase (in.)	118.9	118.9	118.9	118.9	118.9
Price	$2-4,000	$3-5,000	$4-6,000	$5-7,000	$7-9,000
OVERALL■	Poor	Poor	Poor	Good	Average

■Cars without crash tests do not receive an overall rating.

134

1997 Ford Aerostar

Look for models with the 3-liter V6 and, if you often carry heavy loads, the 4-liter V6. The ride is fairly good. Pass on the electronic dashboard, which is standard on the Eddie Bauer model. Fold out child restraints are an excellent option from 1993 on. The brakes are poor, especially on wet roads; the Aerostar really needs 4-wheel ABS to compete in this tough market. Early models had lots of mechanical problems, so get the latest model you can afford.

	1998	1999	2000	2001	2002
Size Class					
Drive					
Crash Test					
Airbags					
ABS					
Parts Cost					
Complaints					
Insurance					
Fuel Econ.					
Theft Rating			NO MODEL PRODUCED		
Bumpers					
Recalls					
Trn. Cir. (ft.)					
Weight (lbs.)					
Whlbase (in.)					
Price					
OVERALL■					

Ford Bronco 1993-96, Expedition 1997-2002

The Bronco represents Ford's first foray into what was to become modern day sport utilities. New in 1997 was the Expedition, the replacement for the Bronco.

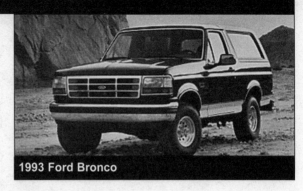

1993 Ford Bronco

The Expedition is designed to compete with the successful Chevy Suburban, although slightly smaller. The Bronco received extensive facelifts in 1992. A driver's side airbag was finally added in 1994; dual airbags are standard for the Expedition and optional front side airbags are offered for 2002. Rear-wheel ABS was available in 1990; 4-wheel ABS has

	1993	1994	1995	1996	1997
Size Class	Sp. Util.	Sp. Util.	Sp. Util.	Sp. Util.	Sp. Util.
Drive	Rear/4	Rear/4	Rear/4	Rear/4	Rear/4
Crash Test	Very Good	Very Good	Very Good	Very Good	Very Good
Airbags	None	Driver	Driver	Driver	Dual
ABS	4-Whl	4-Whl	4-Whl	4-Whl	4-Whl
Parts Cost	Low	Low	Low	High	Average
Complaints	Very Poor	Very Poor	Poor	Good	Very Poor
Insurance	Discount	Discount	Discount	Regular	Regular
Fuel Econ.	13	13	14	14	14
Theft Rating	Very High	Very High	Very High	Very High	Very High
Bumpers					
Recalls	5	4	0	0	3
Trn. Cir. (ft.)	36.6	36.6	36.6	36.6	36.6
Weight (lbs.)	4587	4587	4587	4500	4500
Whlbase (in.)	104.7	104.7	104.7	104.7	119
Price	$7-9,000	$9-11,000	$11-12,000	$12-14,000	$15-17,000
OVERALL■	Poor	Average	Good	Average	Poor

■Cars without crash tests do not receive an overall rating.*Optional **Estimate

2002 Ford Expedition

been standard since 1993.

Both the 5-liter and 5.8-liter V8s available through-out the Bronco's recent history are adequate, though the 5.8 accelerates significantly better. The gas mileage with either engine is dreadful on this heavy vehicle. The Expedition comes with either a 4.6-liter V8 or a larger 5.4-liter engine. You'll find the handling is cumbersome. The Bronco's rear seat won't be comfortable on long trips, but it does improve on the Expedition.

	1998	1999	2000	2001	2002
Size Class	Sp. Util.	Sp. Util.	Sp. Util.	Sp. Util.	Sp. Util.
Drive	Rear/4	Rear/4	Rear/4	Rear/4	Rear/4
Crash Test	Very Good	Very Good	Very Good	Very Good	Very Good
Airbags	Dual	Dual	Dual	Dual	Dl./Sd.(F)*
ABS	4-Whl	4-Whl	4-Whl	4-Whl	4-Whl
Parts Cost	Average	High	High	High	High
Complaints	Poor	Poor	Average	Very Good	Poor
Insurance	Regular	Regular	Discount	Discount	Discount
Fuel Econ.	15	15	15	15	15
Theft Rating	High	High	High	High**	High**
Bumpers					
Recalls	3	1	2	3	0
Trn. Cir. (ft.)	40.4	40.4	40.4	40.4	40.4
Weight (lbs.)	4500	4500	4500	4500	4500
Whlbase (in.)	119.1	119.1	119.1	119.1	119.1
Price	$18-20,000	$19-21,000	$24-26,000	$25-29,000	$32-34,000
OVERALL■	Average	Average	Good	Very Good	Good

Ford Contour/Mercury Mystique 1995-2000

The Ford Contour and Mercury Mystique are the American versions of Ford's "world car"—representing Ford's efforts to enter the lucrative global auto market. The Contour/Mystique

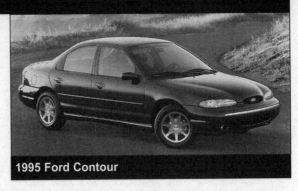

1995 Ford Contour

is marketed to a broader audience. Dual airbags have been standard since their 1995 introduction; ABS is still optional so know what you are buying. The Mystique is the more upscale version and has a softer ride, while the Contour tends to be more utilitarian and aimed towards a broader audience. The base GL on the Contour is basic,

	1993	1994	1995	1996	1997
Size Class			Compact	Compact	Compact
Drive			Front	Front	Front
Crash Test			Good	Good	Good
Airbags			Dual	Dual	Dual
ABS			4-Whl*	4-Whl*	4-Whl*
Parts Cost			Average	Average	Low
Complaints			Very Poor	Very Poor	Average
Insurance			Regular	Regular	Regular
Fuel Econ.			23	23	24
Theft Rating			Very Low	Very Low	Very Low
Bumpers			Weak	Weak	Weak
Recalls			8	5	4
Trn. Cir. (ft.)			36.5	36.5	36.5
Weight (lbs.)			2831	2831	2831
Whlbase (in.)			106.5	106.5	106.5
Price			$4-6,000	$5-7,000	$6-8,000
OVERALL■			Poor	Poor	Good

Center columns 1993/1994: NO MODEL PRODUCED

■Cars without crash tests do not receive an overall rating.*Optional

138

1999 Mercury Mystique

the LX is plusher. Both come with a 2-liter engine, barely adequate— the Mystique's base GS and mid-level LS also come with this engine. The Contour's sporty SE has a 2.5-liter V6, which is powerful and quiet. The 2.5-liter engine is optional for the Mystique. Ford guarantees these engines won't need a tune-up for the first 100,000 miles. The Contour will save you about $1,000 over the Mystique. Your best bet may be to look for an SE with the larger engine and other optional features.

	1998	1999	2000	2001	2002
Size Class	Compact	Compact	Compact		
Drive	Front	Front	Front		
Crash Test	Very Good	Very Good	Very Good		
Airbags	Dual	Dual/Side	Dual/Side		
ABS	4-Whl*	4-Whl*	4-Whl*		
Parts Cost	Low	Low	Low		
Complaints	Very Poor	Average	Good		
Insurance	Regular	Regular	Regular		
Fuel Econ.	24	24	24		
Theft Rating	Average	Low	Low		
Bumpers	Weak				
Recalls	7	2	1		
Trn. Cir. (ft.)	36.5	36.5	36.5		
Weight (lbs.)	2811	2769	2769		
Whlbase (in.)	106.5	106.5	106.5		
Price	$7-9,000	$8-10,000	$10-12,000		
OVERALL■	Average	**BEST BET**	**BEST BET**		

NO MODEL PRODUCED

Ford Crown Victoria 1993-2002, Mercury Grand Marquis 1993-2002

The Crown Victoria and Grand Marquis are almost identical and basically cheap versions of the Lincoln Town Car. In 1992, a major restyling occurred when Ford put an aero-

1993 Ford Crown Victoria

dynamic body on the old chassis. These big Fords got standard driver airbags for 1990; dual front airbags became optional in 1992, standard on 1994 and later models. Front side airbags became optional in 2002. ABS is optional starting in 1991 for Ford, 1992 for Mercury. Also, crash severity sensors, seat position sensors, and seat

	1993	1994	1995	1996	1997
Size Class	Large	Large	Large	Large	Large
Drive	Rear	Rear	Rear	Rear	Rear
Crash Test	Good	Very Good	Very Good	Very Good	Very Good
Airbags	Driver#	Dual	Dual	Dual	Dual
ABS	4-Whl*	4-Whl*	4-Whl*	4-Whl*	4-Whl*
Parts Cost	Low	Low	Low	Low	Average
Complaints	Poor	Poor	Poor	Poor	Average
Insurance	Discount	Discount	Regular	Discount	Discount
Fuel Econ.	18	18	17	17	17
Theft Rating	Very Low	Very Low	Very Low	Very Low	Very Low
Bumpers					
Recalls	4	3	8	4	2
Trn. Cir. (ft.)	39.1	39.1	39.1	40.3	40.3
Weight (lbs.)	3776	3786	3762	3780	3797
Whlbase (in.)	114.4	114.4	114.4	114.4	114.4
Price	$3-4,000	$4-6,000	$6-8,000	$7-9,000	$9-11,000
OVERALL■	Good	Very Good	Average	Very Good	Very Good

■Cars without crash tests do not receive an overall rating.#Passenger Side Optional *Optional **Estimate

2002 Ford Crown Victoria

belt pretensioners are all standard for 2001.

The modular 4.6-liter V8 engine is responsive with decent gas mileage. For 1996, you have the choice of an upgrade on the 4.6 V8, which will deliver 20 more horses. 1992 models and on got a tighter base suspension, which handles better. Go for the later versions with the best crash test results and more standard features. There's ample room for six plus luggage.

	1998	1999	2000	2001	2002
Size Class	Large	Large	Large	Large	Large
Drive	Rear	Rear	Rear	Rear	Rear
Crash Test	Very Good	Very Good	Very Good	Very Good	Very Good
Airbags	Dual	Dual	Dual	Dual	Dual
ABS	4-Whl*	4-Whl*	4-Whl*	4-Whl*	4-Whl*
Parts Cost	Average	Average	Very Good	Very Good	Very Good
Complaints	Good	Good	Very Good	Very Good	Poor
Insurance	Discount	Discount	Discount	Discount	Discount
Fuel Econ.	17	17	17	20	20
Theft Rating	Very Low	Very Low	Very Low**	Very Low**	Very Low**
Bumpers		Strong	Strong	Strong	Strong
Recalls	1	1	3	3	0
Trn. Cir. (ft.)	40.3	40.3	40.3	40.3	40.3
Weight (lbs.)	3917	3917	3917	3917	3942
Whlbase (in.)	114.7	114.7	114.7	114.7	114.7
Price	$11-13,000	$13-15,000	$15-17,000	$17-19,000	$24-26,000
OVERALL■	BEST BET	BEST BET	BEST BET	BEST BET	BEST BET

Ford Escort 1993-2001

The Ford Escort has had many upgrades and style changes since its introduction to the car market in 1981 as the Pinto replacement. In mid-1990 Ford introduced an all-new

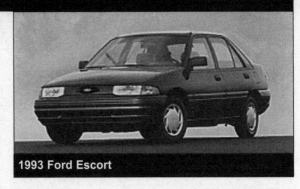

1993 Ford Escort

Escort and its twin, the Mercury Tracer, both based on the Mazda Protégé. Finally, in 1997, the Escort went through its greatest change of all, as the vehicle was completely redesigned. The 1997 model has much rounder and smoother lines than previous models. Watch out for 1990-96 Escorts with motorized shoulder belts and

	1993	1994	1995	1996	1997
Size Class	Subcomp.	Subcomp.	Subcomp.	Subcomp.	Subcomp.
Drive	Front	Front	Front	Front	Front
Crash Test	Very Good	Good	Average	Average	Average
Airbags	None	Driver	Dual	Dual	Dual
ABS	None	None	4-Whl*	4-Whl*	4-Whl*
Parts Cost	Low	Low	Low	Low	Average
Complaints	Poor	Good	Poor	Good	Average
Insurance	Surcharge	Surcharge	Surcharge	Surcharge	Surcharge
Fuel Econ.	25	25	30	25	26
Theft Rating	Very Low	Low	Average	Very Low	Very Low
Bumpers	Weak	Weak	Weak	Weak	Weak
Recalls	2	1	4	0	0
Trn. Cir. (ft.)	31.5	31.5	31.5	31.5	31.5
Weight (lbs.)	2419	2325	2355	2378	2457
Whlbase (in.)	98.4	98.4	98.4	98.4	98.4
Price	<$3,000	< $3,000	$3-5,000	$4-6,000	$5-7,000
OVERALL▪	Poor	Average	Poor	Good	Average

▪Cars without crash tests do not receive an overall rating.*Optional **Estimate

2001 Ford Escort

separate lap belts; it's very easy to forget the lap belt. The 1994 models have a standard driver's airbag, and 1995 models added a passenger airbag. ABS was finally available beginning in 1995. The Escort has offered several 4-cylinder engines; base engines are adequate. New engines for 1997 provide more power. Comfort is good in front, only adequate in back; but both improved with the 1991 changeover. While not that flashy, Escorts are a good, solid buy. For 2001, they are only available for fleet sales.

	1998	1999	2000	2001	2002
Size Class	Subcomp.	Subcomp.	Subcomp.	Subcomp.	
Drive	Front	Front	Front	Front	
Crash Test	Average	Average	Average	Average	
Airbags	Dual	Dual	Dual	Dual	
ABS	4-Whl*	4-Whl*	4-Whl*	4-Whl*	
Parts Cost	Very Low	Very Low	Very Low	Very Low	
Complaints	Average	Good	Very Good	Very Good	
Insurance	Surcharge	Surcharge	Surcharge	Surcharge	
Fuel Econ.	28	28	28	28	
Theft Rating	Very Low**	Very Low**	Very Low**	Very Low**	
Bumpers	Weak				
Recalls	0	0	0	0	
Trn. Cir. (ft.)	31.5	31.5	31.5	31.5	
Weight (lbs.)	2468	2468	2468	2468	
Whlbase (in.)	98.4	98.4	98.4	98.4	
Price	$6-8,000	$8-10,000	$9-11,000	$10-12,000	
OVERALL■	Good	Very Good	BEST BET	BEST BET	

The "2002" column reads vertically: NO MODEL PRODUCED

143

Ford Explorer 1993-2002

The Ford Explorer has been the segment leader for years, and its redesign in 1995 strengthened that position. The Explorer comes in two body styles, 2- or 4-door; the longer 4-door has

1993 Ford Explorer

more room for adults in the back. The Explorer had no airbags or other passive restraints until the 1995 redesign which, thankfully, brought dual airbags and front side airbags as optional for 2001. 1993 Explorers have rear-wheel ABS; later models come with 4-wheel ABS. The Explorer's engine is a 4-liter V6 with 5-speed man-

	1993	1994	1995	1996	1997
Size Class	Sp. Util.	Sp. Util.	Sp. Util.	Sp. Util.	Sp. Util.
Drive	Rear/4	Rear/4	Rear/4	Rear/4	Rear/4
Crash Test	Average	Average	Good	Good	Good
Airbags	None	None	Dual	Dual	Dual
ABS	2-Whl	4-Whl	4-Whl	4-Whl	4-Whl
Parts Cost	Very Low	Very Low	Very Low	Very Low	Average
Complaints	Very Poor	Very Poor	Poor	Very Poor	Very Poor
Insurance	Discount	Discount	Regular	Discount	Discount
Fuel Econ.	17	17	15	18	16
Theft Rating	Very Low	Average	Very Low	Low	Low
Bumpers				Weak	Weak
Recalls	8	11	6	6	5
Trn. Cir. (ft.)		35.6	37.3	37.3	34.6
Weight (lbs.)	3890	3844	4189	4150	3707
Whlbase (in.)	102.1	102.1	111.5	111.5	111.5
Price	$3-5,000	$5-7,000	$7-9,000	$9-11,000	$11-13,000
OVERALL■	Poor	Poor	Good	Good	Average

■Cars without crash tests do not receive an overall rating.*Optional **Estimate

144

2002 Ford Explorer

ual or automatic overdrive, and 2- or part-time 4-wheel drive. A 5.0-liter V8 is also available. On both vehicles, power is adequate, and the gas mileage is better than most large utility vehicles, but still worse than many full-size cars. In general, the handling is unresponsive and the ride is rough. Up to four adults will be comfortable inside. The Explorer's front end was restyled for 1999 and the front bumper was lowered in 2002 to match the height of passenger cars.

	1998	1999	2000	2001	2002
Size Class	Sp. Util.	Sp. Util.	Sp. Util.	Sp. Util.	Sp. Util.
Drive	Rear/4	Rear/4	Rear/4	Rear/4	Rear/4
Crash Test	Average	Average	Average	Average	Average
Airbags	Dual	Dual	Dual/Side*	Dual/Side	Dl./Sd.(F)*
ABS	4-Whl	4-Whl	4-Whl	4-Whl	4-Whl
Parts Cost	Average	Very Poor	Low	Low	Very Low
Complaints	Very Poor	Very Poor	Average	Good	Very Poor
Insurance	Discount	Regular	Regular	Discount	Discount
Fuel Econ.	16	16	16	15	17
Theft Rating	Average	High	Average	Average**	Average**
Bumpers	Weak				
Recalls	3	2	0	2	3
Trn. Cir. (ft.)	37.3	37.3	37.3	37.3	37.3
Weight (lbs.)	3707	3707	3707	4250	4250
Whlbase (in.)	111.5	111.5	111.5	111.6	111.6
Price	$13-15,000	$14-16,000	$16-19,000	$18-20,000	$25-27,000
OVERALL■	Poor	Very Poor	Good	Very Good	Good

Ford Festiva 1993, Aspire 1994-98

The Festiva is a Mazda-designed car built by Kia, which began exporting its own cars to America in 1994. The Festiva appeared in early 1987 as a 1988 model and scarcely changed since

1993 Ford Festiva

then until it was replaced in mid-1994 by the more rounded Aspire. The 1990-93 Festivas have annoying motorized belts—you must remember to fasten the lap belts separately. The mid-1994 changeover to the Aspire brought standard dual airbags and optional ABS. The Festiva/Aspire's 1.3 liter 4-cylinder engine provides ade-

	1993	1994	1995	1996	1997
Size Class	Subcomp.	Subcomp.	Subcomp.	Subcomp.	Subcomp.
Drive	Front	Front	Front	Front	Front
Crash Test	N/A	Average	Average	Average	Average
Airbags	None	Dual	Dual	Dual	Dual
ABS	None	4-Whl*	4-Whl*	4-Whl*	4-Whl*
Parts Cost	High	High	Low	Very High	Very High
Complaints	Average	Poor	Average	Good	Poor
Insurance	Surcharge	Regular	Regular	Surcharge	Surcharge
Fuel Econ.	35	36	36	34	34
Theft Rating	Very Low	Very Low	Very Low	Very Low	Very Low
Bumpers	Weak				
Recalls	1	2	0	0	0
Trn. Cir. (ft.)	28.9	29.5	29.5	30.8	29.5
Weight (lbs.)	1797	2004	2004	2004	2056
Whlbase (in.)	90.2	90.7	90.7	90.7	90.7
Price	<$3,000	< $3,000	< $3,000	$2-4,000	$4-6,000
OVERALL■	Very Poor	Average	Very Good	Average	Poor

■Cars without crash tests do not receive an overall rating.*Optional

146

1997 Ford Aspire

quate power, though more so for the lighter Festiva than for the Aspire. You are better off with the 5-speed transmission—it allows better acceleration and fuel economy, and lets the engine run slower on the highway, reducing noise and improving engine life. The body leans during hard cornering, but handling is generally good. The Festiva comes in several trim levels; you have to get a GL in order to get items like air conditioning and rear wiper.

	1998	1999	2000	2001	2002
Size Class					
Drive					
Crash Test					
Airbags					
ABS					
Parts Cost					
Complaints					
Insurance					
Fuel Econ.					
Theft Rating					
Bumpers					
Recalls					
Trn. Cir. (ft.)					
Weight (lbs.)					
Whlbase (in.)					
Price					
OVERALL■					

NO MODEL PRODUCED

Ford F-Series 1993-2002

The long-running Ford F-Series still remains the best selling pickup in the United States. It does consecutively well in crash tests, scoring a "very good" for over a decade.

1993 Ford F-Series

The F-150 offered a driver's airbag until 1996, when it became standard. Only a year later, in 1997, dual airbags became standard. ABS is standard on two wheels, but 4-wheel ABS is optional.

A 4.2-liter V6 powers the F-150, but 4.6- and 5.4-liter engines are

	1993	1994	1995	1996	1997
Size Class	Truck	Truck	Truck	Truck	Truck
Drive	Rear/4	Rear/4	Rear/4	Rear/4	Rear/4
Crash Test	Very Good	Very Good	Very Good	Very Good	Very Good
Airbags	Driver*	Driver*	Driver*	Driver	Dual
ABS	4-Whl	4-Whl	4-Whl	4-Whl	4-Whl
Parts Cost	Average	Average	Low	Low	Average
Complaints	Poor	Average	Average	Very Good	Very Poor
Insurance	Discount	Discount	Discount	Discount	Regular
Fuel Econ.	16	16	16	15	17
Theft Rating	Average	Average	Average	Average	Average
Bumpers					
Recalls	11	13	9	5	16
Trn. Cir. (ft.)	33.9	33.9	33.9	33.9	40.5
Weight (lbs.)	4065	4065	4065	4065	3075
Whlbase (in.)	116.8	116.8	116.8	116.8	120.2
Price	$4-6,000	$6-8,000	$7-9,000	$8-10,000	$10-12,000
OVERALL■	Good	Very Good	Very Good	**BEST BET**	Poor

■Cars without crash tests do not receive an overall rating.*Optional **Estimate

2002 Ford F-Series

available. There are also many different trim lines and cab configurations to choose from. Fuel economy is very poor, which is typical of standard trucks. Go for the later models with standard dual airbags. Overall the F-150 is a very solid vehicle, with low maintenance costs, very good front and side crash tests and many options to fit your every need.

	1998	1999	2000	2001	2002
Size Class	Truck	Truck	Truck	Truck	Truck
Drive	Rear/4	Rear/4	Rear/4	Rear/4	Rear/4
Crash Test	Very Good	Very Good	Very Good	Very Good	Very Good
Airbags	Dual	Dual	Dual	Dual	Dual
ABS	4-Whl	4-Whl	4-Whl	4-Whl	4-Whl
Parts Cost	Low	Average	Very Low	Very Low	Very Low
Complaints	Average	Poor	Average	Good	Very Good
Insurance	Regular	Regular	Regular	Discount	Discount
Fuel Econ.	17	16	17	17	17
Theft Rating	Average	Average	Average	Average**	Average**
Bumpers					
Recalls	8	16	9	9	1
Trn. Cir. (ft.)	40.5	40.5	40.5	40.5	40.5
Weight (lbs.)	3075	3075	3075	3075	3075
Whlbase (in.)	120.2	120.2	120.2	120.2	120.2
Price	$11-13,000	$13-15,000	$14-16,000	$15-17,000	$19-21,000
OVERALL■	Good	Average	Very Good	BEST BET	BEST BET

Ford Mustang 1993-2002

The Mustang remained virtually the same for over twenty years. It has competed with other pony cars, now only the Chevrolet Camaro and Pontiac Firebird, and done quite well for

1993 Ford Mustang

itself. The Mustang received a complete restyling for 1994, on an improved version of the old chassis. Beginning in 1990, Mustangs have a standard driver's airbag; dual airbags arrived for 1994. ABS was not available until 1994. Engine choices on later models are extreme: a 2.3-liter 4 and a 5-liter V8, both with 5-speed manual or

	1993	1994	1995	1996	1997
Size Class	Intermd.	Intermd.	Intermd.	Intermd.	Intermd.
Drive	Rear	Rear	Rear	Rear	Rear
Crash Test	Very Good[1]	Good	Good	Good[1]	Good[1]
Airbags	Driver	Dual	Dual	Dual	Dual
ABS	None	4-Whl*	4-Whl*	4-Whl*	4-Whl*
Parts Cost	Low	Low	Very Low	Average	High
Complaints	Average	Poor	Very Poor	Poor	Average
Insurance	Surcharge	Regular	Surcharge	Surcharge	Surcharge
Fuel Econ.	22	20	20	20	20
Theft Rating	Very High	Very High	Very High	Very High	Very High
Bumpers					
Recalls	2	5	7	3	2
Trn. Cir. (ft.)	37.4	38.3	38.3	38.3	38.3
Weight (lbs.)	2775	3065	3077	3065	3084
Whlbase (in.)	100.5	101.3	101.3	101.3	101.3
Price	$3-5,000	$5-7,000	$7-9,000	$9-11,000	$10-12,000
OVERALL"	Average	Average	Poor	Very Poor	Poor

"Cars without crash tests do not receive an overall rating. [1]Data given for coupe. Crash test for convertible 1993 is Good; 1996-97 is Very Good. *Optional **Estimate

150

2002 Ford Mustang

automatic. The 1994-95 Mustang offers a 3.8-liter V6 or the 5.0 V8. A smaller and smoother 4.6-liter V8 arrives in 1996, and is almost an economy car; the 3.8 V6 is much peppier. The 3.8-liter V6 actually meets Low Emission Vehicle requirements. Handling is responsive, but with the V8 it's easy to get the car's rear end to swing out. Great crash tests and safety features make this a good choice for an affordable convertible.

	1998	1999	2000	2001	2002
Size Class	Intermd.	Intermd.	Intermd.	Intermd.	Intermd.
Drive	Rear	Rear	Rear	Rear	Rear
Crash Test	Very Good	Very Good	Very Good	Very Good	Very Good
Airbags	Dual	Dual	Dual	Dual	Dual
ABS	4-Whl*	4-Whl*	4-Whl*	4-Whl*	4-Whl*
Parts Cost	Average	Average	Low	Very Low	Very Low
Complaints	Poor	Average	Average	Very Good	Poor
Insurance	Surcharge	Surcharge	Surcharge	Surcharge	Surcharge
Fuel Econ.	20	20	20	20	23
Theft Rating	Average	Average	Average	Average**	Average**
Bumpers		Strong	Strong	Strong	Strong
Recalls	4	1	3	1	0
Trn. Cir. (ft.)	40.8	37.9	37.9	37.9	37.1
Weight (lbs.)	3065	3069	3069	3069	3066
Whlbase (in.)	101.3	101.3	101.3	101.3	101.3
Price	$12-14,000	$13-15,000	$14-16,000	$16-18,000	$19-22,000
OVERALL■	Poor	Average	Average	**BEST BET**	Good

Ford Probe 1993-97

The Probe was originally supposed to replace the Ford Mustang, but the Mustang's popularity and fresh new look changed Ford's mind. The Probe and its close relative, the Mazda

1993 Ford Probe

MX-6, were all-new in 1993, when they were given a more modern, rounded styling. Stay away from anything before 1993 due to motorized shoulder seat belts. The 1993 Probes have regular front belts and a driver's airbag; the 1994 models got a passenger airbag. ABS is optional throughout the model's history.

	1993	1994	1995	1996	1997
Size Class	Compact	Compact	Compact	Compact	Compact
Drive	Front	Front	Front	Front	Front
Crash Test	Average	Very Good	Very Good	Very Good	Very Good
Airbags	Driver	Dual	Dual	Dual	Dual
ABS	4-Whl*	4-Whl*	4-Whl*	4-Whl*	4-Whl*
Parts Cost	Very High	Very High	Very High	Very High	Very High
Complaints	Very Poor	Poor	Poor	Average	Average
Insurance	Regular	Surcharge	Surcharge	Surcharge	Surcharge
Fuel Econ.	24	22	21	26	26
Theft Rating	Average	Average	Average	Average	Average
Bumpers					
Recalls	1	1	1	1	1
Trn. Cir. (ft.)	34.8	35.8	35.8	35.8	35.8
Weight (lbs.)	2619	2690	2921	2690	2690
Whlbase (in.)	102.9	102.8	102.8	102.8	102.8
Price	<$3,000	$2-4,000	$4-6,000	$5-7,000	$7-9,000
OVERALL"	Very Poor	Poor	Poor	Average	Average

"Cars without crash tests do not receive an overall rating.*Optional

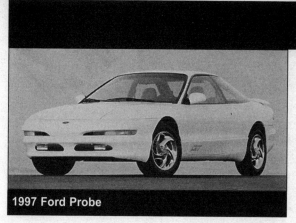

1997 Ford Probe

The 1990-92 Probes have a 2.2-liter 4-cylinder, turbo-charged on GT models; a 3-liter V6 came standard on the 1990-92 LX. The engines for 1993-96 are a bit smaller, a 2-liter 4-cylinder or a 2.5-liter V6, though both are as powerful as the two they replace. The 5-speed is the better transmission choice; it's more enjoyable in daily use than the automatic. Like other sporty cars, the Probe is really a 2-seater with a back seat for occasional use.

	1998	1999	2000	2001	2002
Size Class					
Drive					
Crash Test					
Airbags					
ABS					
Parts Cost					
Complaints					
Insurance					
Fuel Econ.					
Theft Rating			NO MODEL PRODUCED		
Bumpers					
Recalls					
Trn. Cir. (ft.)					
Weight (lbs.)					
Whlbase (in.)					
Price					
OVERALL■					

Ford Ranger 1993-2002

One of the first compact trucks to be created, the Ford Ranger continues to be a serious competitor to the Chevy S-Series and Dodge Dakota. The Ranger has had very few changes

1993 Ford Ranger

since its debut, with the most recent redesign in 1998. Airbags were not available until a driver's airbag became standard in 1995. Dual airbags became an option a year later and have been standard since 1997. Four-wheel ABS remained an option until it became standard

	1993	1994	1995	1996	1997
Size Class	Cmpct. Truck	Cmpct. Truck	Cmpct. Truck	Cmpct. Truck	Cmpct. Truck
Drive	Front/4	Front/4	Front/4	Front/4	Front/4
Crash Test	Good	Good	Good	Good	Good
Airbags	None	None	Driver	Dual*	Dual
ABS	4-Whl*	4-Whl*	4-Whl*	4-Whl*	4-Whl*
Parts Cost	Very Low	Very Low	Very Low	Low	High
Complaints	Good	Average	Good	Average	Average
Insurance	Surcharge	Surcharge	Surcharge	Surcharge	Regular
Fuel Econ.	19	18	19	19	17
Theft Rating	Low	Low	Very Low	Low	Very Low
Bumpers					
Recalls	3	4	0	1	0
Trn. Cir. (ft.)	41.6	41.6	41.6	41.6	41.6
Weight (lbs.)	2849	2849	2849	2849	2849
Whlbase (in.)	113.9	113.9	113.9	113.9	113.9
Price	$2-4,000	$4-6,000	$5-7,000	$6-8,000	$7-9,000
OVERALL■	Average	Poor	Good	Average	Average

■Cars without crash tests do not receive an overall rating.*Optional **Estimate

154

2002 Ford Ranger

in 2001.

The 2.5-liter engine on the 2WD is strong, but you'll want to opt for the 4WD's 3.0-liter. Better yet, the V6 upgrades are best for serious load carrying. The Ranger performed very well on frontal and side crash tests and is worth checking out.

	1998	1999	2000	2001	2002
Size Class	Cmpct. Truck	Cmpct. Truck	Cmpct. Truck	Cmpct. Truck	Cmpct. Truck
Drive	Front/4	Front/4	Front/4	Front/4	Front/4
Crash Test	Very Good	Very Good	Very Good	Very Good	Very Good
Airbags	Dual	Dual	Dual	Dual	Dual
ABS	4-Whl*	4-Whl*	4-Whl*	4-Whl	4-Whl
Parts Cost	Very Low	Low	Average	High	Very High
Complaints	Poor	Poor	Average	Very Good	Average
Insurance	Regular	Regular	Regular	Regular	Surcharge
Fuel Econ.	17	18	18	22	19
Theft Rating	Average	Average	Average	Average**	Average**
Bumpers					
Recalls	4	3	2	2	1
Trn. Cir. (ft.)	39.1	39.1	39.1	39.1	39.1
Weight (lbs.)	2036	2036	2036	2036	2036
Whlbase (in.)	111.6	111.6	111.6	111.6	111.6
Price	$8-10,000	$10-12,000	$11-13,000	$12-14,000	$14-16,000
OVERALL■	Good	Good	Good	Very Good	Poor

Ford Taurus 1993-2002

The Taurus, introduced in 1986 with its twin, the Mercury Sable, popularized aerodynamic car design. Though widely imitated, the Taurus still holds its own; its redesign in 1996

1993 Ford Taurus

only strengthened its industry leading position. The Taurus original-ly came in L, GL, MT-5, and LX models and as a 4-door sedan or 4-door station wagon. For 1996, the Taurus received a total makeover. In 1990, a driver's airbag was added; a passenger airbag became optional in 1992, and standard in 1994, while optional front side and

	1993	1994	1995	1996	1997
Size Class	Intermd.	Intermd.	Intermd.	Intermd.	Intermd.
Drive	Front	Front	Front	Front	Front
Crash Test	Good[1]	Good	Good	Very Good	Very Good
Airbags	Driver[#]	Dual	Dual	Dual	Dual
ABS	4-Whl*	4-Whl*	4-Whl*	4-Whl*	4-Whl*
Parts Cost	Low	Low	Low	Low	Low
Complaints	Very Poor	Very Poor	Very Poor	Poor	Poor
Insurance	Discount	Discount	Discount	Discount	Discount
Fuel Econ.	21	19	20	20	20
Theft Rating	Very Low	Very Low	Low	Very Low	Very Low
Bumpers	Weak	Weak	Weak	Strong	Strong
Recalls	8	4	4	6	3
Trn. Cir. (ft.)	38.6	38.6	38.6	38	38
Weight (lbs.)	3253	3104	3118	3326	3326
Whlbase (in.)	106	106	106	108.5	108.5
Price	<$3,000	$3-5,000	$4-6,000	$6-8,000	$7-8,000
OVERALL■	Average	Average	Average	Very Good	Very Good

■Cars without crash tests do not receive an overall rating. [1]Data given for sedan. Crash test for wagon is Very Good. [#]Passenger Side Option-al. *Optional **Estimate

156

2002 Ford Taurus

head airbags became optional in 2002. ABS is optional on sedans from 1990 on, and on wagons from 1991. It has typically done well on government crash tests. The now standard 140 hp 3-liter V6 engine, is more powerful and economical than its 2.5-liter 4-cylinder engine predecessor. A 3.8-liter is optional on 1990-95 SHO models. The SHO's handling is precise. The 1996 model features a longer wheelbase, which added more room and made seating more comfortable than on past models.

	1998	1999	2000	2001	2002
Size Class	Intermd.	Intermd.	Intermd.	Intermd.	Intermd.
Drive	Front	Front	Front	Front	Front
Crash Test	Very Good	Very Good	Very Good	Very Good	Very Good
Airbags	Dual	Dual	Dual	Dual	Dl./Sd.(F)*/Hd.*
ABS	4-Whl*	4-Whl*	4-Whl*	4-Whl*	4-Whl*
Parts Cost	Average	Low	Low	Low	Very Low
Complaints	Average	Good	Good	Very Good	Average
Insurance	Discount	Discount	Discount	Discount	Discount
Fuel Econ.	20	20	20	20	23
Theft Rating	Low	Very Low	Low	Very Low**	Very Low**
Bumpers	Strong	Strong	Strong	Strong	Strong
Recalls	2	3	2	2	0
Trn. Cir. (ft.)	38	38	39.8	39.8	39.8
Weight (lbs.)	3294	3329	3368	3368	3336
Whlbase (in.)	108.5	108.5	108.5	108.5	108.5
Price	$9-11,000	$10-12,000	$11-13,000	$13-15,000	$19-22,000
OVERALL■	Very Good	BEST BET	BEST BET	BEST BET	BEST BET

Ford Thunderbird 1993-97, 2002

The Thunderbird's redesign brings us back to 1955, when the Thunderbird was introduced. Much safer than the cars of the 50's, the Thunderbird comes standard with dual, front

1993 Ford Thunderbird

side and head airbags as well as 4-wheel ABS. The new Thunderbird comes with a high performance 3.9-liter 252 hp V8. The older Ford Thunderbird shares a body and chassis with the Mercury Cougar, but the Thunderbird was given a facelift in 1996 with a fresh, new look and redone front and back ends. Look out for 1993

	1993	1994	1995	1996	1997
Size Class	Large	Large	Large	Large	Large
Drive	Rear	Rear	Rear	Rear	Rear
Crash Test	Very Good	Very Good	Very Good	Very Good	Very Good
Airbags	None	Dual	Dual	Dual	Dual
ABS	4-Whl*	4-Whl*	4-Whl*	4-Whl*	4-Whl*
Parts Cost	Low	Low	Low	Average	High
Complaints	Very Poor	Very Poor	Very Poor	Very Poor	Poor
Insurance	Discount	Regular	Discount	Discount	Regular
Fuel Econ.	17	18	19	19	18
Theft Rating	Average	Average	Average	Average	Average
Bumpers					
Recalls	2	0	0	2	0
Trn. Cir. (ft.)	36.6	36.6	36.6	36.6	36.5
Weight (lbs.)	3575	3570	3536	3536	3561
Whlbase (in.)	113	113	113	113	113
Price	$4-6,000	$5-7,000	$6-8,000	$7-8,000	$8-10,000
OVERALL■	Average	Good	Very Good	Good	Average

■Cars without crash tests do not receive an overall rating.*Optional

2002 Ford Thunderbird

T-birds which have motorized front shoulder belts and manual lap belts. The 1994 models have dual airbags and conventional belts. ABS was optional until 1997. The old Thunderbirds have a regular or supercharged V6 or V8 and the standard 6-cylinder is adequate. The ride in older Thunderbirds is comfortable, but base models handling isn't as crisp as it should be. Keep your eye out for the all-new 2002 T-bird—the new look is very stylish.

	1998	1999	2000	2001	2002
Size Class					Compact
Drive					Rear
Crash Test					N/A
Airbags					Dl./Sd.(F)
ABS					4-Whl
Parts Cost					Average
Complaints					Average
Insurance					Regular
Fuel Econ.			NO MODEL PRODUCED		19
Theft Rating					
Bumpers					
Recalls					0
Trn. Cir. (ft.)					
Weight (lbs.)					3775
Whlbase (in.)					108.5
Price					$36-38,000
OVERALL■					

159

Ford Windstar 1995-2002

Ford unveiled the Windstar in 1995, in an attempt to stop the Chrysler mini-van juggernauts— otherwise known as the Dodge Caravan and the Plymouth Voyager.

1995 Ford Windstar

The Windstar did receive outstanding crash test ratings and offered standard dual airbags and 4-wheel ABS with optional built-in child seats. Plus, the Windstar came with more interior space than the Grand Caravan/Voyager. The Windstar's design was not revolutionary; however, a slight change in 1998 helped.

	1993	1994	1995	1996	1997
Size Class			Minivan	Minivan	Minivan
Drive			Front	Front	Front
Crash Test			Very Good	Very Good	Very Good
Airbags			Dual	Dual	Dual
ABS			4-Whl	4-Whl	4-Whl
Parts Cost			Average	Average	High
Complaints			Very Poor	Very Poor	Good
Insurance			Discount	Discount	Discount
Fuel Econ.			17	17	17
Theft Rating			Very Low	Very Low	Very Low
Bumpers			Fair	Fair	Fair
Recalls			5	5	2
Trn. Cir. (ft.)			40.3	40.3	40.3
Weight (lbs.)			3733	3733	3733
Whlbase (in.)			120.7	120.7	120.7
Price			$5-7,000	$6-8,000	$8-10,000
OVERALL▪			Good	Good	Very Good

NO MODEL PRODUCED

▪Cars without crash tests do not receive an overall rating.*Optional **Estimate

160

2002 Ford Windstar

The base GL comes standard with the same 3-liter V6 available on the Aerostar and Ranger. A more powerful 3.8-liter V6 engine is optional, standard on the LX models. With contemporary styling and decent handling, the Windstar provided a good challenge to the Chrysler minivans, but a high number of complaints lowers its overall ratings somewhat. Ride is good, and the cargo area is large and well designed. It added dual sliding doors for 1999.

	1998	1999	2000	2001	2002
Size Class	Minivan	Minivan	Minivan	Minivan	Minivan
Drive	Front	Front	Front	Front	Front
Crash Test	Very Good	Very Good	Very Good	Very Good	Very Good
Airbags	Dual	Dual	Dual	Dual	Dl./Sd.(F)*/Hd.*
ABS	4-Whl	4-Whl	4-Whl	4-Whl	4-Whl
Parts Cost	High	High	Very Low	Very Low	Low
Complaints	Very Poor	Poor	Average	Very Good	Very Poor
Insurance	Discount	Discount	Discount	Discount	Discount
Fuel Econ.	18	17	17	17	19
Theft Rating	Average	Very Low	Very Low	Very Low**	Very Low**
Bumpers	Fair	Strong	Strong	Strong	Strong
Recalls	6	2	5	6	0
Trn. Cir. (ft.)	40.3	40.3	40.3	40.3	40.3
Weight (lbs.)	3733	3733	3733	3733	4017
Whlbase (in.)	120.7	120.7	120.7	120.7	120.7
Price	$11-13,000	$14-16,000	$17-19,000	$18-20,000	$21-23,000
OVERALL■	Average	Good	**BEST BET**	**BEST BET**	**BEST BET**

Geo Metro 1993-97, Chevrolet Metro 1998-2000, Suzuki Swift 1993-2001

A Geo Metro convertible arrived during 1990 and lasted until 1993. Convertibles have a driver's airbag with regular lap-shoulder belts in front. Other Metros and Swifts

1993 Geo Metro

through 1994 have the less-than-desirable door-mounted seat belts, with no airbags or ABS. In 1995, a redesign brought more modern styling, more headroom, dual airbags, conventional seat belts, optional ABS, and daytime running lights. Metros and Sprints have

	1993	1994	1995	1996	1997
Size Class	Subcomp.	Subcomp.	Subcomp.	Subcomp.	Subcomp.
Drive	Front	Front	Front	Front	Front
Crash Test	Average	Average	Good	Good	Good
Airbags	None[1]	None[1]	Dual	Dual	Dual
ABS	None	None	4-Whl*	4-Whl*	4-Whl*
Parts Cost	High	Very High	High	Very High	Very High
Complaints	Average	Average	Poor	Average	Poor
Insurance	Surcharge	Surcharge	Surcharge	Surcharge	Surcharge
Fuel Econ.	36	39	44	39	44
Theft Rating	Low	Low	Low	Very Low	Very Low
Bumpers	Weak	Weak			
Recalls	1	0	1	0	2
Trn. Cir. (ft.)	30.2	31.5	31.5	31.5	31.5
Weight (lbs.)	1694	1699	1751	1808	1878
Whlbase (in.)	89.2	89.2	93.1	93.1	93.1
Price	<$3,000	< $3,000	< $3,000	< $3,000	$3-4,000
OVERALL▪	Very Poor	Very Poor	Average	Good	Average

▪Cars without crash tests do not receive an overall rating.[1]Data given for sedan/coupe. Convertible is Driver. *Optional **Estimate

2001 Suzuki Swift

a 1-liter 3-cylinder engine; Swifts get a 1.3-liter 4-cylinder with up to 100 horsepower, which it also shares with the 1995 Metro 4-door. The Metro and Swift have been among the industry fuel economy leaders for years. Stick to the standard 5-speed for best performance and gas mileage. In the hatchback, room for two is tight; the rear seat is for kids. Handling is quick and precise, but crosswinds and large trucks can blow the car off course.

	1998	1999	2000	2001	2002
Size Class	Subcomp.	Subcomp.	Subcomp.	Subcomp.	
Drive	Front	Front	Front	Front	
Crash Test	Good	Good	Good	Good	
Airbags	Dual	Dual	Dual	Dual	
ABS	4-Whl*	4-Whl*	4-Whl*	4-Whl*	
Parts Cost	Very High	Very High	Very High	Very High	
Complaints	Poor	Average	Very Good	Very Good	
Insurance	Surcharge	Surcharge	Surcharge	Surcharge	
Fuel Econ.	41	39	41	30	
Theft Rating	Very Low	Very Low**	Very Low**	Very Low**	
Bumpers					
Recalls	0	0	0	0	
Trn. Cir. (ft.)	31.5	31.5	31.5	31.5	
Weight (lbs.)	1895	1895	1895	1895	
Whlbase (in.)	93.1	93.1	93.1	93.1	
Price	$4-6,000	$5-7,000	$6-8,000	$7-8,000	
OVERALL■	Average	Good	Very Good	Good	

NO MODEL PRODUCED (spanning the 2002 column)

Geo Prizm 1993-97, Chevrolet Prizm 1998-2002

The Prizm is a clone of Toyota's popular Corolla, but it never sold as well due to Toyota's better reputation. The Prizm comes with two trim levels and only in a sedan. The 1993

1993 Geo Prizm

Prizm has a drivers airbag, added a passenger airbag in '94 and finally got front side airbags as an option in 2000. ABS first became optional in 1993.

The standard Prizm engine, a 1.6-liter 4-cylinder, is adequate. The larger engine on 1993-97 models, with either a five-speed or auto-

	1993	1994	1995	1996	1997
Size Class	Subcomp.	Subcomp.	Subcomp.	Compact	Compact
Drive	Front	Front	Front	Front	Front
Crash Test	Average	Good	Good	Good	Good
Airbags	Driver	Dual	Dual	Dual	Dual
ABS	4-Whl*	4-Whl*	4-Whl*	4-Whl*	4-Whl*
Parts Cost	High	High	Average	Average	Very High
Complaints	Poor	Average	Average	Good	Good
Insurance	Regular	Regular	Surcharge	Surcharge	Surcharge
Fuel Econ.	26	26	27	31	30
Theft Rating	Very Low	Very Low	Low	Very Low	Very Low
Bumpers					
Recalls	1	3	3	0	2
Trn. Cir. (ft.)	31.5	31.5	31.5	31.5	31.5
Weight (lbs.)	2348	2355	2359	2359	2359
Whlbase (in.)	97	97	97	97.1	97.1
Price	<$3,000	$3-5,000	$4-6,000	$5-7,000	$6-8,000
OVERALL"	Poor	Average	Average	Good	Average

"Cars without crash tests do not receive an overall rating.*Optional **Estimate

2002 Chevrolet Prizm

matic overdrive, is quieter and peppier, and gas mileage is equivalent. With the demise of the Geo nameplate, the Prizm fell under the Chevrolet name starting in 1998. If you are looking for a Toyota Corolla and can live without the Toyota name, the Prizm is still a good choice. Go with the later models with side airbags if your budget allows.

	1998	1999	2000	2001	2002
Size Class	Compact	Compact	Compact	Compact	Compact
Drive	Front	Front	Front	Front	Front
Crash Test	Good	Good	Good	Good	Good
Airbags	Dual/Side*	Dual/Side*	Dual/Side*	Dual/Side*	Dl./Sd.(F)
ABS	4-Whl*	4-Whl*	4-Whl*	4-Whl*	4-Whl
Parts Cost	Very High	High	High	High	High
Complaints	Very Good	Very Good	Very Good	Very Good	Very Good
Insurance	Surcharge	Surcharge	Surcharge	Surcharge	Surcharge
Fuel Econ.	31	31	31	31	34
Theft Rating	Very Low	Very Low	Very Low	Very Low**	Very Low**
Bumpers	Weak		Strong	Strong	Strong
Recalls	0	0	0	0	0
Trn. Cir. (ft.)	34	34	34	34	34
Weight (lbs.)	2403	2403	2403	2403	2398
Whlbase (in.)	97	97.1	97.1	97.1	97.1
Price	$7-9,000	$8-10,000	$9-11,000	$11-13,000	$15-17,000
OVERALL▪	Good	Very Good	Very Good	Very Good	**BEST BET**

Geo Tracker 1993-97, Chevrolet Tracker 1998-2002, Suzuki Sidekick 1991-98

The Tracker is one of the smaller sport utility vehicles. The Tracker is available as a hardtop or convertible and only has 2 doors but can carry up to four people. All Trackers have

1993 Geo Tracker

conventional lap-shoulder belts in front. Airbags come standard on the 1996 Tracker. 2-wheel ABS, available beginning in 1993, operates only on the rear wheels, but you can choose 4-wheel ABS starting in 1996. Until its makeover in 1999, Trackers had a 1.6-liter single-cam 4-cylinder, with either a standard 5-speed manual or option-

	1993	1994	1995	1996	1997
Size Class	Sp. Util.	Sp. Util.	Sp. Util.	Sp. Util.	Sp. Util.
Drive	Rear/4	Rear/4	Rear/4	Rear/4	Rear/4
Crash Test	Very Poor	Very Poor	Poor	Poor	Poor
Airbags	None	None	None	Dual	Dual
ABS	2-Whl	2-Whl	2-Whl	2-Whl[1]	2-Whl[1]
Parts Cost	Very High	High	High	High	Very High
Complaints	Very Good	Average	Poor	Poor	Very Good
Insurance	Surcharge	Surcharge	Surcharge	Surcharge	Surcharge
Fuel Econ.	24	23	24	23	24
Theft Rating	Very High	Very High	Very High	Very High	Very High
Bumpers					
Recalls	2	4	0	2	0
Trn. Cir. (ft.)	32.2	32.2	32.2	32.2	32.2
Weight (lbs.)	2270	2238	2246	2339	2339
Whlbase (in.)	86.6	86.6	86.6	86.6	86.6
Price	<$3,000	< $3,000	$3-5,000	$4-6,000	$5-7,000
OVERALL■	Very Poor	Very Poor	Very Poor	Very Poor	Poor

■Cars without crash tests do not receive an overall rating.[1]Optional 4-Wheel. *Optional **Estimate

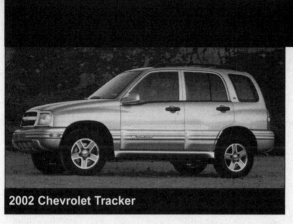

2002 Chevrolet Tracker

al 3-speed automatic and 2- or 4-wheel drive. Now Trackers come standard with a 2.0-liter 4-cylinder engine or an optional 2.5-liter V6. As with many subcompacts, the Tracker's fuel economy, performance, and noise improve with the 5-speed. Accommodations are OK in front for two, but tight for two in back. The instrument panel and controls are functional and simple. Along with the rest of the Geo lineup, the Tracker became a Chevrolet in 1998, when the Geo name was dropped.

	1998	1999	2000	2001	2002
Size Class	Sp. Util.	Sp. Util.	Sp. Util.	Sp. Util.	Sp. Util.
Drive	Rear/4	Rear/4	Rear/4	Rear/4	Rear/4
Crash Test	Poor	Good	Good	Good	Good
Airbags	Dual	Dual	Dual	Dual	Dual
ABS	4-Whl*	4-Whl*	4-Whl*	4-Whl*	4-Whl
Parts Cost	Very High	Very High	Very High	Very Low	Very High
Complaints	Very Good	Good	Good	Very Good	Average
Insurance	Surcharge	Surcharge	Surcharge	Surcharge	Surcharge
Fuel Econ.	23	23	23	23	24
Theft Rating	High	Very High	Very High	Very High**	Very High**
Bumpers					
Recalls	0	0	0	0	0
Trn. Cir. (ft.)	34.4	31.5	31.5	31.5	31.5
Weight (lbs.)	2339	2596	2596	2596	2690
Whlbase (in.)	86.6	86.6	86.6	86.6	86.6
Price	$6-8,000	$9-11,000	$10-12,000	$13-15,000	$16-18,000
OVERALL■	Poor	Poor	Poor	Very Good	Poor

Honda Accord 1993-2002

The Accord first showed up in American showrooms almost 20 years ago. For the past decade, it has battled for the top sales spot with the Ford Taurus. The Accord has undergone a redesign

1993 Honda Accord

for the most part every four years since 1982. For 1996, Honda gave it a slightly redesigned front and rear, creating a more rounded appearance, and the Accord received its most dramatic makeover in its 22-year history in 1998. At that time, changes were made to structure, engine, suspension, interior room and trunk space. All

	1993	1994	1995	1996	1997
Size Class	Intermd.	Intermd.	Intermd.	Intermd.	Intermd.
Drive	Front	Front	Front	Front	Front
Crash Test	Very Good	Average	Average	Average	Average
Airbags	Driver#	Dual	Dual	Dual	Dual
ABS	4-Whl*	4-Whl*	4-Whl*	4-Whl*	4-Whl*
Parts Cost	Average	Average	Average	Average	High
Complaints	Good	Average	Average	Good	Good
Insurance	Regular	Regular	Regular	Regular	Discount
Fuel Econ.	22	23	25	25	25
Theft Rating	Very High	Very High	Very High	Average	Very High
Bumpers	Strong	Weak	Weak	Weak	Weak
Recalls	3	1	2	1	1
Trn. Cir. (ft.)	36.1	36.1	36.1	36.7	36.1
Weight (lbs.)	2778	2800	2877	3219	2855
Whlbase (in.)	107.1	106.9	106.9	106.9	106.9
Price	$4-6,000	$6-8,000	$8-10,000	$9-11,000	$11-13,000
OVERALL■	Good	Average	Average	Good	Good

■Cars without crash tests do not receive an overall rating.#Passenger Side Optional. *Optional **Estimate

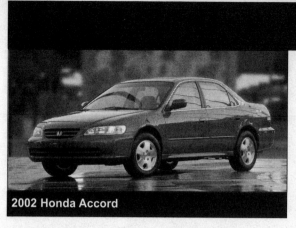
2002 Honda Accord

1992-93 Accords have a driver's airbag and conventional belts and the 1993 SE sedan adds a passenger airbag. For 1994, all Accords have dual airbags and 2002 models have front side airbags. ABS became available in 1991. The 4-cylinder engines are lively and, with the 5-speed, economical. The Accord is competent and popular and a consistently good crash test performer. Just watch out for thieves who are after the versatile parts on early models.

	1998	1999	2000	2001	2002
Size Class	Intermd.	Intermd.	Intermd.	Intermd.	Intermd.
Drive	Front	Front	Front	Front	Front
Crash Test	Very Good	Very Good	Very Good	Very Good	Very Good
Airbags	Dual	Dual	Dual	Dual	Dl./Sd.(F)
ABS	4-Whl*	4-Whl*	4-Whl*	4-Whl*	4-Whl
Parts Cost	Average	Average	Low	Low	Low
Complaints	Average	Very Good	Good	Very Good	Good
Insurance	Discount	Discount	Regular	Regular	Regular
Fuel Econ.	25	25	25	25	26
Theft Rating	Average	Average	Average	Average**	Average**
Bumpers	Strong	Strong	Strong	Strong	Strong
Recalls	2	0	2	1	0
Trn. Cir. (ft.)	36.1	36.1	36.1	36.1	36.1
Weight (lbs.)	2943	2943	3020	3031	2967
Whlbase (in.)	106.9	105.1	105.1	105.1	105.1
Price	$13-15,000	$15-17,000	$16-18,000	$18-20,000	$19-21,000
OVERALL■	BEST BET	BEST BET	BEST BET	BEST BET	BEST BET

Honda Civic 1993-2002

The Civic first appeared in the United States in 1973 and there have been a lot of changes since then. Honda dropped the wagon and the sporty CRX from the redesigned 1992

1993 Honda Civic

lineup, but added a stylish coupe and the sporty targa-top del Sol for 1993. For 1996, the Civic was all-new, as Honda gave it a new look, a stronger body, and a firmer suspension. The Civic was redesigned again in 2001. Dual airbags became standard on all models beginning in 1994 and front side airbags became optional in 2001. ABS is

	1993	1994	1995	1996	1997
Size Class	Subcomp.	Subcomp.	Subcomp.	Subcomp.	Subcomp.
Drive	Front	Front	Front	Front	Front
Crash Test	Average	Average	Average	Good	Good
Airbags	Driver	Dual	Dual	Dual	Dual
ABS	4-Whl*	4-Whl*	4-Whl*	4-Whl*	4-Whl*
Parts Cost	Average	Low	Average	Average	Average
Complaints	Average	Good	Good	Average	Good
Insurance	Regular	Regular	Surcharge	Surcharge	Surcharge
Fuel Econ.	40	29	34	33	29
Theft Rating	Very High	Average	High	High	Very High
Bumpers	Weak	Weak	Weak	Weak	Weak
Recalls	1	2	0	1	1
Trn. Cir. (ft.)	32.8	32.1	32.1	32.8	32.8
Weight (lbs.)	2094	2108	2178	2262	2238
Whlbase (in.)	101.3	101.3	101.3	103.2	103.2
Price	<$3,000	$3-5,000	$5-7,000	$6-8,000	$7-9,000
OVERALL▪	Average	Good	Average	Average	Average

▪Cars without crash tests do not receive an overall rating.*Optional **Estimate

2002 Honda Civic

optional starting in 1992. It is hard to do better than a Civic when it comes to fuel economy. The 5-speed shifts smoothly; the automatic isn't as pleasant. After its redesign in 2001, the Civic gained a new 1.7-liter engine and more interior space. The Civic ranks among the best subcompacts.

	1998	1999	2000	2001	2002
Size Class	Subcomp.	Subcomp.	Subcomp.	Subcomp.	Subcomp.
Drive	Front	Front	Front	Front	Front
Crash Test	Good	Good	Good	Very Good	Very Good
Airbags	Dual	Dual	Dual	Dual	Dl./Sd.(F)*
ABS	4-Whl*	4-Whl*	4-Whl*	4-Whl*	4-Whl*
Parts Cost	Very Low	Low	Low	Low	Average
Complaints	Good	Very Good	Very Good	Good	Average
Insurance	Surcharge	Surcharge	Surcharge	Surcharge	Surcharge
Fuel Econ.	33	32	32	32	34
Theft Rating	High	Very High	Very High	Very High**	Very High**
Bumpers	Weak	Strong	Strong	Strong	Strong
Recalls	1	0	1	4	1
Trn. Cir. (ft.)	32.8	32.8	32.8	34.1	34.1
Weight (lbs.)	2238	2339	2339	2421	2405
Whlbase (in.)	103.2	103.2	103.2	103.1	103.1
Price	$9-11,000	$10-12,000	$11-13,000	$13-15,000	$14-16,000
OVERALL▪	Very Good	Very Good	Very Good	Very Good	Very Good

Honda Odyssey/Isuzu Oasis 1995-2002

1996 Isuzu Oasis

In 1995, Honda introduced the Odyssey, an interesting as well as uniquely designed minivan, with high hopes of cashing in on the hot selling minivan market. Isuzu simply took the Odyssey and rebadged it into the Oasis. Prior to 1999, the Odyssey was lower and narrower than most minivans, making it easier to maneuver and handle, but after it was redesigned in 1999 it became wider. Rather than sliding doors, the rear passengers used to have two sedan type doors but now has two sliding doors as many of its

	1993	1994	1995	1996	1997
Size Class	NO MODEL PRODUCED		Minivan	Minivan	Minivan
Drive			Front	Front	Front
Crash Test			Good	Good	Good
Airbags			Dual	Dual	Dual
ABS			4-Whl	4-Whl	4-Whl
Parts Cost			Average	Very High	Very High
Complaints			Poor	Average	Good[1]
Insurance			Discount	Discount	Discount
Fuel Econ.			20	21	21
Theft Rating			Average	Average	Average
Bumpers				Weak	Weak
Recalls			0	0	0
Trn. Cir. (ft.)			37.6	37.6	37.6
Weight (lbs.)			3450	3473	3473
Whlbase (in.)			111.4	111.4	111.4
Price			$10-12,000	$12-14,000	$14-16,000
OVERALL▪			Very Good	Good	Very Good

▪Cars without crash tests do not receive an overall rating. [1]Odyssey received Very Good in 1997. **Estimate

2002 Honda Odyssey

competitors. Dual airbags and ABS were standard from their introduction in 1995 and front side airbags have since become available. A 2.2-liter, 4-cylinder engine found on the Accord used to power this minivan, but since its redesign it has been powered by a 3.5-liter V6. The Odyssey/Oasis performed well in government crash tests and comes with 5 mph bumpers. A full array of custom features, and interior size and space has increased the popularity of this vehicle.

	1998	1999	2000	2001	2002
Size Class	Minivan	Minivan	Minivan	Minivan	Minivan
Drive	Front	Front	Front	Front	Front
Crash Test	Good	Very Good	Very Good	Very Good	Very Good
Airbags	Dual	Dual	Dual	Dual	Dl./Sd.(F)
ABS	4-Whl	4-Whl	4-Whl	4-Whl	4-Whl
Parts Cost	High	High	High	High	Average
Complaints	Average	Very Poor	Poor	Good	Very Poor
Insurance	Discount	Discount	Discount	Discount	Discount
Fuel Econ.	20	21	21	21	21
Theft Rating	Very Low	Very Low	Very Low	Very Low**	Very Low**
Bumpers	Weak	Strong	Strong	Strong	Strong
Recalls	0	1	4	0	0
Trn. Cir. (ft.)	37.6	37.7	37.7	37.7	37.7
Weight (lbs.)	3450	4233	4233	4233	4299
Whlbase (in.)	111.4	118.1	118.1	118.1	118.1
Price	$17-19,000	$19-21,000	$21-23,000	$23-25,000	$25-27,000
OVERALL■	Good	Good	Good	**BEST BET**	**BEST BET**

Honda Passport 1994-2002

The Passport, which represents Honda's first entry in the highly competitive U.S. sport utility market, is based on the Isuzu Rodeo. This sport utility was intended to compete with

1994 Honda Passport

vehicles like the Jeep Grand Cherokee, but it always seemed to be a step behind. The Passport had no airbags until 1996, and in 2002 they received head airbags. ABS is standard beginning in 1992, but only on the rear wheels. From 1996 until 1998, you have to pay

	1993	1994	1995	1996	1997
Size Class		Sp. Util.	Sp. Util.	Sp. Util.	Sp. Util.
Drive		Rear/4	Rear/4	Rear/4	Rear/4
Crash Test		N/A	N/A	Average	Average
Airbags		None	None	Dual	Dual
ABS		2-Whl	2-Whl	2-Whl#	4-Whl
Parts Cost		Low	Low	Very Low	Average
Complaints		Poor	Average	Good	Poor
Insurance		Regular	Regular	Regular	Regular
Fuel Econ.		17	19	17	17
Theft Rating		High	High	Very High	Very High
Bumpers					
Recalls		1	0	0	0
Trn. Cir. (ft.)		38.1	38.1	38.1	38.1
Weight (lbs.)		4105	4105	4105	4105
Whlbase (in.)		108.5	108.5	108.5	108.5
Price		$3-5,000	$4-6,000	$6-8,000	$8-10,000
OVERALL*				Good	Poor

NO MODEL PRODUCED

*Cars without crash tests do not receive an overall rating. #4-Whl. Optional. **Estimate

174

2002 Honda Passport

extra for 4-wheel ABS, but from 1999 on, it is standard.

Available in 2- or 4-wheel drive and with automatic or manual transmission, the ride and handling are adequate. The Passport is powered by a 3.2-liter V6, which should provide enough power, but expect to pay quite a bit at the pump. The cargo space is small and the payload is low. The Passport is not a strong competitor against Jeep Grand Cherokee or later Expeditions and Explorers.

	1998	1999	2000	2001	2002
Size Class	Sp. Util.	Sp. Util.	Sp. Util.	Sp. Util.	Sp. Util.
Drive	Rear/4	Rear/4	Rear/4	Rear/4	Rear/4
Crash Test	Average	Average	Average	Average	Average
Airbags	Dual	Dual	Dual	Dual	Dual
ABS	4-Whl	4-Whl	4-Whl	4-Whl	4-Whl
Parts Cost	Average	Very High	Low	Low	Low
Complaints	Very Poor	Very Poor	Good	Very Good	Very Poor
Insurance	Regular	Regular	Regular	Regular	Regular
Fuel Econ.	17	18	18	19	19
Theft Rating	Very High	Very High	Very High	Very High**	Very High
Bumpers					
Recalls	2	1	0	1	0
Trn. Cir. (ft.)	38.4	38.4	38.4	38.4	38.4
Weight (lbs.)	3966	3966	3968	3968	3968
Whlbase (in.)	106.4	106.4	106.4	106.4	106.4
Price	$10-12,000	$12-14,000	$14-16,000	$16-18,000	$25-27,000
OVERALL■	Very Poor	Very Poor	Good	Very Good	Poor

Honda Prelude 1993-2001

The first Preludes were not much bigger than a Civic. In 1983, the Prelude grew in length, weight, wheelbase, and sales. In 1989, 4-wheel steering (4WS) was optional, but was

1993 Honda Prelude

dropped for 1995. For 1992, the Prelude received new, controversial styling with a strong GM influence on the dashboard and back end. In 1997, the Prelude was restyled and once again, its style was controversial. The 1992-93 models have a standard driver's airbag and optional passenger airbag (except S models). From 1994 on, models

	1993	1994	1995	1996	1997
Size Class	Compact	Compact	Compact	Compact	Compact
Drive	Front	Front	Front	Front	Front
Crash Test	Very Good	Very Good	Very Good	Very Good	N/A
Airbags	Driver#	Dual	Dual	Dual	Dual
ABS	4-Whl*	4-Whl*	4-Whl*	4-Whl*	4-Whl*
Parts Cost	High	High	Very High	High	Very High
Complaints	Good	Very Good	Very Good	Very Good	Poor
Insurance	Surcharge	Surcharge	Surcharge	Surcharge	Surcharge
Fuel Econ.	22	22	22	22	22
Theft Rating	Very High	Very High	Very High	Very High	Very High
Bumpers					
Recalls	0	0	0	0	0
Trn. Cir. (ft.)	34.8	35.9	35.9	35.9	35.6
Weight (lbs.)	2765	2900	2866	2809	2954
Whlbase (in.)	100.4	100.4	100.4	100.4	101.8
Price	$4-6,000	$6-8,000	$8-10,000	$11-13,000	$14-16,000
OVERALL■	Average	Good	Good	Good	

■Cars without crash tests do not receive an overall rating.#Passenger Side Optional. *Optional **Estimate

2001 Honda Prelude

have standard dual airbags. ABS is optional until 1998. The standard 4-cylinder is powerful enough, but if you want more horses, the Si and VTEC offer them. The Prelude's 5-speed is smooth, and automatic overdrive is excellent. The panel on 1992-96 Preludes is quite busy; the 1997 panel is better.

	1998	1999	2000	2001	2002
Size Class	Compact	Compact	Compact	Compact	
Drive	Front	Front	Front	Front	
Crash Test	N/A	N/A	N/A	N/A	
Airbags	Dual	Dual	Dual	Dual	
ABS	4-Whl*	4-Whl	4-Whl	4-Whl	
Parts Cost	High	High	High	High	
Complaints	Poor	Average	Very Good	Very Good	
Insurance	Surcharge	Surcharge	Regular	Regular	
Fuel Econ.	22	22	22	22	
Theft Rating	Very High	Very High**	Very High**	Very High**	
Bumpers		Strong	Strong	Strong	
Recalls	0	0	0	0	
Trn. Cir. (ft.)	36.1	36.1	36.1	36.1	
Weight (lbs.)	2954	2954	2954	2954	
Whlbase (in.)	101.8	101.8	101.8	101.8	
Price	$16-18,000	$17-19,000	$19-21,000	$21-23,000	
OVERALL■					

NO MODEL PRODUCED (2002 column)

Hyundai Accent 1995-2002

New Accents start around $10-12,000, so you should have little trouble finding an Accent to fit your budget. In 1995, Hyundai replaced the Excel with the Accent, a front wheel drive car

1995 Hyundai Accent

with many improvements over the Excel. The Accent was redesigned in 2000 and given a more sophisticated look. The Accent has more interior room and horsepower than the Excel. Dual airbags are standard and ABS is optional. A tiny 1.5-liter 4-cylinder engine is adequate to move this small car. Fuel economy is good, though

	1993	1994	1995	1996	1997
Size Class			Subcomp.	Subcomp.	Subcomp.
Drive			Front	Front	Front
Crash Test			Average	Average	Average
Airbags			Dual	Dual	Dual
ABS			4-Whl*	4-Whl*	4-Whl*
Parts Cost			Low	Low	Low
Complaints			Very Poor	Poor	Average
Insurance			Surcharge	Surcharge	Surcharge
Fuel Econ.			27	28	28
Theft Rating			Average	Average	Average
Bumpers					
Recalls			4	3	2
Trn. Cir. (ft.)			31.8	31.8	31.8
Weight (lbs.)			2101	2101	2101
Whlbase (in.)			94.5	94.5	94.5
Price			< $3,000	$3-5,000	$4-6,000
OVERALL■			Poor	Poor	Average

NO MODEL PRODUCED

■Cars without crash tests do not receive an overall rating.*Optional **Estimate

2002 Hyundai Accent

not on par with misers like the Geo Metro. Compared to the Tercel, the Accent is just as powerful and roomy, but the Metro and Swift offer more interior room.

Front seat passengers will be comfy in the Accent, but the back seat is cramped. After its redesign in 2000, it is accompanied by an unbeatable 10-year/100,000 mile powertrain warranty along with second generation depowered airbags and belt pretensioners to keep you safe.

	1998	1999	2000	2001	2002
Size Class	Subcomp.	Subcomp.	Subcomp.	Subcomp.	Subcomp.
Drive	Front	Front	Front	Front	Front
Crash Test	Average	Average	Very Good	Very Good	Very Good
Airbags	Dual	Dual	Dual	Dual	Dual
ABS	4-Whl*	4-Whl*	4-Whl*	4-Whl*	4-Whl*
Parts Cost	Very Low	Very Low	Low	Low	Very Low
Complaints	Average	Good	Good	Good	Good
Insurance	Surcharge	Surcharge	Surcharge	Surcharge	Surcharge
Fuel Econ.	28	28	28	18	31
Theft Rating	Very Low	Low	Very Low**	Average**	Average**
Bumpers		Strong	Strong	Strong	Strong
Recalls	0	0	3	1	0
Trn. Cir. (ft.)	31.8	31.8	32.5	32.5	32.5
Weight (lbs.)	2101	2101	2240	2240	2339
Whlbase (in.)	94.5	94.5	96.1	96.1	96.1
Price	$5-7,000	$6-8,000	$7-9,000	$8-10,000	$10-12,000
OVERALL"	Good	Very Good	Very Good	Very Good	**BEST BET**

179

Hyundai Elantra 1993-2002

Around since 1992, the Elantra made its first real impact on the automotive world in 1996 with its first redesign since its inception. The 1996 redesign introduced a more

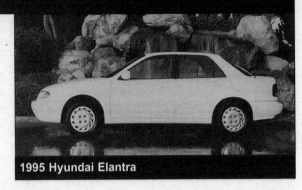

1995 Hyundai Elantra

rounded look and an improved interior. Pre-1996 models tend to feel outdated. Hyundai has positioned the Elantra between the cheaper Accent, the more expensive Sonata, and, new for 1997, the sporty Tiburon. Watch out for door-mounted lap/shoulder belts, which appear in pre-1996 models. A driver's airbag first appears in 1994;

	1993	1994	1995	1996	1997
Size Class	Compact	Compact	Compact	Compact	Compact
Drive	Front	Front	Front	Front	Front
Crash Test	Very Poor	Very Poor	Very Poor	Average	Average
Airbags	None	Driver	Driver	Dual	Dual
ABS	None	4-Whl*	4-Whl*	4-Whl*	4-Whl*
Parts Cost	Low	Very Low	Very Low	Very Low	Low
Complaints	Average	Poor	Very Poor	Very Poor	Very Poor
Insurance	Surcharge	Surcharge	Surcharge	Surcharge	Surcharge
Fuel Econ.	22	23	22	22	24
Theft Rating	Low	Very Low	Low	Very Low	Very Low
Bumpers				Weak	Weak
Recalls	0	2	1	1	1
Trn. Cir. (ft.)	33.8	33.8	34	34	32.5
Weight (lbs.)	2452	2540	2500	2458	2458
Whlbase (in.)	98.4	98.4	98.4	100.4	100.4
Price	<$3,000	< $3,000	$3-5,000	$4-6,000	$5-7,000
OVERALL■	Very Poor	Very Poor	Very Poor	Poor	Poor

■Cars without crash tests do not receive an overall rating.*Optional **Estimate

2002 Hyundai Elantra

dual airbags become standard in 1996 and side airbags are standard with the 2001 redesign. 4-wheel ABS is optional starting in 1994. 1992-95 models come standard with a 1.6-liter 4-cylinder engine, which delivers adequate power with average fuel economy. The optional 1.8-liter engine on these models is slightly more powerful. You will be able to find some great standard features for such an inexpensive car, such as leather seats, a CD player and seat belt pretensioners.

	1998	1999	2000	2001	2002
Size Class	Compact	Compact	Compact	Compact	Compact
Drive	Front	Front	Front	Front	Front
Crash Test	Average	Average	Average	VeryGood	Very Good
Airbags	Dual	Dual	Dual	Dual/Side	Dual/Side
ABS	4-Whl*	4-Whl*	4-Whl*	4-Whl*	4-Whl*
Parts Cost	Very Low	Very Low	Low	Low	Low
Complaints	Average	Good	Average	Very Good	Average
Insurance	Surcharge	Surcharge	Surcharge	Surcharge	Surcharge
Fuel Econ.	24	24	24	25	28
Theft Rating	Low	Very Low	Average	Average**	Average**
Bumpers	Weak	Strong	Strong	Strong	
Recalls	0	1	2	1	0
Trn. Cir. (ft.)	32.5	32.5	32.5	37.5	37.5
Weight (lbs.)	2458	2458	2458	2635	2698
Whlbase (in.)	100.4	100.4	100.4	102.7	102.7
Price	$6-8,000	$7-9,000	$9-11,000	$11-13,000	$13-15,000
OVERALL"	Good	Very Good	Average	BEST BET	Very Good

Hyundai Sonata 1993-2002

The Sonata, Hyundai's mid-size car, went six years without a major change—an unusually long time in this competitive market. The 1995 Sonata, new from the ground up,

1995 Hyundai Sonata

replaced the old model in the spring of 1994 and brought with it more contemporary styling and a longer wheelbase that translates into more legroom. 2001 brought yet another redesign and great safety features, such as standard front airbags. The Sonata, unfortunately, has motorized front shoulder belts and separate lap belts as

	1993	1994	1995	1996	1997
Size Class	Compact	Compact	Intermd.	Intermd.	Intermd.
Drive	Front	Front	Front	Front	Front
Crash Test	Poor	Poor	Average	Average	Average
Airbags	None	None	Dual	Dual	Dual
ABS	4-Whl*	4-Whl*	4-Whl*	4-Whl*	4-Whl*
Parts Cost	Very Low	Very Low	Very Low	Low	Low
Complaints	Very Poor	Very Good	Very Poor	Poor	Average
Insurance	Surcharge	Surcharge	Surcharge	Surcharge	Surcharge
Fuel Econ.	20	20	21	22	21
Theft Rating	High	Low	Low	Very High	Low
Bumpers	Weak	Weak	Weak	Weak	Weak
Recalls	1	1	1	2	1
Trn. Cir. (ft.)	35.7	35.7	34.6	34.6	34.6
Weight (lbs.)	2723	2850	2864	2964	2935
Whlbase (in.)	104.3	104.3	106.3	106.3	106.3
Price	<$3,000	< $3,000	$3-5,000	$4-6,000	$5-7,000
OVERALL■	Very Poor	Poor	Poor	Poor	Average

■Cars without crash tests do not receive an overall rating.*Optional **Estimate

182

2002 Hyundai Sonata

passive restraints in lieu of airbags through 1994; the 1995 model finally gets dual airbags, but you're still stuck with motorized belts. And to get ABS, available beginning in 1992, you'll have to look for the more expensive GL or GLS models. Ride isn't as smooth or quiet as on other mid-size cars; handling, though, is pretty good. Interior room and comfort are good—comparable to other mid-size cars. Trunk space is adequate; the dashboard is easy to use.

	1998	1999	2000	2001	2002
Size Class	Intermd.	Intermd.	Intermd.	Intermd.	Intermd.
Drive	Front	Front	Front	Front	Front
Crash Test	Average	Average	Average	Average	N/A
Airbags	Dual	Dual	Dual	Dual	Dl./Sd.(F)
ABS	4-Whl*	4-Whl*	4-Whl*	4-Whl*	4-Whl
Parts Cost	Low	Low	Low	Low	Low
Complaints	Poor	Average	Good	Very Good	Average
Insurance	Surcharge	Surcharge	Surcharge	Surcharge	Surcharge
Fuel Econ.	21	21	21	21	25
Theft Rating	Average**	Average**	Average**	Average**	Average**
Bumpers		Strong	Strong	Strong	Strong
Recalls	1	1	3	2	0
Trn. Cir. (ft.)	34.6	34.6	34.6	34.6	34.4
Weight (lbs.)	2935	2935	3072	3072	3217
Whlbase (in.)	106.3	106.3	106.3	106.3	106.3
Price	$7-9,000	$9-11,000	$11-13,000	$12-14,000	$16-18,000
OVERALL■	Poor	Average	Average	Good	Poor

Hyundai Tiburon 1997-2002

The Tiburon remains the sportiest car among the Hyundai offerings. Competing in the saturated compact sports car market, the Tiburon offers standard dual

1997 Hyundai Tiburon

airbags, ABS and seat belt pretensioners—a significant assortment of standard features for such a low priced sports car.

The 2.0-liter 4-cylinder engine is quick and produces 140hp, but the handling and suspension are superior. The Porsche-designed sus-

	1993	1994	1995	1996	1997
Size Class					Compact
Drive					Front
Crash Test					N/A
Airbags					Dual
ABS					4-Whl*
Parts Cost					Very Low
Complaints					Very Poor
Insurance					Regular
Fuel Econ.		NO MODEL PRODUCED			23
Theft Rating					
Bumpers					Strong
Recalls					3
Trn. Cir. (ft.)					34.1
Weight (lbs.)					2597
Whlbase (in.)					97.4
Price					$4-6,000
OVERALL■					

■Cars without crash tests do not receive an overall rating. *Optional **Estimate

184

pension system provides a smooth ride, which is rare in sports cars. The controls are well placed and easy-to-read.

2002 Hyundai Tiburon

	1998	1999	2000	2001	2002
Size Class	Compact	Compact	Compact	Compact	Compact
Drive	Front	Front	Front	Front	Front
Crash Test	N/A	N/A	N/A	N/A	N/A
Airbags	Dual	Dual	Dual	Dual	Dual
ABS	4-Whl*	4-Whl*	4-Whl*	4-Whl*	4-Whl
Parts Cost	Very Low	Very Low	Very Low	Low	Very Low
Complaints	Very Poor	Poor	Poor	Very Good	Very Poor
Insurance	Regular	Regular	Regular	Regular	Regular
Fuel Econ.	25	25	25	25	26
Theft Rating	Average	Average	Average	Average**	Average**
Bumpers	Strong	Strong	Strong	Strong	Strong
Recalls	1	3	1	1	0
Trn. Cir. (ft.)	34.1	34.1	34.1	34.1	34.1
Weight (lbs.)	2597	2597	2597	2597	2597
Whlbase (in.)	97.4	97.4	97.4	97.4	97.4
Price	$5-7,000	$7-9,000	$9-11,000	$10-12,000	$14-16,000
OVERALL■					

Infiniti G20 1993-96, 1999-2002

Styling is pretty bland on the G20 compared to the other Infiniti models, but it's certainly on par with its American competitors. The G20 is clearly less of a status symbol, and, if you can live without the nameplate, you might want to consider a Nissan Sentra with all the options for less money. Conventional belts and dual airbags became standard midway through the 1993 model year. ABS has been standard throughout the G20's history. After being discontinued in 1997, the G20 came back in '99 with standard side

1993 Infiniti G20

	1993	1994	1995	1996	1997
Size Class	Compact	Compact	Compact	Compact	
Drive	Front	Front	Front	Front	
Crash Test	N/A	N/A	N/A	N/A	
Airbags	Dual	Dual	Dual	Dual	
ABS	4-Whl	4-Whl	4-Whl	4-Whl	
Parts Cost	Low	Low	High	Average	
Complaints	Average	V ery Good	Average	Good	
Insurance	Regular	Regular	Regular	Discount	
Fuel Econ.	22	22	24	24	
Theft Rating	Average	Average	Average	Average	
Bumpers					
Recalls	3	2	1	1	
Trn. Cir. (ft.)	35.4	35.4	35.4	35.4	
Weight (lbs.)	2745	2877	2877	2877	
Whlbase (in.)	100.4	100.4	100.4	100.4	
Price	$6-8,000	$7-9,000	$8-10,000	$9-11,000	
OVERALL■					

NO MODEL PRODUCED

■Cars without crash tests do not receive an overall rating. **Estimate

2002 Infiniti G20

airbags. The G20 shares its 4-cylinder 145 hp engine with the Sentra SE; you'll probably be happier with the 5-speed manual transmission than with the 4-speed automatic, and you'll get better mileage. Ride is firm and handling can be a bit challenging in sudden high speed maneuvers, but otherwise it's predictable and responsive. The instrument panel is a pleasure to use, but the car is small for four adults.

	1998	1999	2000	2001	2002
Size Class		Compact	Compact	Compact	Compact
Drive		Front	Front	Front	Front
Crash Test		N/A	N/A	N/A	N/A
Airbags		Dual/Side	Dual/Side	Dual/Side	Dl./Sd.(F)
ABS		4-Whl	4-Whl	4-Whl	4-Whl
Parts Cost	NO MODEL PRODUCED	High	Average	High	Very High
Complaints		Very Good	Very Good	Good	Very Good
Insurance		Regular	Regular	Regular	Regular
Fuel Econ.		23	23	24	26
Theft Rating		Average**	Average**	Average**	Average**
Bumpers			Strong	Strong	Strong
Recalls		0	0	0	0
Trn. Cir. (ft.)		37.4	37.4	37.4	37.4
Weight (lbs.)		2913	2913	2913	2913
Whlbase (in.)		102.4	102.4	102.4	102.4
Price		$16-18,000	$18-20,000	$19-21,000	$22-24,000
OVERALL■					

Infiniti I30 1996-2001, Infiniti I35 2002

In 2000, the all-new second generation I30 had a revised version of the 3.0-liter V6 that produces 227 horsepower, but the I30 was redesigned again in 2002 and renamed the I35.

1996 Infiniti I30

The new engine packs more punch with a 270-hp, 3.4-liter V6. The exterior has new styling, including increased dimensions, and interior is all-new as well. In addition to standard ABS and driver and front passenger airbags and side airbags, there is now head protec-

	1993	1994	1995	1996	1997
Size Class				Large	Large
Drive				Front	Front
Crash Test				N/A	N/A
Airbags				Dual	Dual
ABS				4-Whl	4-Whl
Parts Cost				Very High	Very High
Complaints		NO MODEL PRODUCED		Good	Very Good
Insurance				Surcharge	Surcharge
Fuel Econ.				21	21
Theft Rating				Very High	Very High
Bumpers					
Recalls				0	0
Trn. Cir. (ft.)				34.8	34.8
Weight (lbs.)				3090	3090
Whlbase (in.)				106.3	106.3
Price				$12-14,000	$14-16,000
OVERALL■					

■Cars without crash tests do not receive an overall rating.**Estimate

2002 Infiniti I35

tion. It also has rear child seat tethers, which ensure your child seat is secured properly. The optional navigation system is 3D and rises from the dash for easy visibility. Essentially an upscale Nissan Maxima, the I30 received minor changes through 1998-99. If you can live without the nameplate, consider a fully loaded Maxima and save a couple thousand dollars.

	1998	1999	2000	2001	2002
Size Class	Large	Large	Large	Large	Large
Drive	Front	Front	Front	Front	Front
Crash Test	N/A	N/A	N/A	N/A	N/A
Airbags	Dual/Side	Dual/Side	Dual/Side	Dual/Side	Dual/Side
ABS	4-Whl	4-Whl	4-Whl	4-Whl	4-Whl
Parts Cost	Very High	Very High	Very High	Very High	Very High
Complaints	Good	Very Good	Very Good	Very Good	Average
Insurance	Surcharge	Surcharge	Surcharge	Surcharge	Regular
Fuel Econ.	21	21	20	18	22
Theft Rating	Very High	Average	Average[**]	Average[**]	Average[**]
Bumpers		Strong	Strong	Strong	Strong
Recalls	0	0	0	0	1
Trn. Cir. (ft.)	34.8	34.8	35.4	35.4	40
Weight (lbs.)	3090	3150	3342	3342	
Whlbase (in.)	106.3	106.3	108.3	108.3	108.3
Price	$17-19,000	$19-21,000	$23-25,000	$24-26,000	$28-30,000
OVERALL■					

Infiniti Q45 1993-2002

The Q45 is Infiniti's biggest and most impressive model. The Q45 was among Infiniti's first ventures as the premium car division of Nissan, and the Q45 continues to be Infiniti's flag-

Infiniti Q45

ship. The Q45 got a new front end treatment, including a small, chrome grille in 1995, and it was all-new for 1997 and again in 2002. All Q45 models have a driver's airbag and ABS is standard. The 1994 models added a passenger airbag, the 1998 models added side airbags and the 2002 models come standard with head airbags.

	1993	1994	1995	1996	1997
Size Class	Large	Large	Large	Large	Large
Drive	Rear	Rear	Rear	Rear	Rear
Crash Test	N/A	N/A	N/A	N/A	N/A
Airbags	Driver	Dual	Dual	Dual	Dual
ABS	4-Whl	4-Whl	4-Whl	4-Whl	4-Whl
Parts Cost	Very High	High	High	High	Very High
Complaints	Very Good	Very Poor	Good	Average	Good
Insurance	Discount	Discount	Discount	Discount	Regular
Fuel Econ.	17	17	17	17	18
Theft Rating	High	Very High	Very High	Very High	Very High
Bumpers					Weak
Recalls	0	0	0	0	1
Trn. Cir. (ft.)	37.4	37.4	37.4	37.4	36.1
Weight (lbs.)	3929	4039	4039	4039	3879
Whlbase (in.)	113.2	113.2	113.4	113.4	111.4
Price	$10-12,000	$12-14,000	$14-16,000	$16-18,000	$21-23,000
OVERALL■					

■Cars without crash tests do not receive an overall rating.**Estimate

2002 Infiniti Q45

The new Q45's 4.5-liter 274 hp V8 with automatic overdrive used to be a terrible gas guzzler, but since its redesign, it has become even more efficient than previously offered 4.1-liter engine. The Q45 comes with just about everything you could imagine; you can find cars with active suspension (Q45a), a touring package (Q45t), or traction control, which is worth looking for. Handling is excellent. The ride is generally smooth, but more sensitive than most other luxury cars.

	1998	1999	2000	2001	2002
Size Class	Large	Large	Large	Large	Large
Drive	Rear	Rear	Rear	Rear	Rear
Crash Test	N/A	N/A	N/A	N/A	N/A
Airbags	Dual/Side	Dual/Side	Dual/Side	Dual/Side	Dl./Sd./Hd.
ABS	4-Whl	4-Whl	4-Whl	4-Whl	4-Whl
Parts Cost	Very High	Very High	Very High	Very High	Very High
Complaints	Very Good	Very Good	Very Good	Very Good	Average
Insurance	Regular	Regular	Discount	Discount	Discount
Fuel Econ.	18	17	17	17	20
Theft Rating	Very High**	Very High**	Very High**	Very High**	Very High**
Bumpers	Weak	Strong	Strong	Strong	Strong
Recalls	0	0	0	0	0
Trn. Cir. (ft.)	36.1	36.1	36.1	36.1	37.4
Weight (lbs.)	3879	4007	4007	4007	
Whlbase (in.)	111.4	111.4	111.4	111.4	113
Price	$24-26,000	$29-31,000	$34-36,000	$38-40,000	$49-51,000
OVERALL■					

Infiniti QX4 1997-2002

Created to be an upscale Nissan Pathfinder, the Infiniti QX4 is more luxurious and significantly more expensive. Dual airbags have come standard on the QX4 since its creation in 1997

1997 Infiniti QX4

and in 2000, side airbags were added. Four-wheel ABS has always been standard.

Only one engine is available on the QX4: a 3.3-liter V6. The engine is powerful enough to comfortably power the mid-size sport

	1993	1994	1995	1996	1997
Size Class					Sp. Util.
Drive					4-Whl
Crash Test					Very Good
Airbags					Dual
ABS					4-Whl
Parts Cost					High
Complaints					Good
Insurance					Regular
Fuel Econ.					16
Theft Rating					Very High
Bumpers		NO MODEL PRODUCED			
Recalls					2
Trn. Cir. (ft.)					39.5
Weight (lbs.)					4275
Whlbase (in.)					106.3
Price					$8-20,000
OVERALL■					Average

■Cars without crash tests do not receive an overall rating. **Estimate

2002 Infiniti QX4

utility, but it isn't ideal for towing heavy loads. The high price tag was meant to compete with other luxury vehicles, such as the Mercedes-Benz M-Class or the BMW X5, but it doesn't offer as many luxury gadgets or safety features. Most of the safety features found on the QX4 come standard on the Pathfinder, so it isn't worth the extra money to splurge on the QX4.

	1998	1999	2000	2001	2002
Size Class	Sp. Util.	Sp. Util.	Sp. Util.	Sp. Util.	Sp. Util.
Drive	4-Whl	4-Whl	4-Whl	4-Whl	4-Whl
Crash Test	Very Good	Very Good	Very Good	Very Good	Very Good
Airbags	Dual	Dual	Dual/Side	Dual/Side	Dual/Side
ABS	4-Whl	4-Whl	4-Whl	4-Whl	4-Whl
Parts Cost	Very High	Very High	Very High	Very High	High
Complaints	Good	Very Good	Very Good	Good	Very Good
Insurance	Regular	Regular	Regular	Discount	Discount
Fuel Econ.	16	16	16	16	16
Theft Rating	Very High	Very High	Very High	Very High	Very High**
Bumpers					
Recalls	4	4	2	2	0
Trn. Cir. (ft.)	39.5	39.5	39.5	39.5	39.5
Weight (lbs.)	4275	4275	4275	4275	4320
Whlbase (in.)	106.3	106.3	106.3	106.3	106.3
Price	$20-23,000	$23-25,000	$27-29,000	$28-30,000	$34-36,000
OVERALL*	Average	Average	Good	Very Good	**BEST BET**

Isuzu Amigo 1993-95, 1998-1999

Based on the Isuzu pickup chassis, this 2-door sport utility has changed little since its introduction in 1989. From the doors forward, it is identical to the pickup, but the

1993 Isuzu Amigo

rear is chopped off and the partial hardtop roof ends with a soft top portion above the rear seats/cargo area. The Amigo lagged behind its competition by never offering airbags. ABS started in 1993, but only on the rear wheels. The Amigo weighs a lot for such a small vehicle, so the 3.2-liter 4-cylinder engine for 2000 has a lot of work

	1993	1994	1995	1996	1997
Size Class	Sp. Util.	Sp. Util.	Sp. Util.		
Drive	Rear/4	Rear/4	Rear/4		
Crash Test	Poor	Poor	Poor		
Airbags	None	None	None		
ABS	2-Whl	2-Whl	2-Whl		
Parts Cost	Very Low	Very Low	Very Low		
Complaints	Good	Average	Very Good		
Insurance	Surcharge	Surcharge	Surcharge		
Fuel Econ.	18	16	16		
Theft Rating	Very High	Very High	Very High		
Bumpers					
Recalls	0	1	0		
Trn. Cir. (ft.)	33.5	33.5	33.5		
Weight (lbs.)	2905	2905	2905		
Whlbase (in.)	91.7	91.7	91.7		
Price	<$3,000	$3-5,0000	$5-7,000		
OVERALL■	Poor	Very Poor	Poor		

Column for 1996-1997: NO MODEL PRODUCED

■Cars without crash tests do not receive an overall rating.

1999 Isuzu Amigo

to do. It puts out 130 hp and can tow 4,500 pounds. As a result, gas mileage suffers. Because of the Amigo's short wheelbase, the ride is rougher than other Isuzu light trucks. Handling is pretty good, but take those corners slowly. The instrument panel is poorly designed with too many buttons and knobs. Being a relatively tall vehicle with a narrow track width, the Amigo is quite unstable—so be careful. Overall, you can find a much better vehicle to spend your money on.

	1998	1999	2000	2001	2002
Size Class	Sp. Util.	Sp. Util.			
Drive	Rear/4	Rear/4			
Crash Test	N/A	N/A			
Airbags	Dual	Dual			
ABS	4-Whl	4-Whl			
Parts Cost	Average	Average			
Complaints	Very Poor	Very Poor			
Insurance	Surcharge	Surcharge			
Fuel Econ.	20	20			
Theft Rating	Very High	Very High			
Bumpers					
Recalls	4	0			
Trn. Cir. (ft.)	34.1	34.1			
Weight (lbs.)	3329	3329			
Whlbase (in.)	96.9	96.9			
Price	$10-12,000	$11-13,000			
OVERALL■	Very Poor	Very Poor			

NO MODEL PRODUCED

Isuzu Rodeo 1993-2002

1993 Isuzu Rodeo

Cheaper than its twin, the Honda Passport, the Rodeo comes with many of the same features, but the overall performance is disappointing. The Rodeo had no airbags until 1996, and in 2002 they received head airbags. ABS is standard beginning in 1992, but only on the rear wheels. From 1996 until 1998, you have to pay extra for 4-wheel ABS, but from 1999 on, it is standard.

	1993	1994	1995	1996	1997
Size Class	Sp. Util.	Sp. Util.	Sp. Util.	Sp. Util.	Sp. Util.
Drive	Rear/4	Rear/4	Rear/4	Rear/4	Rear/4
Crash Test	Poor	Poor	Poor	Average	Average
Airbags	None	None	None	Dual	Dual
ABS	2-Whl	2-Whl	2-Whl	4-Whl*	4-Whl*
Parts Cost	Low	Low	Low	Very Low	High
Complaints	Average	Average	Very Poor	Average	Average
Insurance	Regular	Regular	Surcharge	Surcharge	Regular
Fuel Econ.	18	16	16	16	16
Theft Rating	Average	High	Average	Average	Average
Bumpers				Weak	Weak
Recalls	0	1	4	2	0
Trn. Cir. (ft.)	37.7	37.7	37.7	37.7	37.7
Weight (lbs.)	3470	3490	3545	3593	3705
Whlbase (in.)	108.7	108.7	108.7	108.7	108.7
Price	$3-5,000	$5-7,000	$7-9,000	$9-11,000	$12-14,000
OVERALL■	Poor	Very Poor	Very Poor	Poor	Poor

■Cars without crash tests do not receive an overall rating.*Optional **Estimate

2002 Isuzu Rodeo

Two-wheel drive models come with a standard in-line 4-cylinder that is not powerful enough, even with only two passengers aboard. The 4-wheel drive models are better equipped with a more powerful V6. The sloping roof cuts down on cargo space and there is a lot of interior noise.

	1998	1999	2000	2001	2002
Size Class	Sp. Util.	Sp. Util.	Sp. Util.	Sp. Util.	Sp. Util.
Drive	Rear/4	Rear/4	Rear/4	Rear/4	Rear/4
Crash Test	Average	Average	Average	Average	Average
Airbags	Dual	Dual	Dual	Dual	Dual/Head
ABS	4-Whl*	4-Whl	4-Whl	4-Whl	4-Whl
Parts Cost	High	High	Very Low	Low	Average
Complaints	Very Poor	Very Poor	Average	Good	Very Poor
Insurance	Regular	Regular	Regular	Regular	Regular
Fuel Econ.	16	16	16	17	19
Theft Rating	High	High	High	Very High**	Very High**
Bumpers	Weak	Weak	Weak	Weak	Weak
Recalls	0	4	0	0	0
Trn. Cir. (ft.)	38.4	38.4	38.4	38.4	38.4
Weight (lbs.)	3860	3860	3848	3848	3848
Whlbase (in.)	106.4	106.4	106.4	106.4	106.4
Price	$13-15,000	$15-17,000	$19-21,000	$20-23,000	$25-27,000
OVERALL■	Very Poor	Very Poor	Good	Good	Poor

Isuzu Trooper 1993-2002

The Trooper is the original and largest sport utility vehicle. Isuzu introduced the 2-door in 1993. A 4x2 version was introduced in 2000, as well as a fresh new style with new features,

1993 Isuzu Trooper

new colors and a new trim level, yet prices did not rise. Troopers didn't have airbags or passive belts through 1994, but 1995 and later models have dual airbags, a welcome addition. 4-wheel ABS is available on certain Troopers beginning in 1994, standard in 1997. The older 4-cylinder or turbo-diesel engines struggled with any sig-

	1993	1994	1995	1996	1997
Size Class	Sp. Util.	Sp. Util.	Sp. Util.	Sp. Util.	Sp. Util.
Drive	All	All	All	All	Front/All
Crash Test	Poor	Poor	Average	Average	Average
Airbags	None	None	Dual	Dual	Dual
ABS	2-Whl	4-Whl*	4-Whl*	4-Whl*	4-Whl
Parts Cost	High	Low	Low	Average	Very High
Complaints	Poor	Average	Poor	Very Poor	Good
Insurance	Regular	Discount	Regular	Discount	Discount
Fuel Econ.	15	15	15	16	14
Theft Rating	Low	Average	Average	Average	Average
Bumpers					
Recalls	1	1	0	4	4
Trn. Cir. (ft.)	32.8	32.8	32.8	38.1	38.1
Weight (lbs.)	4210	4155	4060	4315	4315
Whlbase (in.)	91.71	91.71	91.71	91.71	91.71
Price	$5-7,000	$7-9,000	$9-11,000	$11-13,000	$13-15,000
OVERALL■	Very Poor	Average	Average	Poor	Average

■Cars without crash tests do not receive an overall rating.*Optional **Estimate

198

2002 Isuzu Trooper

nificant load, but the now standard V6, first offered in 1989, provides more power. The V6, even the twin-cam version, is barely enough power for such a heavy vehicle. It is no surprise that gas mileage is poor with the V6. Engines come with 5-speed manual or automatic overdrive, and part-time 4-wheel drive. The handling is worse than average for sport utility vehicles. The ride is poor on all Troopers, but fairly quiet on newer models. It has not been crash tested in recent years.

	1998	1999	2000	2001	2002
Size Class	Sp. Util.	Sp. Util.	Sp. Util.	Sp. Util.	Sp. Util.
Drive	Front/All	Front/All	Front/All	Front/All	Front/All
Crash Test	N/A	N/A	N/A	N/A	N/A
Airbags	Dual	Dual	Dual	Dual	Dual/Head
ABS	4-Whl	4-Whl	4-Whl	4-Whl	4-Whl
Parts Cost	Very High	Very High	Very High	Very High	High
Complaints	Good	Good	Good	Very Good	Average
Insurance	Discount	Discount	Discount	Discount	Discount
Fuel Econ.	16	16	16	16	17
Theft Rating	Average	Average**	Average**	Average**	Average**
Bumpers					
Recalls	1	0	1	0	0
Trn. Cir. (ft.)	38.1	38.1	38.1	38.1	38.1
Weight (lbs.)	4540	4540	4465	4465	4465
Whlbase (in.)	108.7	108.7	108.7	108.7	108.7
Price	$14-16,000	$16-18,000	$17-19,000	$19-21,000	$28-30,000
OVERALL■					

Jeep Cherokee 1993-2001

The Jeep Cherokee pioneered and popularized 4-door sport utility vehicles. Originally slated to be replaced by the modern Grand Cherokee in 1993, Jeep decided to

1993 Jeep Cherokee

keep both models around, and the Cherokee has carried on. Cherokees sport a standard 2.5-liter 4-cylinder engine, which is slow but economical. A 2.8-liter V6 was optional for several years, but it was replaced in 1989 with a 4-liter 6. In 2001, you had the option of the 4-liter inline-6 offered on the Grand Cherokee. With either engine,

	1993	1994	1995	1996	1997
Size Class	Sp. Util.	Sp. Util.	Sp. Util.	Sp. Util.	Sp. Util.
Drive	Rear/4	Rear/4	Rear/4	Rear/4	Rear/4
Crash Test	Average	Average	Good	Good	Poor
Airbags	None	None	Driver	Driver	Dual
ABS	4-Whl*	4-Whl*	4-Whl*	4-Whl*	4-Whl*
Parts Cost	Very Low	Very Low	Very Low	Very Low	Low
Complaints	Very Poor	Very Poor	Very Poor	Very Poor	Very Poor
Insurance	Regular	Regular	Regular	Discount	Discount
Fuel Econ.	17	15	17	19	19
Theft Rating	Very High	Very High	High	VeryHigh	Very High
Bumpers					
Recalls	3	3	4	4	3
Trn. Cir. (ft.)	35.9	35.9	35.9	35.9	35.9
Weight (lbs.)	2808	2932	2932	2905	2947
Whlbase (in.)	101.4	101.4	101.4	101.4	101.4
Price	<$3,000	$3-5,000	$5-7,000	$6-8,000	$9-11,000
OVERALL■	Very Poor	Very Poor	Poor	Average	Poor

■Cars without crash tests do not receive an overall rating.*Optional **Estimate

2001 Jeep Cherokee

you can find a 5-speed manual or an automatic, and you can choose between a 2-wheel drive or two 4-wheel drive systems. The Cherokee's handling is pretty good. For the future, keep your eye out for the all-new Jeep Liberty that hopes to carry on the popularity of the now-retired Cherokee.

	1998	1999	2000	2001	2002
Size Class	Sp. Util.	Sp. Util.	Sp. Util.	Sp. Util.	
Drive	Rear/4	Rear/4	Rear/4	Rear/4	
Crash Test	Poor	Poor	Poor	Poor	
Airbags	Dual	Dual	Dual	Dual	
ABS	4-Whl*	4-Whl*	4-Whl*	4-Whl*	
Parts Cost	Very Low	Very Low	Very Low	Very Low	
Complaints	Poor	Average	Average	Average	
Insurance	Discount	Discount	Discount	Discount	
Fuel Econ.	19	19	19	19	
Theft Rating	Very High	Very High	Very High	Very High**	
Bumpers					
Recalls	2	0	1	2	
Trn. Cir. (ft.)	35.1	35.1	35.1	35.1	
Weight (lbs.)	3150	3150	3150	3150	
Whlbase (in.)	101.4	101.4	101.4	101.4	
Price	$11-13,000	$13-15,000	$14-16,000	$16-18,000	
OVERALL■	Good	Very Good	Good	Good	

NO MODEL PRODUCED

Jeep Grand Cherokee 1993-2002

The Jeep Grand Cherokee, one of the better sport utilities on the market, was originally scheduled to replace the Cherokee. With its redesign in 1993, it was given rounded corners,

1993 Jeep Grand Cherokee

a better suspension, and a more modern interior design than the boxy, rough-and-tumble Cherokee. It was introduced in the spring of 1992 as a 1993 model, but did not end up replacing the Cherokee. A driver's airbag and 4-wheel ABS became standard with the 1993 redesign. Starting in 1996, dual airbags were standard and now

	1993	1994	1995	1996	1997
Size Class	Sp. Util.	Sp. Util.	Sp. Util.	Sp. Util.	Sp. Util.
Drive	Rear/4	Rear/4	Rear/4	Rear/4	Rear/4
Crash Test	Average	Average	Average	Average	Average
Airbags	Driver	Driver	Driver	Dual	Dual
ABS	4-Whl	4-Whl	4-Whl	4-Whl	4-Whl
Parts Cost	Low	Average	Very Low	Very Low	Very Low
Complaints	Very Poor	Very Poor	Poor	Very Poor	Very Poor
Insurance	Regular	Regular	Regular	Discount	Discount
Fuel Econ.	16	15	15	15	15
Theft Rating	Very High	Very High	Very High	Very High	Very High
Bumpers				Weak	Weak
Recalls	8	2	3	4	5
Trn. Cir. (ft.)	36.6	36.6	36.6	36.6	37.5
Weight (lbs.)	3449	3530	3567	3614	3609
Whlbase (in.)	105.9	105.9	105.9	105.9	105.9
Price	$5-7,000	$6-8,000	$7-9,000	$10-12,000	$11-13,000
OVERALL■	Very Poor	Very Poor	Poor	Average	Average

■Cars without crash tests do not receive an overall rating.**Estimate

2002 Jeep Grand Cherokee

both side and head airbags are standard. The 1993-97 Grand Cherokees have a powerful 4-liter 190 hp engine or an optional 5.2-liter 220 hp V8 with automatic overdrive. All Grand Cherokees are available in both rear- and 4-wheel drive, and Jeep gives you three different 4-wheel drive systems to meet your demands. Gas mileage is about what you'd expect from a sport utility vehicle, and cargo room is adequate.

	1998	1999	2000	2001	2002
Size Class	Sp. Util.	Sp. Util	Sp. Util	Sp. Util	Sp. Util.
Drive	Rear/4	Rear/4	Rear/4	Rear/4	Rear/4
Crash Test	Average	Average	Average	Average	Average
Airbags	Dual	Dual	Dual	Dual	Dl./Sd./Hd.
ABS	4-Whl	4-Whl	4-Whl	4-Whl	4-Whl
Parts Cost	Very Low	Very Low	Very Low	Very Low	Very Low
Complaints	Very Poor	Very Poor	Average	Good	Poor
Insurance	Discount	Discount	Discount	Discount	Discount
Fuel Econ.	15	15	15	15	17
Theft Rating	High	Average	Average	Average**	Average**
Bumpers	Weak				
Recalls	2	2	1	1	5
Trn. Cir. (ft.)	36.7	36.7	36.7	36.7	37.4
Weight (lbs.)	3800	3800	3800	3800	3791
Whlbase (in.)	105.9	105.9	105.9	105.9	105.9
Price	$14-16,000	$18-20,000	$20-22,000	$21-23,000	$28-30,000
OVERALL■	Average	Good	Very Good	BEST BET	Very Good

Jeep Wrangler 1993-2002

The Wrangler replaced the CJ series Jeeps that were direct descendants of World War II-era Jeeps. The Wrangler is basic transportation in a 4-wheel drive vehicle; other than the

1993 Jeep Wrangler

addition of trim packages and options, it barely changed between 1989 and 1996. A new version debuted in 1997 and is a much better vehicle. Unfortunately, airbags aren't available until 1997. ABS became optional on all models beginning in 1992. The standard 2.5-liter 4-cylinder offers adequate power, or you can choose an option-

	1993	1994	1995	1996	1997
Size Class	Sp. Util.	Sp. Util.	Sp. Util.	Sp. Util.	Sp. Util.
Drive	Rear/4	Rear/4	Rear/4	Rear/4	Rear/4
Crash Test	Average	Poor	Poor	Poor	Very Good
Airbags	None	None	None	None	Dual
ABS	4-Whl*	4-Whl*	4-Whl*	4-Whl*	4-Whl*
Parts Cost	Low	Very Low	Very Low	Very Low	Low
Complaints	Poor	Poor	Poor	Very Good	Very Poor
Insurance	Regular	Regular	Regular	Regular	Surcharge
Fuel Econ.	16	17	19	19	17
Theft Rating	Very High	Very High	Very High	Very High	Very High
Bumpers					
Recalls	3	2	1	0	4
Trn. Cir. (ft.)	32.9	32.9	32.9	32.9	33.6
Weight (lbs.)	3080	2935	2934	2934	3092
Whlbase (in.)	93.4	93.4	93.4	93.4	93.4
Price	$3-5,000	$5-7,000	$7-9,000	$8-10,000	$10-12,000
OVERALL■	Very Poor	Very Poor	Poor	Average	Very Poor

■Cars without crash tests do not receive an overall rating.*Optional **Estimate

al 4-liter 6 that offers more than enough power. Wranglers come with part-time 4-wheel drive and a 5-speed manual or 3-speed automatic. You'll find handling is average for sport utili-

2002 Jeep Wrangler

ty vehicles and notably worse than a typical passenger car's. Ride improves in the 1997 version. The rear seat is definitely cramped and uncomfortable for adults. Interior comfort and weather sealing are minimal with the soft top, but the heater is powerful.

	1998	1999	2000	2001	2002
Size Class	Sp. Util.	Sp. Util.	Sp. Util.	Sp. Util.	Sp. Util.
Drive	Rear/4	Rear/4	Rear/4	Rear/4	Rear/4
Crash Test	Very Good	Very Good	Very Good	Very Good	Very Good
Airbags	Dual	Dual	Dual	Dual	Dual
ABS	4-Whl*	4-Whl*	4-Whl*	4-Whl*	4-Whl*
Parts Cost	Average	Very Low	Very Low	Very Low	Very Low
Complaints	Poor	Good	Poor	Very Good	Poor
Insurance	Surcharge	Surcharge	Surcharge	Surcharge	Surcharge
Fuel Econ.	17	16	16	16	19
Theft Rating	High	High	Average	Average**	Average**
Bumpers					
Recalls	2	0	2	3	2
Trn. Cir. (ft.)	32.8	32.8	32.8	32.8	32.8
Weight (lbs.)	3045	3045	3045	3045	3294
Whlbase (in.)	93.4	93.4	93.4	93.4	93.4
Price	$12-14,000	$13-15,000	$15-17,000	$17-19,000	$18-21,000
OVERALL■	Poor	Very Good	Average	Very Good	Average

Kia Sephia 1994-2001

1995 Kia Sephia

Kia was the first new manufacturer to enter the U.S. auto market in several years. However, they had experience—for years, Kia made Festivas and Aspires for Ford. The Sephia debuted into a very crowded and competitive subcompact market in 1994. During its first year, the Sephia did not offer airbags or ABS, but Kia quickly remedied this in 1995 when Sephias came standard with dual airbags; optional ABS was added in 1996. In 1994, your only engine choice was a meek 88 horsepower 1.6-liter engine;

	1993	1994	1995	1996	1997
Size Class	NO MODEL PRODUCED	Subcomp.	Subcomp.	Subcomp.	Subcomp.
Drive		Front	Front	Front	Front
Crash Test		Average	Average	Average	Average
Airbags		None	None	Dual	Dual
ABS		None	None	4-Whl*	4-Whl*
Parts Cost		High	High	Average	High
Complaints		Poor	Very Poor	Very Poor	Very Poor
Insurance		Surcharge	Surcharge	Surcharge	Surcharge
Fuel Econ.		25	25	29	28
Theft Rating		Average	Average	Average	Very Low
Bumpers				Weak	Weak
Recalls		1	0	0	0
Trn. Cir. (ft.)		33.5	33.5	33.5	33.5
Weight (lbs.)		2405	2405	2476	2476
Whlbase (in.)		98.4	98.4	98.4	98.4
Price		< $3,000	< $3,000	$2-4,000	$4-6,000
OVERALL■		Very Poor	Very Poor	Poor	Very Poor

■Cars without crash tests do not receive an overall rating. *Optional **Estimate

2001 Kia Sephia

however, with the changes in safety features in 1995, Kia also upgraded its engine. For 1995 and later models, the Sephia is equipped with an impressive 1.8-liter 4-cylinder engine which can produce 122 horsepower. Unlike many of Sephia's competitors, Kia only offers one body style, the sedan. You do, however, have several trim levels to choose from. Interior space is adequate, but trunk space is skimpy. With the introduction of the Spectra in 2000, the Sephia was phased out in 2001.

	1998	1999	2000	2001	2002
Size Class	Subcomp.	Subcomp.	Subcomp.	Subcomp.	
Drive	Front	Front	Front	Front	
Crash Test	Good	Good	Good	Good	
Airbags	Dual	Dual	Dual	Dual	
ABS	4-Whl*	4-Whl*	4-Whl*	4-Whl*	
Parts Cost	High	Average	Average	Low	
Complaints	Very Poor	Very Poor	Very Poor	Very Poor	
Insurance	Surcharge	Surcharge	Surcharge	Surcharge	
Fuel Econ.	28	24	23	24	
Theft Rating	Very Low	Very Low	Very Low	Low**	
Bumpers		Strong	Weak	Weak	
Recalls	0	0	0	0	
Trn. Cir. (ft.)	33.5	33.5	32.16	32.16	
Weight (lbs.)	2476	2476	2478	2478	
Whlbase (in.)	98.4	98.4	100.8	100.8	
Price	$5-7,000	$6-8,000	$7-9,000	$9-10,000	
OVERALL■	Poor	Average	Poor	Average	

NO MODEL PRODUCED

Kia Sportage 1995-2002

Kia's small sport utility has been increasing its safety package over the past few years. No airbags were offered until the standard driver's in 1996. In 1998, Kia offered dual airbags as

1995 Kia Sportage

standard. A similar upgrade occurred with ABS: none available in 1995, 2-wheel in 1996, and optional 4-wheel ABS for 1998-2002.

The 2-liter 4-cylinder engine is adequate and fuel economy is average for this segment of vehicle. A more powerful engine would

	1993	1994	1995	1996	1997
Size Class			Sp. Util.	Sp. Util.	Sp. Util.
Drive			Rear/4	Rear/4	Rear/4
Crash Test			N/A	N/A	N/A
Airbags			Driver	Driver	Driver
ABS			2-Whl	2-Whl	2-Whl
Parts Cost			High	High	High
Complaints			Very Poor	Very Poor	Very Poor
Insurance			Discount	Discount	Discount
Fuel Econ.			19	19	19
Theft Rating			Average	Average	Average
Bumpers					
Recalls			1	2	1
Trn. Cir. (ft.)			34.8	34.8	34.8
Weight (lbs.)			3252	3252	3303
Whlbase (in.)			104.4	104.4	104.4
Price			$5-7,000	$6-8,000	$7-9,000
OVERALL■					

(In columns 1993 and 1994: NO MODEL PRODUCED)

■Cars without crash tests do not receive an overall rating.*Optional **Estimate

2002 Kia Sportage

be nice; unfortunately, none is offered. The model lineup is fairly simple, with only a base model and an optional EX package that comes with some luxury amenities. Four-wheel drive is optional. In 1999, Kia introduced 2-door models for the first time and it has been an option ever since.

	1998	1999	2000	2001	2002
Size Class	Sp. Util.	Sp. Util	Sp. Util	Sp. Util	Sp. Util.
Drive	Rear/4	Rear/4	Rear/4	Rear/4	Rear/4
Crash Test	N/A	N/A	N/A	N/A	N/A
Airbags	Dual	Dual	Dual	Dual	Dual
ABS	4-Whl*	4-Whl*	4-Whl*	4-Whl*	4-Whl*
Parts Cost	High	High	High	High	Average
Complaints	Very Poor	Very Poor	Very Poor	Very Poor	Very Poor
Insurance	Discount	Discount	Regular	Surcharge	Surcharge
Fuel Econ.	19	19	19	19	21
Theft Rating	High	High	High	High**	High**
Bumpers			Weak	Weak	Weak
Recalls	1	1	0	0	0
Trn. Cir. (ft.)	34.8	34.8	34.8	34.8	34.8
Weight (lbs.)	3303	3303	3303	3303	3186
Whlbase (in.)	104.3	104.3	104.3	104.3	104.3
Price	$8-10,000	$9-11,000	$10-12,000	$13-15,000	$17-19,000
OVERALL■					

Land Rover Discovery Series 1995-98, Discovery Series II 1999-2002

Land Rover has geared this rugged model to the wealthier sport utility buyer. Although it's slightly smaller than the Range Rover, you should have no problem have no problem doing any neces-

1996 Land Rover Discovery

sary suburban hauling in comfort. And if you're one of the few sport utility owners who actually take the vehicle off the pavement, you'll find the Discovery holds its own. In 1995, Land Rover was one of the first sport utility manufacturers to provide standard dual airbags.

	1993	1994	1995	1996	1997
Size Class			Sp. Util.	Sp. Util.	Sp. Util.
Drive			All	All	All
Crash Test			Average	Average	Average
Airbags			Dual	Dual	Dual
ABS			4-Whl	4-Whl	4-Whl
Parts Cost			Very High	Very High	Very High
Complaints			Very Poor	Very Poor	Poor
Insurance			Regular	Regular	Regular
Fuel Econ.	NO MODEL PRODUCED		13	13	13
Theft Rating			Average	Average	Average
Bumpers					
Recalls			2	4	3
Trn. Cir. (ft.)			39.4	39.4	39.4
Weight (lbs.)			4465	4465	4465
Whlbase (in.)			100	100	100
Price			$13-15,000	$15-17,000	$18-20,000
OVERALL■			Very Poor	Very Poor	Very Poor

■Cars without crash tests do not receive an overall rating.**Estimate

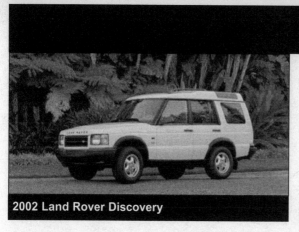

2002 Land Rover Discovery

The Discovery comes with a 3.9-liter V8 engine, standard four-wheel drive, and ABS brakes. You'll want to note the high price of replacement parts, low fuel efficiency, and steady number of recalls in the early years. It also has not been crash tasted since its redesign and name change in 1999. It has been known since then as the Discovery Series II.

	1998	1999	2000	2001	2002
Size Class	Sp. Util.	Sp. Util.	Sp. Util.	Sp. Util.	Sp. Util.
Drive	All	All	All	All	All
Crash Test	Average	N/A	N/A	N/A	N/A
Airbags	Dual	Dual	Dual	Dual	Dual
ABS	4-Whl	4-Whl	4-Whl	4-Whl	4-Whl
Parts Cost	Very High	Very High	Very High	Very High	High
Complaints	Average	Very Good	Very Good	Very Good	Good
Insurance	Regular	Regular	Regular	Regular	Regular
Fuel Econ.	14	14	14	14	15
Theft Rating	Average**	Average**	Average**	Average**	Average**
Bumpers					
Recalls	2	5	3	3	1
Trn. Cir. (ft.)	39.4	39.4	39.4	39.4	39.4
Weight (lbs.)	4465	4465	4465	4465	4576
Whlbase (in.)	100	100	100	100	100
Price	$22-24,000	$25-27,000	$28-30,000	$30-32,000	$35-37,000
OVERALL■	Poor				

Land Rover Range Rover 1993-2002

The Land Rover Range Rover has been around since 1970, before the sport utility fad, but still hasn't been crash tested. The original Range Rover lasted 14 years until a

1993 Land Rover Range Rover

new model was introduced for model year 1995. Like the Discovery, the Range Rover got dual airbags in 1995 and now front side airbags are standard; 4-wheel ABS was an earlier feature. The naming changed slightly after 1995. Prior to the remake, the Classic Range Rover was the only model available and came with a 3.5-liter

	1993	1994	1995	1996	1997
Size Class	Sp. Util.	Sp. Util	Sp. Util.	Sp. Util.	Sp. Util.
Drive	All	All	All	All	All
Crash Test	N/A	N/A	N/A	N/A	N/A
Airbags	None	None	Dual	Dual	Dual
ABS	4-Whl	4-Whl	4-Whl	4-Whl	4-Whl
Parts Cost	Very High	Very High	Very High	Very High	Very High
Complaints	Poor	Poor	Very Poor	Very Poor	Poor
Insurance	Regular	Regular	Regular	Regular	Regular
Fuel Econ.	12	12	12	12	13
Theft Rating	Average	Average	Average	Average	Average
Bumpers					
Recalls	0	0	6	1	1
Trn. Cir. (ft.)	39.4	39.4	39	39	39
Weight (lbs.)	4401	4401	4960	4960	4960
Whlbase (in.)	108	108	108.1	108.1	108.1
Price	$14-16,000	$16-18,000	$18-20,000	$23-25,000	$26-29,000
OVERALL▪					

▪Cars without crash tests do not receive an overall rating.**Estimate

2002 Land Rover Range Rover

V8 engine. The 4.0-liter SE and 4.6-liter HSE became available in 1995. The larger engines mean stronger engines; the 4.6 HSE can tow almost 4 tons. Four-wheel drive and an automatic transmission are both standard. The Range Rover weighs about 4,500 lbs., so acceleration is fairly slow and fuel economy is dismal. Typical of this class of vehicles, the handling is sluggish, though the ride is comfortable. These trucks were made to go off-road, which is why their drive is rougher.

	1998	1999	2000	2001	2002
Size Class	Sp. Util.	Sp. Util.	Sp. Util.	Sp. Util.	Sp. Util.
Drive	All	All	All	All	All
Crash Test	N/A	N/A	N/A	N/A	N/A
Airbags	Dual	Dual	Dual	Dual	Dual
ABS	4-Whl	4-Whl	4-Whl	4-Whl	4-Whl
Parts Cost	Very High	Very High	Very High	Very High	High
Complaints	Very Poor	Very Poor	Good	Very Good	Very Poor
Insurance	Regular	Regular	Regular	Regular	Regular
Fuel Econ.	13	13	13	13	13
Theft Rating	Average	Average**	Average**	Average**	Average**
Bumpers					
Recalls	1	2	3	1	0
Trn. Cir. (ft.)	39	39	39	39	39
Weight (lbs.)	4960	4960	4960	4960	4960
Whlbase (in.)	108.1	108.1	108.1	108.1	108.1
Price	$31-34,000	$36-39,000	$41-43,000	$47-50,000	$67-69,000
OVERALL■					

Lexus ES300 1993-2002

The ES is basically a dressed up version of the Toyota Camry. The ES has most of the Camry's options as standard equipment, including a V6 and stereo with CD player.

1993 Lexus ES300

Styling on the 1992 model was altered slightly, and the ES300 has gotten sleeker over the past decade, with its most recent redesign in 2002. For 1993, dual airbags became standard. Front side airbags became standard in 1998, and in 2002, standard head airbags were added. ABS has always been standard on all 4 wheels. Some models

	1993	1994	1995	1996	1997
Size Class	Large	Large	Large	Large	Large
Drive	Front	Front	Front	Front	Front
Crash Test	Good	Good	Good	Good	Good
Airbags	Dual	Dual	Dual	Dual	Dual
ABS	4-Whl	4-Whl	4-Whl	4-Whl	4-Whl
Parts Cost	High	High	Very High	High	Very High
Complaints	Average	Good	Very Good	Very Good	Very Good
Insurance	Discount	Discount	Discount	Discount	Discount
Fuel Econ.	18	20	20	20	19
Theft Rating	Average	Very High	High	Very High	Very High
Bumpers					
Recalls	0	0	0	0	1
Trn. Cir. (ft.)	36.7	36.7	36.7	36.7	36.7
Weight (lbs.)	3362	3374	3374	3373	3296
Whlbase (in.)	103.1	103.1	103.1	103.1	105.1
Price	$9-11,000	$11-13,000	$13-15,000	$15-17,000	$19-21,000
OVERALL"	Very Good	Very Good	Very Good	Very Good	Very Good

"Cars without crash tests do not receive an overall rating.**Estimate

2002 Lexus ES300

have a smaller engine, but the larger V6 is much more satisfying and just as fuel-efficient. In 1994, Lexus, realizing that someone seeking a luxury car would want an automatic, dropped the manual and in 2002, Lexus added a new automatic five-speed transmission. Handling is adequate, and the ride is pleasantly firm. In front, room is ample, less so in the rear. A good car, but you can save almost $10,000 by buying a well-equipped Camry.

	1998	1999	2000	2001	2002
Size Class	Large	Large	Large	Large	Large
Drive	Front	Front	Front	Front	Front
Crash Test	Very Good	Very Good	Very Good	Very Good	Very Good
Airbags	Dual/Side	Dual/Side	Dual/Side	Dual/Side	Dl./Sd.(F)/Hd.
ABS	4-Whl	4-Whl	4-Whl	4-Whl	4-Whl
Parts Cost	High	High	High	High	
Complaints	Very Good	Very Good	Very Good	Very Good	Average
Insurance	Discount	Discount	Discount	Discount	Discount
Fuel Econ.	19	19	19	19	24
Theft Rating	Very High	Average	Average**	Average**	Average**
Bumpers		Strong	Weak	Weak	Weak
Recalls	0	0	0	0	2
Trn. Cir. (ft.)	36.7	36.7	36.7	36.7	36.1
Weight (lbs.)	3378	3351	3373	3373	3439
Whlbase (in.)	105.1	105.1	105.1	105.1	107.1
Price	$22-24,000	$24-26,000	$28-30,000	$30-32,000	$32-34,000
OVERALL■	BEST BET	BEST BET	BEST BET	BEST BET	Very Good

Lexus GS300/400 1994-2001, Lexus GS300/430 2002

1993 Lexus GS300

Lexus' newest entry into the luxury market was designed to bridge the nearly $20,000 gap between the entry level ES300 and the luxurious LS400. Little has changed on the GS300 since its inception until its full revision in 1999. It got an increased wheelbase, which allows for more interior room and a bigger trunk. As you would expect, dual airbags and ABS have been standard on the GS300 since its inception. Side airbags became standard in 1998 as well and now a head airbag is standard. The

	1993	1994	1995	1996	1997
Size Class	NO MODEL PRODUCED	Large	Large	Large	Large
Drive		Rear	Rear	Rear	Rear
Crash Test		Average	Average	Average	Average
Airbags		Dual	Dual	Dual	Dual
ABS		4-Whl	4-Whl	4-Whl	4-Whl
Parts Cost		Very High	Very High	High	Very High
Complaints		Very Good	Very Good	Average	Very Good
Insurance		Regular	Regular	Regular	Discount
Fuel Econ.		18	18	18	18
Theft Rating		Very Low	Very Low	Very High	Very High
Bumpers					
Recalls		1	0	0	0
Trn. Cir. (ft.)		36.1	36.1	36.1	36.1
Weight (lbs.)		3660	3660	3660	3660
Whlbase (in.)		109.4	109.4	109.4	109.4
Price		$15-17,000	$18-20,000	$21-23,000	$23-25,000
OVERALL■		Good	Good	Poor	Good

■Cars without crash tests do not receive an overall rating.**Estimate

2002 Lexus GS300

GS300 is powered by a very strong but inefficient 3-liter 6-cylinder engine that provides poor gas mileage, but no worse than its corporate siblings, the ES300 and the LS400. A five-speed automatic transmission makes driving enjoyable, and as the GS300 emphasizes a smooth ride. Front occupants will ride in comfort, but the back seat will be cramped for adults. The GS300 is an expensive choice. Before settling on it, keep in mind that you can find less expensive cars with the GS300's same luxurious feel.

	1998	1999	2000	2001	2002
Size Class	Large	Large	Large	Large	Large
Drive	Rear	Rear	Rear	Rear	Rear
Crash Test	N/A	N/A	N/A	N/A	N/A
Airbags	Dual/Side	Dual/Side	Dual/Side	Dual/Side	Dl./Sd.(F)/Hd.
ABS	4-Whl	4-Whl	4-Whl	4-Whl	4-Whl
Parts Cost	High	High	High	High	High
Complaints	Poor	Very Good	Very Good	Very Good	Poor
Insurance	Discount	Discount	Discount	Discount	Discount
Fuel Econ.	20	20	20	20	21
Theft Rating	Very High	Very High	Very High	Very High[**]	Very High[**]
Bumpers			Weak		Strong
Recalls	1	0	0	0	0
Trn. Cir. (ft.)	36.1	37.1	37.1	37.1	37.1
Weight (lbs.)	3635	3638	3638	3638	3638
Whlbase (in.)	110.2	110.2	110.2	110.2	110.2
Price	$27-29,000	$30-32,000	$33-35,000	$35-37,000	$40-42,000
OVERALL■					

Lexus LS400/LS430 1993-2002

The LS400, the flagship sedan, is the biggest, most expensive Lexus you can buy. It received a host of detail improvements and price increases between its 1990 introduction and its

1993 Lexus LS400

redesign in 1995. The 1995 overhaul brought a sleeker, lighter and more powerful model. For 2001, another redesign brings more interior space and a smoother ride along with a new designation, the LS430. All LS400 models have standard driver's airbag and ABS. Dual airbags first became standard in 1993. Standard side airbags

	1993	1994	1995	1996	1997
Size Class	Large	Large	Large	Large	Large
Drive	Rear	Rear	Rear	Rear	Rear
Crash Test	N/A	N/A	N/A	N/A	N/A
Airbags	Dual	Dual	Dual	Dual	Dual
ABS	4-Whl	4-Whl	4-Whl	4-Whl	4-Whl
Parts Cost	Very High	Very High	Very High	Very High	Very High
Complaints	Very Good	Very Good	Very Good	Good	Very Good
Insurance	Regular	Discount	Discount	Discount	Discount
Fuel Econ.	18	18	19	19	19
Theft Rating	High	Average	Average	Very High	Very High
Bumpers					Weak
Recalls	0	0	1	1	1
Trn. Cir. (ft.)	36.1	36.1	34.8	34.8	34.8
Weight (lbs.)	3858	3859	3650	3649	3726
Whlbase (in.)	110.8	110.8	112.2	112.2	112.2
Price	$14-16,000	$17-19,000	$20-22,000	$23-25,000	$28-30,000
OVERALL■					

■Cars without crash tests do not receive an overall rating.**Estimate

2002 Lexus LS430

for both the driver and front passenger appear in 1997 models and the 2001 redesign brings in a standard head airbag. The LS400 has a very smooth, powerful four-cam V8 with automatic overdrive, and the 1995 and later versions are even more powerful. The LS400 is thoroughly equipped in base form, but you should look for a car with optional traction control. Handling isn't quite up to the level of the best sedans. The front seats are outstanding, and the rear seat is nearly as comfortable.

	1998	1999	2000	2001	2002
Size Class	Large	Large	Large	Large	Large
Drive	Rear	Rear	Rear	Rear	Rear
Crash Test	N/A	N/A	N/A	N/A	N/A
Airbags	Dual/Side	Dual/Side	Dual/Side	Dual/Side	Dl./Sd.(F)/Hd.
ABS	4-Whl	4-Whl	4-Whl	4-Whl	4-Whl
Parts Cost	High	High	High	High	High
Complaints	Poor	Very Good	Very Good	Very Good	Average
Insurance	Discount	Discount	Discount	Discount	Regular
Fuel Econ.	19	18	18	18	21
Theft Rating	High	High	High**	High**	High**
Bumpers	Weak	Weak	Strong	Strong	Strong
Recalls	0	0	0	0	0
Trn. Cir. (ft.)	34.8	34.8	34.8	37.4	37.4
Weight (lbs.)	3890	3890	3890	3955	3995
Whlbase (in.)	112.2	112.2	112.2	115.2	115.2
Price	$33-35,000	$38-40,000	$42-44,000	$46-49,000	$54-56,000
OVERALL■					

Lexus SC300/400/430 1993-2002

The SC300 and 400 are nearly identical except for the engines and luxury appointments. The new 2002 Lexus SC 430, however, is a whole new car. Now sporting dual and side

1993 Lexus SC300

airbags as well as 4-wheel ABS and handy gadgets like a DVD Navigations system, the SC430 has designated itself as a true sports car. Powered by a 300 hp 4.3-liter V8, this engine may be a little too powerful. Many of the standard features that you will find on the older SC400 will be optional on the cheaper SC300. 4-wheel ABS is

	1993	1994	1995	1996	1997
Size Class	Large	Large	Large	Large	Large
Drive	Rear	Rear	Rear	Rear	Rear
Crash Test	N/A	N/A	N/A	N/A	N/A
Airbags	Dual	Dual	Dual	Dual	Dual
ABS	4-Whl	4-Whl	4-Whl	4-Whl	4-Whl
Parts Cost	Very High	Very High	Very High	Very High	Very High
Complaints	Good	Very Good	Good	Very Good	Good
Insurance	Discount	Discount	Discount	Regular	Surcharge
Fuel Econ.	18	18	18	18	18
Theft Rating	Very High	Very High	Very High	Very High	Very High
Bumpers					
Recalls	0	0	0	0	1
Trn. Cir. (ft.)	36.1	36.1	36.1	36.1	36.1
Weight (lbs.)	3506	3506	3660	3610	3538
Whlbase (in.)	105.9	105.9	105.9	105.9	105.9
Price	$10-12,000	$15-17,000	$17-20,000	$20-23,000	$23-27,000
OVERALL■					

■Cars without crash tests do not receive an overall rating.**Estimate

2002 Lexus SC430

standard on all models. Dual airbags became standard starting in 1993. The SC400 will cost you more in both sticker price and at the pump. Also, look for a model with traction control; this will help control the engine's power on slippery roads. The front seats are very comfortable; however, the rear seats are cramped and uncomfortable for adults. Because it is a relatively small coupe, the trunk space is below average.

	1998	1999	2000	2001	2002
Size Class	Large	Large	Large	Large	Large
Drive	Rear	Rear	Rear	Rear	Rear
Crash Test	N/A	N/A	N/A	N/A	N/A
Airbags	Dual	Dual	Dual	Dual	Dl./Sd./Hd.
ABS	4-Whl	4-Whl	4-Whl	4-Whl	4-Whl
Parts Cost	Very High	High	High	High	High
Complaints	Very Good	Good	Very Poor	Very Good	Average
Insurance	Surcharge	Surcharge	Regular	Regular	Regular
Fuel Econ.	19	18	18	18	20
Theft Rating	Very High	Very High[**]	Very High[**]	Very High[**]	Very High[**]
Bumpers		Strong	Strong	Strong	Strong
Recalls	1	0	0	0	0
Trn. Cir. (ft.)	36.1	36.1	36.1	36.1	35.4
Weight (lbs.)	3560	3655	3655	3655	3840
Whlbase (in.)	105.9	105.9	105.9	105.9	103.1
Price	$27-33,000	$30-37,000	$34-42,000	$38-47,000	$45-57,000
OVERALL■					

Lincoln Continental 1993-2002

Lincoln has been applying the Continental name to a variety of cars for over fifty years. First based on the Ford Fairmont and then the Taurus and Sable, the Continental has finally

1993 Lincoln Continental

become a car of its own. In 1995, a major redesign with much more modern styling came along, and another revision occurred in 1998. Continentals come in several trim levels, including some designer series. Continentals have dual airbags for 1992-97 and add side airbags in 1998. ABS has been standard since the mid 80's. The

	1993	1994	1995	1996	1997
Size Class	Large	Large	Large	Large	Large
Drive	Front	Front	Front	Front	Front
Crash Test	N/A	N/A	N/A	N/A	N/A
Airbags	Dual	Dual	Dual	Dual	Dual
ABS	4-Whl	4-Whl	4-Whl	4-Whl	4-Whl
Parts Cost	Very High	Very High	High	High	Very High
Complaints	Very Poor	Very Poor	Average	Average	Poor
Insurance	Discount	Discount	Regular	Discount	Discount
Fuel Econ.	17	18	17	17	17
Theft Rating	Average	Low	Low	Average	Average
Bumpers					
Recalls	4	4	2	2	1
Trn. Cir. (ft.)	38.4	38.4	41.1	41.1	41.1
Weight (lbs.)	3595	3576	3969	3911	3884
Whlbase (in.)	109	109	109	109	109
Price	$4-6,000	$6-8,000	$8-10,000	$10-12,000	$13-15,000
OVERALL▪					

▪Cars without crash tests do not receive an overall rating.▪▪Estimate

222

2002 Lincoln Continental

Continental's engines are strong and smooth but hardly economical; the 1995 4.6-liter V8 is particularly powerful, but it was beefed up even more in 2001 and is now 275 hp. The Continental is very quiet and comfortable, though often unresponsive. The muffler was upgraded in 1999 to be quieter. The digital instrument panel shows only one gauge at a time, which can be frustrating. The Continental has plenty of room for six and a large trunk.

	1998	1999	2000	2001	2002
Size Class	Large	Large	Large	Large	Large
Drive	Front	Front	Front	Front	Front
Crash Test	N/A	N/A	N/A	N/A	N/A
Airbags	Dual	Dual/Side	Dual/Side	Dual/Side	Dl./Sd.(F)/Hd.
ABS	4-Whl	4-Whl	4-Whl	4-Whl	4-Whl
Parts Cost	Very High	High	High	High	Very High
Complaints	Poor	Good	Average	Good	Average
Insurance	Discount	Discount	Discount	Discount	Discount
Fuel Econ.	17	17	17	17	20
Theft Rating	Average	Average	Average**	Average**	Average**
Bumpers		Strong	Strong	Strong	Strong
Recalls	2	1	2	1	0
Trn. Cir. (ft.)	41.1	41.1	41.1	41.1	41.1
Weight (lbs.)	3868	3868	3868	3868	3848
Whlbase (in.)	109	109	109	109	109
Price	$17-19,000	$20-22,000	$23-25,000	$27-29,000	$36-38,000
OVERALL■					

Lincoln Mark VIII 1993-98

The Mark series is based on the same chassis as the older Mercury Cougars and Ford Thunderbirds, but it costs substantially more. However, the Mark series does have a dis-

1993 Lincoln Mark VIII

tinctive style all its own and a slightly better ride. For 1993, Lincoln replaced the Mark VII with an all-new Mark VIII, based on the newer 1989 Thunderbird/Cougar chassis. For 1997, the Mark VIII received a fresh new exterior and interior. The Mark VIII went farther than the Mark VII standard driver's airbag, featuring standard

	1993	1994	1995	1996	1997
Size Class	Large	Large	Large	Large	Large
Drive	Rear	Rear	Rear	Rear	Rear
Crash Test	Very Good	Very Good	Very Good	Very Good	Very Good
Airbags	Dual	Dual	Dual	Dual	Dual
ABS	4-Whl	4-Whl	4-Whl	4-Whl	4-Whl
Parts Cost	Average	Average	Average	Average	High
Complaints	Very Poor	Very Poor	Very Poor	Very Poor	Very Poor
Insurance	Regular	Discount	Discount	Discount	Discount
Fuel Econ.	17	18	18	18	18
Theft Rating	Very High	High	High	Very High	Very High
Bumpers					
Recalls	2	1	0	0	0
Trn. Cir. (ft.)	40.1	37.2	37.2	37.2	37.2
Weight (lbs.)	3752	3768	3768	3767	3778
Whlbase (in.)	113	113	113	113	113
Price	$4-6,000	$6-8,000	$9-11,000	$12-14,000	$15-17,000
OVERALL■	Poor	Good	Good	Good	Good

■Cars without crash tests do not receive an overall rating.**Estimate

1998 Lincoln Mark VIII

dual airbags for 1993. All Marks going back to 1986 had standard ABS; it was even available on many 1985 models. Handling is nothing special on the Mark series. Starting in 1993, Lincoln has offered only one version. If you can live without the Lincoln name, the Ford Thunderbird and Mercury Cougar are similar cars at much lower prices.

	1998	1999	2000	2001	2002
Size Class	Large				
Drive	Rear				
Crash Test	Very Good				
Airbags	Dual				
ABS	4-Whl				
Parts Cost	Very High				
Complaints	Very Good				
Insurance	Discount				
Fuel Econ.	18				
Theft Rating	Average**				
Bumpers					
Recalls	0				
Trn. Cir. (ft.)	37.2				
Weight (lbs.)	3765				
Whlbase (in.)	113				
Price	$18-20,000				
OVERALL■	BEST BET				

NO MODEL PRODUCED

Lincoln Navigator 1998-2002

The Lincoln Navigator was created in 1998 to be a luxury large sport utility vehicle and is based on the Ford Expedition. The Navigator has been very successful and continues to

1998 Lincoln Navigator

be one of the two real luxury large SUV's, the second being the Cadillac Escalade. Leather seats, walnut trim, power everything and other amenities set it apart from the other makes in this market. Although it had only dual airbags when it debuted, it now has stan-

	1993	1994	1995	1996	1997
Size Class					
Drive					
Crash Test					
Airbags					
ABS					
Parts Cost					
Complaints					
Insurance					
Fuel Econ.					
Theft Rating		NO MODEL PRODUCED			
Bumpers					
Recalls					
Trn. Cir. (ft.)					
Weight (lbs.)					
Whlbase (in.)					
Price					
OVERALL*					

*Cars without crash tests do not receive an overall rating.**Estimate

2002 Lincoln Navigator

dard side and head airbags. Four-wheel ABS is also standard.

The huge 260-hp 5.4-liter V8 that powers this huge sport utility has notoriously been in the top ten gas guzzlers on the market. Other deterrents include the poor handling and slow acceleration, but both are typical of large SUVs. On the plus side, the Navigator scored very well on the frontal crash test.

	1998	1999	2000	2001	2002
Size Class	Sp. Util.	Sp. Util.	Sp. Util.	Sp. Util.	Sp. Util.
Drive	Front/4	Front/4	Front/4	Front/4	Front/4
Crash Test	Very Good	Very Good	Very Good	Very Good	Very Good
Airbags	Dual	Dual	Dual/Side	Dual/Side	Dl./Sd.(F)/Hd.
ABS	4-Whl	4-Whl	4-Whl	4-Whl	4-Whl
Parts Cost	Average	High	Low	Average	Low
Complaints	Very Poor	Poor	Average	Very Good	Poor
Insurance	Discount	Discount	Discount	Discount	Discount
Fuel Econ.	14	14	14	14	14
Theft Rating	Very High	Very High	Very High	Very High**	Very High**
Bumpers					
Recalls	4	4	2	2	0
Trn. Cir. (ft.)	40.5	40.5	40.5	40.5	40.5
Weight (lbs.)	5424	5424	5424	5424	5424
Whlbase (in.)	119	119	119	119	119
Price	$23-25,000	$26-28,000	$30-32,000	$33-35,000	$45-47,000
OVERALL■	Average	Average	**BEST BET**	**BEST BET**	Very Good

Lincoln Town Car 1993-2002

For many decades now, the Lincoln Town Car has been one of the largest cars you could buy. The largest of Lincoln's cars, it shares the Ford Crown Victoria and Mercury

1993 Lincoln Town Car

Grand Marquis chassis, and it's one of the last rear wheel drive vehicles being produced in the U.S. The edges were smoothed off over the years and it now shares the body style of the Continental. The base model Town Cars are fully equipped, but fancier models have an extra touch of decadence. Dual airbags became standard in

	1993	1994	1995	1996	1997
Size Class	Large	Large	Large	Large	Large
Drive	Rear	Rear	Rear	Rear	Rear
Crash Test	Very Good	Very Good	Very Good	Very Good	Very Good
Airbags	Dual	Dual	Dual	Dual	Dual
ABS	4-Whl	4-Whl	4-Whl	4-Whl	4-Whl
Parts Cost	Low	Low	Very Low	Low	Average
Complaints	Poor	Average	Average	Average	Average
Insurance	Discount	Discount	Discount	Discount	Discount
Fuel Econ.	18	18	17	17	17
Theft Rating	Very High	High	High	Very High	Very High
Bumpers					
Recalls	2	3	6	5	3
Trn. Cir. (ft.)	40	40	40	42	42
Weight (lbs.)	4040	4039	4031	4040	4040
Whlbase (in.)	117.4	117.4	117.4	117.4	117.4
Price	$5-7,000	$7-9,000	$9-11,000	$11-13,000	$14-16,000
OVERALL■	Very Good	Very Good	Very Good	Very Good	Good

■Cars without crash tests do not receive an overall rating.**Estimate

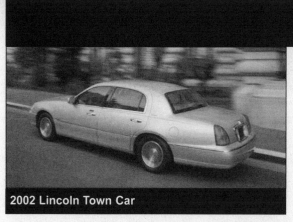
2002 Lincoln Town Car

1992 and side airbags were introduced as standard in 1999. Now head airbags have become standard as well. ABS became standard in 1991. The 1993-2002 models got the 4.6-liter V8, a responsive and fairly fuel efficient power plant. It is now up to 225 horsepower. Typical of American luxury cars, the Town Car rides smoothly, but it protests during corners or sudden maneuvers. Watch out for the digital dashboard, it can be hard to read, but the Town Car is a very good choice.

	1998	1999	2000	2001	2002
Size Class	Large	Large	Large	Large	Large
Drive	Rear	Rear	Rear	Rear	Rear
Crash Test	Very Good	Very Good	Very Good	VeryGood	Very Good
Airbags	Dual	Dual/Side	Dual/Side	Dual/Side	Dl./Sd.(F)/Hd.
ABS	4-Whl	4-Whl	4-Whl	4-Whl	4-Whl
Parts Cost	Average	Very High	Low	Very Low	Very Low
Complaints	Average	Good	Good	Good	Good
Insurance	Discount	Discount	Discount	Discount	Discount
Fuel Econ.	17	17	17	18	19
Theft Rating	Average	Average	Average**	Average**	Average**
Bumpers		Strong	Strong	Strong	Strong
Recalls	2	2	5	5	0
Trn. Cir. (ft.)	42.2	42	42	42	42
Weight (lbs.)	3860	4015	4015	4015	4047
Whlbase (in.)	117.7	117.7	117.7	117.7	117.7
Price	$17-19,000	$20-22,000	$23-25,000	$26-28,000	$40-42,000
OVERALL■	Very Good	Very Good	**BEST BET**	**BEST BET**	**BEST BET**

Mazda 323 1993-94, Protegé 1993-2002

For 1990, Mazda restyled its subcompact and split off the sedans (under the name Protegé) from the 323 hatchback coupe. In 1995, the 323 was discontinued, and the 4-door

1993 Mazda Protegé

Protegé was slightly redesigned. In 1999, the Protegé underwent another restyling and emerged as a hipper and sporty sedan. The 1990-94 323 and Protegé have motorized front shoulder belts and separate lap belts. 1995 was the first year optional ABS was offered on upper level models and dual airbags were standard on all models.

	1993	1994	1995	1996	1997
Size Class	Subcomp.	Subcomp.	Subcomp.	Subcomp.	Subcomp.
Drive	Front	Front	Front	Front	Front
Crash Test	Average	Average	N/A	N/A	N/A
Airbags	None	None	Dual	Dual	Dual
ABS	None	None	4-Whl*	4-Whl*	4-Whl*
Parts Cost	Low	Average[1]	Average	Average	High
Complaints	Average	Average	Very Poor	Poor	Average
Insurance	Surcharge	Surcharge	Surcharge	Surcharge	Surcharge
Fuel Econ.	28	26	31	32	30
Theft Rating	Low	Low	Very Low	Very Low	Very Low
Bumpers*					
Recalls	1	1	2	0	0
Trn. Cir. (ft.)	31.5	31.5	34.8	33.4	33.4
Weight (lbs.)	2238	2238	2445	2385	2385
Whlbase (in.)	98.43	98.43	102.6	102.6	102.6
Price	<$3,000	$2-4,000	$4-6,000	$5-7,000	$6-8,000
OVERALL■	Poor	Very Poor			

■Cars without crash tests do not receive an overall rating.[1]Data given for Protegé. Parts Cost for 323 is Low. *Optional **Estimate

2002 Mazda Protegé

Side airbags became on option in 1999. The 1.5-liter 4-cylinder engine is fairly weak, so consider the optional 2.0-liter 130 hp engine. The 323 and Protegé fall behind other sub-compacts in high speed handling, which can be erratic. The interior has enough room for four, though the 1995 and later models are somewhat more spacious. Trunk space is adequate, and front seat comfort is reasonably good. The ride and noise are typical of sub-compacts.

	1998	1999	2000	2001	2002
Size Class	Subcomp.	Subcomp.	Subcomp.	Subcomp.	Subcomp.
Drive	Front	Front	Front	Front	Front
Crash Test	N/A	Good	Good	Good	Good
Airbags	Dual	Dual	Dual	Dual	Dual/Sd.(F)*
ABS	4-Whl*	4-Whl*	4-Whl*	4-Whl*	4-Whl*
Parts Cost	High	High	High	High	High
Complaints	Good	Good	Good	Very Good	Average
Insurance	Surcharge	Surcharge	Surcharge	Surcharge	Surcharge
Fuel Econ.	30	29	29	29	27
Theft Rating	Very Low	Low	Low**	Low**	Low**
Bumpers					Strong
Recalls	0	0	0	0	0
Trn. Cir. (ft.)	33.4	33.4	34.1	34.1	34.1
Weight (lbs.)	2385	2385	2434	2434	2687
Whlbase (in.)	102.6	102.6	102.6	102.6	102.8
Price	$7-9,000	$8-10,000	$10-12,000	$12-14,000	$14-16,000
OVERALL■		Good	Good	Good	Good

Mazda 626 1993-2002

Mazda restyled the 626 again for 1993 and dropped the hatchback model. Minor cosmetic changes were done to the 626 in 1996 and again in 2000. The 1993 626 has a driver's airbag

1993 Mazda 626

and conventional belts; 1994 models added a passenger airbag. With its redesign in 2000, optional front side airbags were added. ABS can be found on various models beginning in 1991. The base 4-cylinder is lively enough and reasonably economical. For more power but higher fuel costs, consider the turbocharged 4-cylinder or

	1993	1994	1995	1996	1997
Size Class	Compact	Compact	Compact	Compact	Compact
Drive	Front	Front	Front	Front	Front
Crash Test	Good	Good	Good	Good	Good
Airbags	Driver	Dual	Dual	Dual	Dual
ABS	4-Whl*	4-Whl*	4-Whl*	4-Whl*	4-Whl*
Parts Cost	High	High	High	High	Average
Complaints	Poor	Very Poor	Very Poor	Very Poor	Poor
Insurance	Surcharge	Regular	Regular	Surcharge	Surcharge
Fuel Econ.	23	23	23	26	26
Theft Rating	Very Low	Average	Very Low	Very Low	Very Low
Bumpers	Weak	Weak	Weak	Weak	Weak
Recalls	0	0	2	1	2
Trn. Cir. (ft.)	35.4	35.4	34.8	34.8	34.8
Weight (lbs.)	2606	2606	2743	2828	2749
Whlbase (in.)	102.8	102.8	102.8	102.8	102.8
Price	$2-4,000	$3-5,000	$5-7,000	$6-8,000	$7-9,000
OVERALL■	Poor	Poor	Poor	Very Poor	Poor

■Cars without crash tests do not receive an overall rating.*Optional **Estimate

2002 Mazda 626

the 2.5-liter V6. The 626's automatic, which shifts harshly and often, is the car's worst feature. While the handling is fairly precise, the body tends to lean. Like most Japanese mid-sized cars, the base 626 has plenty of standard equipment. The interior and trunk areas are spacious, functional, and comfortable for four. With a good crash test, later models are a solid choice.

	1998	1999	2000	2001	2002
Size Class	Compact	Compact	Compact	Compact	Compact
Drive	Front	Front	Front	Front	Front
Crash Test	Good	Good	Very Good	Very Good	Very Good
Airbags	Dual	Dual	Dual/Side	Dual/Side	Dl./Sd.(F)*
ABS	4-Whl*	4-Whl*	4-Whl*	4-Whl*	4-Whl*
Parts Cost	Low	Average	Average	Average	Very Good
Complaints	Average	Good	Very Good	Very Good	Good
Insurance	Surcharge	Surcharge	Surcharge	Surcharge	Surcharge
Fuel Econ.	26	26	26	26	24
Theft Rating	Average	Average	Average	Average**	Average**
Bumpers		Strong	Strong	Strong	Strong
Recalls	2	1	1	0	0
Trn. Cir. (ft.)	34.8	34.8	36.1	36.1	36.1
Weight (lbs.)	2749	2749	2749	2749	2961
Whlbase (in.)	102.8	102.8	105.1	105.1	105.1
Price	$9-11,000	$11-13,000	$13-15,000	$15-17,000	$20-22,000
OVERALL■	Average	Good	BEST BET	BEST BET	BEST BET

Mazda Miata 1993-2002

The Miata was an amazing phenomenon for Mazda when introduced early in the summer of 1989 and is still going strong in its fourteenth year. The Miata is a modern, Japanese

1996 Mazda Miata

rendition of a traditional English sports car with all the fun, while adding improved comfort and a minimum of reliability problems. When the Miata first went on sale, you had to wait in line and pay well above sticker price in most cities in order to get one. The body was redesigned in 1999 to give it a more modern look. All Miatas

	1993	1994	1995	1996	1997
Size Class	Subcomp.	Subcomp.	Subcomp.	Subcomp.	Subcomp.
Drive	Rear	Rear	Rear	Rear	Rear
Crash Test	Average	Average	Average	Average	Average
Airbags	Driver	Dual	Dual	Dual	Dual
ABS	4-Whl*	4-Whl*	4-Whl*	4-Whl*	4-Whl*
Parts Cost	Average	Low	Average	High	High
Complaints	Very Good	Very Good	Average	Good	Good
Insurance	Regular	Regular	Regular	Regular	Regular
Fuel Econ.	24	23	23	23	23
Theft Rating	Low	Average	Average	Low	Average
Bumpers					
Recalls	1	0	0	0	0
Trn. Cir. (ft.)	30.8	30	30	30	30
Weight (lbs.)	2222	2293	2293	2293	2293
Whlbase (in.)	89.2	89.2	89.2	89.2	89.2
Price	$4-6,000	$6-8,000	$8-10,000	$9-11,000	$11-13,000
OVERALL"	Good	Very Good	Average	Good	Average

"Cars without crash tests do not receive an overall rating.*Optional **Estimate

2002 Mazda Miata

have a driver's airbag. For 1994, the passenger gets an airbag, too. ABS is available beginning with 1991 models, but it comes only with one of the expensive options packages. All 1990-93 Miatas have a twin-cam 1.6-liter 4-cylinder engine. For 1994, the Miata gets a more powerful 1.8-liter twin-cam 4 with 170 hp, but the gas mileage drops with the larger engine. Don't expect a quiet ride, spacious interior, or oversize trunk in a Miata. The Miata is a good choice in a sports car and it did very well in crash tests.

	1998	1999	2000	2001	2002
Size Class	Subcomp.	Subcomp.	Subcomp.	Subcomp.	Subcomp.
Drive	Rear	Rear	Rear	Rear	Rear
Crash Test	Average	Very Good	Very Good	Very Good	Very Good
Airbags	Dual	Dual	Dual	Dual	Dual
ABS	4-Whl*	4-Whl*	4-Whl*	4-Whl*	4-Whl*
Parts Cost	Average	High	High	High	High
Complaints	Very Good	Very Poor	Average	Very Good	Poor
Insurance	Regular	Regular	Regular	Regular	Regular
Fuel Econ.	23	25	25	25	25
Theft Rating	Average	Average	Average	Average**	Average**
Bumpers					Weak
Recalls	0	1	1	1	0
Trn. Cir. (ft.)	30	30.2	30.2	30.2	30.2
Weight (lbs.)	2293	2299	2299	2299	2387
Whlbase (in.)	89.2	89.2	89.2	89.2	89.2
Price	$13-15,000	$15-17,000	$18-20,000	$19-21,000	$22-24,000
OVERALL■	Very Good	Average	Good	Very Good	Average

Mazda Millenia 1995-2002

In 1995, the Millenia was introduced and billed as a performance luxury sedan with subtle styling. Dual airbags and ABS were standard from the start.

1995 Mazda Millenia

When the 929 was discontinued in 1996, the Millenia was moved to the forefront to pick up the lost 929 sales. For '97, slight interior and exterior changes were made. In 1999, the Millenia was restyled in hopes that it would be a winner in the competitive intermediate market and in 2001, it was given another facelift. The standard 2.5-liter V6 engine

	1993	1994	1995	1996	1997
Size Class			Intermd.	Intermd.	Intermd.
Drive			Front	Front	Front
Crash Test			Very Good	Very Good	Very Good
Airbags			Dual	Dual	Dual
ABS			4-Whl	4-Whl	4-Whl
Parts Cost			Very High	Very High	Very High
Complaints			Poor	Good	Very Good
Insurance			Regular	Regular	Regular
Fuel Econ.			20	20	20
Theft Rating			High	High	High
Bumpers			Weak	Weak	Weak
Recalls			0	0	0
Trn. Cir. (ft.)			37.4	37.4	37.4
Weight (lbs.)			3216	3216	3216
Whlbase (in.)			108.3	108.3	108.3
Price			$8-10,000	$10-12,000	$12-14,000
OVERALL■			Poor	Good	Good

(Columns 1993 and 1994: NO MODEL PRODUCED)

■Cars without crash tests do not receive an overall rating.**Estimate

236

2002 Mazda Millenia

on the base model is more than adequate; however, the Millenia S model comes with a more powerful and responsive "Miller cycle," a supercharged version of the same engine. Performance is the difference, as the S model is meant to appeal to younger drivers. The base can get by on regular fuel, but the S engine requires premium fuel, increasing operating costs. In government crash tests, the Millenia performed excellently. Overall, the Millenia is a good choice in a crowded luxury market.

	1998	1999	2000	2001	2002
Size Class	Intermd.	Intermd.	Intermd.	Intermd.	Intermd.
Drive	Front	Front	Front	Front	Front
Crash Test	Very Good	Very Good	Very Good	Very Good	Very Good
Airbags	Dual	Dual	Dual	Dual	Dl./Sd.(F)
ABS	4-Whl	4-Whl	4-Whl	4-Whl	4-Whl
Parts Cost	Very High	Very High	Very High	Very High	Very High
Complaints	Good	Good	Very Good	Very Good	Good
Insurance	Regular	Regular	Surcharge	Surcharge	Surcharge
Fuel Econ.	20	20	20	20	22
Theft Rating	Very High	Very High**	Very High**	Very High**	Very High**
Bumpers	Weak	Weak	Weak	Weak	Weak
Recalls	0	0	0	0	0
Trn. Cir. (ft.)	37.4	37.4	34.1	34.1	34.1
Weight (lbs.)	3216	3216	3241	3241	3358
Whlbase (in.)	108.3	108.3	108.3	108.3	108.3
Price	$14-16,000	$16-18,000	$18-20,000	$21-23,000	$29-31,000
OVERALL■	Average	Average	Average	Average	Average

Mazda MPV 1993-2002

The Mazda MPV, multipurpose passenger vehicle, takes its name from a U.S. government regulatory classification. The MPV didn't change at all from its introduction through

1993 Mazda MPV

1995. However, it was all-new in '96. There wasn't an official 1999 model year and it was introduced as all-new for 2000. A driver's airbag is standard beginning in 1993, and dual airbags become standard in 1996. ABS is standard on the rear wheels in 1990-95, but 4-wheel ABS is not available until 1996. Optional side airbags were

	1993	1994	1995	1996	1997
Size Class	Minivan	Minivan	Minivan	Minivan	Minivan
Drive	Rear/4	Rear/4	Rear/4	Rear/4	Rear/4
Crash Test	Average	Average	Average	Very Good	Very Good
Airbags	Driver	Driver	Driver	Dual	Dual
ABS	2-Whl	2-Whl	2-Whl	4-Whl	4-Whl
Parts Cost	Average	Average	Average	High	High
Complaints	Poor	Poor	Good	Average	Average
Insurance	Regular	Regular	Regular	Discount	Regular
Fuel Econ.	16	16	16	16	16
Theft Rating	Average	Average	Average	Very High	Average
Bumpers		Weak	Weak	Weak	Weak
Recalls	0	0	0	0	0
Trn. Cir. (ft.)	36.1	36.1	36.1	36.1	36.1
Weight (lbs.)	3515	3595	3745	3730	3790
Whlbase (in.)	110.4	110.4	110.4	110.4	110.4
Price	$5-7,000	$6-8,000	$7-9,000	$9-11,000	$12-14,000
OVERALL■	Poor	Very Poor	Average	Good	Average

■Cars without crash tests do not receive an overall rating. *Optional **Estimate

238

2002 Mazda MPV

available in 2000. The new 2000 model has a 2.5-liter V6 and less space than some of its competitors. The 4-cylinder engine was discontinued for 1995 along with the five person seating configuration, leaving customers with the more powerful V6 and seven person seating. Brakes, handling, and ride are inferior to most minivans. Not an outstanding vehicle; you'll likely be happier and better off with one of Chrysler's minivans.

	1998	1999	2000	2001	2002
Size Class	Minivan		Minivan	Minivan	Minivan
Drive	Rear/4		Rear/4	Rear/4	Rear/4
Crash Test	Very Good		Good	Good	Good
Airbags	Dual		Dual	Dual	Dl./Sd.(F)*
ABS	4-Whl	No Model Produced	4-Whl	4-Whl	4-Whl
Parts Cost	Very High		High	High	High
Complaints	Average		Poor	Very Good	Average
Insurance	Regular		Regular	Regular	Discount
Fuel Econ.	16		16	16	20
Theft Rating	Average		Average**	Average**	Low**
Bumpers	Weak		Weak	Weak	Weak
Recalls	0		1	1	1
Trn. Cir. (ft.)	36.1		37.4	37.4	37.4
Weight (lbs.)	3790		3657	3657	3662
Whlbase (in.)	110.4		111.8	111.8	111.8
Price	$13-15,000		$17-19,000	$19-21,000	$22-24,000
OVERALL■	Average		Poor	Good	Good

Mazda Truck (B-Series) 1993-2002

Based on the Ford Ranger, the Mazda Truck (or Mazda B-Series) was created to be a sportier alternative. A CD player, power door locks and windows, cruise control and a theft deterrent system are a few of the available options. Four-wheel ABS is also optional, but dual airbags have been standard since 1998.

1994 Mazda B-Series Truck

The B-Series comes with three different engine options: a 4.0-liter V8, a 3.0-liter V6 or a base 2.5-liter 4-cylinder. Mazda also

	1993	1994	1995	1996	1997
Size Class	Cmpct. Truck	Cmpct. Truck	Cmpct. Truck	Cmpct. Truck	Cmpct. Truck
Drive	Rear/4	Rear/4	Rear/4	Rear/4	Rear/4
Crash Test	N/A	Good	Good	Good	Good
Airbags	None	None	Driver	Driver	Driver
ABS	4-Whl*	4-Whl*	4-Whl*	4-Whl*	4-Whl*
Parts Cost	Very Low	Very Low	Very Low	Low	Very Low
Complaints	Very Good	Average	Poor	Poor	Good
Insurance	Surcharge	Surcharge	Surcharge	Surcharge	Surcharge
Fuel Econ.#	23	22	22	22	23
Theft Rating	Very Low	Very Low	Very Low	Very Low	Very Low
Bumpers					
Recalls	0	9	0	0	0
Trn. Cir. (ft.)	36.5	37.3	37.3	37.3	37.3
Weight (lbs.)	2660	3208	3208	3208	3208
Whlbase (in.)	108.7	107.9	107.9	107.9	107.9
Price	$3-5,000	$4-6,000	$5-7,000	$6-8,000	$7-9,000
OVERALL■		Poor	Average	Average	Very Good

■Cars without crash tests do not receive an overall rating.#Based on 4x2 Version. *Optional **Estimate

2002 Mazda Truck

offers both regular and extended cabs. The regular cab has done very well in crash tests, and although the extended cab has not done as well, it is still a good choice.

	1998	1999	2000	2001	2002
Size Class	Cmpct. Truck	Cmpct. Truck	Cmpct. Truck	Cmpct. Truck	Cmpct. Truck
Drive	Rear/4	Rear/4	Rear/4	Rear/4	Rear/4
Crash Test	Very Good	Very Good	Very Good	Very Good	Very Good
Airbags	Dual	Dual	Dual	Dual	Dual
ABS	4-Whl*	4-Whl*	4-Whl*	4-Whl*	4-Whl
Parts Cost	Very Low	Very Low	Low	Average	Average
Complaints	Very Good	Poor	Poor	Good	Very Good
Insurance	Surcharge	Surcharge	Surcharge	Surcharge	Surcharge
Fuel Econ.	22	19	18	18	18
Theft Rating	Low	Low	Low	Low**	Low**
Bumpers					
Recalls	2	1	1	1	0
Trn. Cir. (ft.)	37.3	37.3	37.3	37.3	37.3
Weight (lbs.)	3433	3433	3433	3433	3433
Whlbase (in.)	111.6	111.6	111.6	111.6	111.6
Price	$8-10,000	$9-11,000	$10-12,000	$11-13,000	$14-16,000
OVERALL■	BEST BET	Good	Average	Good	Very Good

Mercedes-Benz C-Class 1994-2002

The C-Class has managed to make a name for itself as the least expensive member, though it still may not be considered affordable by some. The C-Class, which debuted in 1994

1994 Mercedes-Benz C-Class

as the replacement for the 190E, competes mainly with the cheaper luxury offerings from Infiniti (I30) and Lexus (ES300). As with other luxury models from Mercedes, the C-Class comes with a large list of standard features, including dual airbags and 4-wheel ABS. The C-Class is all-new for 2001 and gains more interior space and

	1993	1994	1995	1996	1997
Size Class		Intermd.	Intermd.	Intermd.	Intermd.
Drive		Rear	Rear	Rear	Rear
Crash Test		Good	Good	Good	Good
Airbags		Dual	Dual	Dual	Dual
ABS		4-Whl	4-Whl	4-Whl	4-Whl
Parts Cost		Very High	Very High	Very High	Very High
Complaints		Good	Very Good	Very Good	Very Good
Insurance		Regular	Discount	Discount	Discount
Fuel Econ.	NO MODEL PRODUCED	23	23	23	23
Theft Rating		High	High	High	Very High
Bumpers					
Recalls		1	0	1	0
Trn. Cir. (ft.)		35.2	35.2	35.2	35.2
Weight (lbs.)		3150	3150	3150	3195
Whlbase (in.)		105.9	105.9	105.9	105.9
Price		$13-15,000	$15-17,000	$17-19,000	$18-20,000
OVERALL■		Average	Very Good	Very Good	Very Good

■Cars without crash tests do not receive an overall rating.**Estimate

2002 Mercedes-Benz C-Class

head airbags to complement the side airbags. Like the E-Class, the C stands for the car's platform, while the number following it tells you which engine the car has. The standard offering is a 2.2-liter 4-cylinder engine (C220), which will deliver average power and average gas mileage. The 2.2 was replaced in 1997 with a larger 2.3-liter engine. The front seats are firm and comfortable, but the back is cramped with three adults.

	1998	1999	2000	2001	2002
Size Class	Intermd.	Intermd.	Intermd.	Intermd.	Intermd.
Drive	Rear	Rear	Rear	Rear	Rear
Crash Test	Good	Good	Average	N/A	N/A
Airbags	Dual/Side	Dual/Side	Dual/Side	Dual/Side	Dl./Sd./Hd.
ABS	4-Whl	4-Whl	4-Whl	4-Whl	4-Whl
Parts Cost	Very High	Very High	Very High	Very High	Very High
Complaints	Average	Poor	Very Good	Very Good	Average
Insurance	Discount	Discount	Discount	Discount	Regular
Fuel Econ.	23	21	21	22	22
Theft Rating	Average	Average	Average**	Average**	Average**
Bumpers					
Recalls	1	1	1	0	1
Trn. Cir. (ft.)	35.2	35.2	35.2	35.3	35.3
Weight (lbs.)	3250	3316	3316	3310	3360
Whlbase (in.)	105.9	105.9	105.9	106.9	106.9
Price	$21-23,000	$24-26,000	$26-28,000	$28-30,000	$30-32,000
OVERALL■	Very Good	Good	Very Good		

Mercedes-Benz E-Class 1993-2002

The E-Class, Mercedes' mid-level series, received new, aerodynamic styling for 1996 that was a sweeping departure from the tradition-al Mercedes look and feel. Body

1993 Mercedes-Benz E-Class

choices on early models include convertible, coupe, wagon and sedan. Only the sedan is available for 1996 and 1997. All E-Class models have a driver's airbag (dual airbags are standard in 1993), and side and head airbags are now standard as well as four-wheel ABS. The E-Class has offered a diesel 5-cylinder, several in-line 6-

	1993	1994	1995	1996	1997
Size Class	Large	Large	Large	Large	Large
Drive	Rear	Rear	Rear	Rear	Rear
Crash Test	N/A	N/A	N/A	N/A	N/A
Airbags	Dual	Dual	Dual	Dual	Dual
ABS	4-Whl	4-Whl	4-Whl	4-Whl	4-Whl
Parts Cost	Very High	Very High	Very High	Very High	Very High
Complaints	Very Good	Very Good	Very Good	Very Good	Very Good
Insurance	Discount	Discount	Discount	Discount	Discount
Fuel Econ.	20	18	20	28	26
Theft Rating	High	Very High	Very High	Very High	Very High
Bumpers					
Recalls	1	1	1	1	0
Trn. Cir. (ft.)	37	37	37	37.1	37.1
Weight (lbs.)	3390	3525	3525	3538	3538
Whlbase (in.)	110.2	110.2	110.2	111.5	111.5
Price	$14-16,000	$16-18,000	$19-21,000	$23-25,000	$27-29,000
OVERALL▪					

▪Cars without crash tests do not receive an overall rating.**Estimate

2002 Mercedes-Benz E-Class

cylinders, roughly 3-liters in size, and the V8-powered 400E, 420E, and 500E, which are now called the E300, E320 and E430. The basic 6 is certainly satisfactory. A few early E-Class sedans have a 5-speed manual; most have automatic overdrive. Since the V8 models cost nearly as much as three or four compact cars, most E-Class buyers concentrate on the E300 sedan or wagon. The front seats are outstanding—firm, yet relaxing on long drives. Thoughtful attention to safety and detail abound.

	1998	1999	2000	2001	2002
Size Class	Large	Large	Large	Large	Large
Drive	Rear	Rear	Rear	Rear	Rear
Crash Test	N/A	N/A	N/A	N/A	N/A
Airbags	Dual/Side	Dual/Side	Dual/Side	Dual/Side	Dl./Sd./Hd.
ABS	4-Whl	4-Whl	4-Whl	4-Whl	4-Whl
Parts Cost	Very High	Very High	Very High	Very High	Very High
Complaints	Very Good	Very Good	Very Good	Very Good	Very Good
Insurance	Discount	Discount	Discount	Discount	Discount
Fuel Econ.	21	21	21	23	23
Theft Rating	Very High	High	Very High	Very High**	Very High**
Bumpers		Weak	Weak	Weak	Weak
Recalls	0	2	2	0	0
Trn. Cir. (ft.)	37.1	37.1	37.1	37.1	37.1
Weight (lbs.)	3460	3525	3525	3525	3823
Whlbase (in.)	111.5	111.5	111.5	111.5	111.5
Price	$31-34,000	$35-38,000	$41-43,000	$45-49,000	$48-51,000
OVERALL■					

Mercedes-Benz M-Class 1998-2002

Created in 1998 to compete in the growing SUV market, the M-Class has made a name for itself and done quite well. With a price tag comparable to an upscale luxury sedan, the M-

1998 Mercedes-Benz M-Class

Class is full of safety features and electronic options. The M-Class contains dual, side and head airbags, pretensioners, belt adjusters and 4-wheel ABS.

While the ML320 comes with an adequate V6, the ML430 comes

	1993	1994	1995	1996	1997
Size Class					
Drive					
Crash Test					
Airbags					
ABS					
Parts Cost					
Complaints		NO MODEL PRODUCED			
Insurance					
Fuel Econ.					
Theft Rating					
Bumpers					
Recalls					
Trn. Cir. (ft.)					
Weight (lbs.)					
Whlbase (in.)					
Price					
OVERALL■					

■Cars without crash tests do not receive an overall rating.**Estimate

2002 Mercedes-Benz M-Class

with a very powerful 5.0-liter V8 with 288 hp. The M-Class is comparable to other luxury SUV's in its class, such as the BMW X5 or the Lexus RX300. All have similar features and both the Lexus RX300 and the Mercedes M-Class have done very well in frontal crash tests.

	1998	1999	2000	2001	2002
Size Class	Sp. Util.	Sp. Util.	Sp. Util.	Sp. Util.	Sp. Util.
Drive	4-Whl	4-Whl	4-Whl	4-Whl	4-Whl
Crash Test	Very Good	Very Good	Very Good	Very Good	Very Good
Airbags	Dual/Side	Dual/Side	Dual/Side	Dual/Side	Dl./Sd./Hd.
ABS	4-Whl	4-Whl	4-Whl	4-Whl	4-Whl
Parts Cost	Very High	Very High	Very High	High	Very High
Complaints	Poor	Average	Very Good	Very Good	Poor
Insurance	Discount	Discount	Discount	Discount	Discount
Fuel Econ.	18	16	17	17	17
Theft Rating	Average	Average	Average	Average**	Average**
Bumpers					
Recalls	2	1	2	1	4
Trn. Cir. (ft.)	37	37	37	37	37
Weight (lbs.)	4552	4552	4552	4552	4552
Whlbase (in.)	111	111	111	111	111
Price	$25-27,000	$28-30,000	$34-36,000	$36-38,000	$38-40,000
OVERALL■	Good	Very Good	BEST BET	BEST BET	Average

Mercury Cougar 1993-2002

The Mercury Cougar used to share the same chassis as the old Ford Thunderbird and Lincoln cars, but with its redesign in 1999, it has now established itself as a sports sedan. Dual

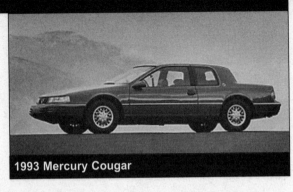

1993 Mercury Cougar

airbags were added to the 1994 models, but current models boast both side and head airbags models. ABS is optional from 1992.

Newer Cougars have a base 2.0-liter 4-cylinder engine, but a 2.5-liter V6 is optional. Older Cougars come with a standard V6 engine.

	1993	1994	1995	1996	1997
Size Class	Large	Large	Large	Large	Large
Drive	Rear	Rear	Rear	Rear	Rear
Crash Test	Very Good	Very Good	Very Good	Very Good	Very Good
Airbags	None	Dual	Dual	Dual	Dual
ABS	4-Whl*	4-Whl*	4-Whl*	4-Whl*	4-Whl*
Parts Cost	Low	Low	Low	Average	High
Complaints	Very Poor	Poor	Poor	Average	Average
Insurance	Discount	Discount	Discount	Discount	Regular
Fuel Econ.	17	19	19	19	18
Theft Rating	Low	Low	Average	Average	Low
Bumpers					
Recalls	2	0	0	2	0
Trn. Cir. (ft.)	36.6	36.6	36.6	36.6	36.5
Weight (lbs.)	3512	3564	3533	3559	3536
Whlbase (in.)	113	113	113	113	113
Price	$3-5,000	$4-6,000	$6-8,000	$7-9,000	$8-10,000
OVERALL■	Average	BEST BET	Very Good	Very Good	Good

■Cars without crash tests do not receive an overall rating.*Optional **Estimate

2002 Mercury Cougar

In general, the ride is comfortable and the new smaller Cougars have much better handling. The 1992-98 Cougar, like the T-bird, has enough room for four plus luggage.

	1998	1999	2000	2001	2002
Size Class	Large	Large	Large	Large	Large
Drive	Rear	Rear	Rear	Rear	Rear
Crash Test	Very Good	N/A	N/A	N/A	N/A
Airbags	Dual	Dual	Dual	Dual	Dl./Sd(F)/Hd.
ABS	4-Whl*	4-Whl	4-Whl	4-Whl	4-Whl
Parts Cost	High	High	Very Low	Very Low	Very Low
Complaints	Very Good	Very Poor	Poor	Good	Very Poor
Insurance	Regular	Surcharge	Surcharge	Surcharge	Regular
Fuel Econ.	18	23	23	23	23
Theft Rating	Low	Average	Average**	Average**	Average**
Bumpers					
Recalls	0	1	0	0	0
Trn. Cir. (ft.)	36.5	37	37	37	37
Weight (lbs.)	3536	2892	2892	2892	2861
Whlbase (in.)	113	106.4	106.4	106.4	106.4
Price	$10-12,000	$12-14,000	$13-15,000	$15-17,000	$17-19,000
OVERALL■	Very Good				

Mercury Sable 1993-2001

1993 Mercury Sable

This twin of the popular Taurus emphasizes luxury, even in base GS form. The Taurus and Sable, available as either a 4-door sedan or wagon, popularized aerodynamic car design, and both became Ford's savior from financial disaster. Though widely imitated, these cars have held their own against tough competition; a redesign for the 1996 model year only strengthened that position. Mercury started back in 1993 with dual front airbags, but ABS is only optional beginning in 1991. From 1989 on, all Sables have a

	1993	1994	1995	1996	1997
Size Class	Intermd.	Intermd.	Intermd.	Intermd.	Intermd.
Drive	Front	Front	Front	Front	Front
Crash Test	Good[1]	Good	Good	Very Good	Very Good
Airbags	Dual	Dual	Dual	Dual	Dual
ABS	4-Whl*	4-Whl*	4-Whl*	4-Whl*	4-Whl*
Parts Cost	Low	Low	Low	Low	Low
Complaints	Very Poor	Very Poor	Very Poor	Very Poor	Average
Insurance	Discount	Discount	Discount	Discount	Discount
Fuel Econ.	21	20	20	20	20
Theft Rating	Very Low	Very Low	Very Low	Very Low	Very Low
Bumpers	Weak	Weak	Weak	Strong	Strong
Recalls	8	4	4	5	3
Trn. Cir. (ft.)	38.6	38.6	38.6	38	38
Weight (lbs.)	3122	3275	3144	3388	3388
Whlbase (in.)	106	106	106	108.5	108.5
Price	$3-5,000	$4-6,000	$5-7,000	$6-8,000	$7-9,000
OVERALL■	Good	Average	Average	Very Good	BEST BET

■Cars without crash tests do not receive an overall rating.[1]Data given for sedan. Crash test for wagon is Very Good. *Optional **Estimate

250

2001 Mercury Sable

140 hp 3.0 V6 or the optional 3.8-liter V6, also 140 hp. The base engine is peppy; the 3.8-liter offers more torque for towing or heavy loads. With standard suspension, Sable rides smoother but corners less precisely than the Taurus. The optional suspension improves handling but makes the ride stiffer. Replace the general tires with ones better suited for handling. Inside, Sable's dashboard is easy to read, and four adults will have ample room and comfort.

	1998	1999	2000	2001	2002
Size Class	Intermd.	Intermd.	Intermd.	Intermd.	
Drive	Front	Front	Front	Front	
Crash Test	Very Good	Very Good	Very Good	Very Good	
Airbags	Dual	Dual	Dual	Dual	
ABS	4-Whl*	4-Whl*	4-Whl*	4-Whl*	
Parts Cost	Average	Very Low	Very Low	Very Low	
Complaints	Average	Average	Poor	Good	
Insurance	Discount	Discount			
Fuel Econ.	20	20	20	20	
Theft Rating	Low	Very Low	Very Low	Very Low**	
Bumpers		Strong	Strong		
Recalls	2	3	2	1	
Trn. Cir. (ft.)	38	38	39.8	39.8	
Weight (lbs.)	3299	3302	3302	3302	
Whlbase (in.)	108.5	108.5	108.5	108.5	
Price	$9-11,000	$10-12,000	$12-14,000	$14-16,000	
OVERALL■	Very Good	BEST BET	Good	Very Good	

NO MODEL PRODUCED

Mercury Villager/Nissan Quest 1993-2002

The Villager differs from its near twin, the Nissan Quest, only in standard equipment. Ford turned the design work over to Nissan, and Ford builds them in Ohio. With minor

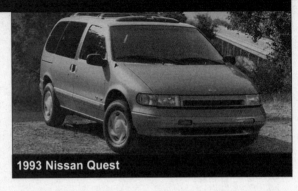

1993 Nissan Quest

cosmetic touchups, the Villager remains the same since 1993 when driver airbags were introduced. Passenger airbags were added in 1996, but now both front side and head airbags are standard. The awkward motorized shoulder belts with separate lap belts were standard through 1995. The 4-wheel ABS is optional on the Villager and

	1993	1994	1995	1996	1997
Size Class	Minivan	Minivan	Minivan	Minivan	Minivan
Drive	Front	Front	Front	Front	Front
Crash Test	Average	Average	Average	Good	Good
Airbags	Driver	Driver	Driver	Dual	Dual
ABS	4-Whl[1]	4-Whl[1]	4-Whl[1]	4-Whl[1]	4-Whl[1]
Parts Cost	Low	Low	Low	Average	High
Complaints[#]	Very Poor	Very Poor	Very Poor	Very Poor	Poor
Insurance	Discount	Discount	Discount	Discount	Discount
Fuel Econ.	17	17	17	17	17
Theft Rating	Low	Very Low	Very Low	Very Low	Very Low
Bumpers	Weak	Weak	Weak	Weak	Weak
Recalls	0	8	2	5	4
Trn. Cir. (ft.)	38.7	38.7	38.7	38.7	38.7
Weight (lbs.)	3015	3015	3015	2876	2865
Whlbase (in.)	112.2	112.2	112.2	112.2	112.2
Price	$5-7,000	$6-8,000	$7-9,000	$8-10,000	$10-12,000
OVERALL[**]	Average	Poor	Average	Average	Average

[**]Cars without crash tests do not receive an overall rating. [1]Data given for Villager, is optional on the Quest. [#]Complaints for Villager. Quest scores Poor in '95, Average in '99. [**]Estimate

2002 Mercury Villager

the Quest.

Both vehicles have an adequate 151 hp, 3-liter V6 that gets overwhelmed with too much towing, but the optional towing package helps. The handling is only average. However, it can be firmed up with the optional "handling package" suspension; you'll find these minivans ride remarkably like passenger cars. They were crash tested in 2001 and did extremely well.

	1998	1999	2000	2001	2002
Size Class	Minivan	Minivan	Minivan	Minivan	Minivan
Drive	Front	Front	Front	Front	Front
Crash Test	Good	Very Good	Very Good	Very Good	Very Good
Airbags	Dual	Dual	Dual	Dual	Dl./Sd.(F)/Hd.
ABS	4-Whl	4-Whl	4-Whl	4-Whl	4-Whl
Parts Cost	Average	Low	Low	Low	Very Low
Complaints	Poor	Poor	Good	Very Good	Average
Insurance	Discount	Discount	Discount	Discount	Discount
Fuel Econ.	17	17	17	17	19
Theft Rating	Average	Low	Low	Low[**]	Low[**]
Bumpers	Weak	Strong	Strong	Strong	Strong
Recalls	2	1	1	1	0
Trn. Cir. (ft.)	38.7	38.7	38.7	38.7	39.9
Weight (lbs.)	3865	3830	3830	3830	3997
Whlbase (in.)	112.2	112.2	112.2	112.2	112.2
Price	$12-14,000	$15-17,000	$17-19,000	$19-21,000	$22-24,000
OVERALL■	Average	Very Good	BEST BET	BEST BET	BEST BET

Mitsubishi Diamante 1993-2002

The Mitsubishi Diamante was introduced in 1992 and was targeted at the sports sedan buyer who wants lots of technical gadgetry. A lower level wagon is available through 1995;

1993 Mitsubishi Diamante

Mitsubishi dropped the LS and wagon in 1996 and refocused on the luxury sedan market. In an effort to increase sales, Mitsubishi revamped the 1997 Diamante, increasing interior room and rounding out the edges. In 1999, it was reduced to only one trim level. A driver airbag was added in 1993, a second airbag in 1994. Four-wheel

	1993	1994	1995	1996	1997
Size Class	Large	Large	Large	Large	Large
Drive	Front	Front	Front	Front	Front
Crash Test	Good	Good	Good	Good	N/A
Airbags	Driver	Dual	Dual	Dual	Dual
ABS	4-Whl*	4-Whl*	4-Whl*	4-Whl*	4-Whl*
Parts Cost	Very High	Very High	Very High	Very High	Very High
Complaints	Poor	Poor	Average	Very Good	Very Poor
Insurance	Regular	Regular	Regular	Regular	Regular
Fuel Econ.	18	18	18	18	18
Theft Rating	Very High	Very High	High	Very High	Very High
Bumpers					
Recalls	4	3	1	0	0
Trn. Cir. (ft.)	36.7	36.7	36.7	36.7	36.7
Weight (lbs.)	3483	3483	3505	3483	3363
Whlbase (in.)	107.1	107.1	107.1	107.1	107.1
Price	$3-5,000	$5-7,000	$7-9,000	$9-11,000	$13-15,000
OVERALL"	Very Poor	Very Poor	Poor	Good	

"Cars without crash tests do not receive an overall rating.*Optional **Estimate

2002 Mitsubishi Diamante

ABS has been available since the Diamante's introduction. In 2002, a more powerful 3.5-liter V6 is introduced, but the previous 3-liter V6 is powerful enough, especially at higher speeds. Fuel economy is average for a car this size. The Diamante handles, rides, accelerates, and brakes adequately, though none of these items surpass other cars in its class. The trunk is spacious and easy to access. Pay the extra money and you'll get a somewhat more sophisticated car with lots of computer wizardry.

	1998	1999	2000	2001	2002
Size Class	Large	Large	Large	Large	Large
Drive	Front	Front	Front	Front	Front
Crash Test	N/A	N/A	N/A	N/A	N/A
Airbags	Dual	Dual	Dual	Dual	Dual
ABS	4-Whl	4-Whl	4-Whl	4-Whl	4-Whl
Parts Cost	Very High	Very High	Very High	High	Average
Complaints	Poor	Very Good	Poor	Very Good	Poor
Insurance	Regular	Regular	Regular	Regular	Regular
Fuel Econ.	18	18	18	18	20
Theft Rating	Very High**	Very High**	Very High**	Very High**	Very High**
Bumpers		Strong	Strong	Strong	
Recalls	0	1	1	0	1
Trn. Cir. (ft.)	36.7	36.7	36.7	36.7	36.7
Weight (lbs.)	3417	3417	3417	3417	3417
Whlbase (in.)	107.1	107.1	107.1	107.1	107.1
Price	$14-16,000	$15-17,000	$18-20,000	$19-21,000	$26-28,000
OVERALL■					

Mitsubishi Galant 1993-2002

The Galant competes with Toyota's Camry and Avalon, the Honda Accord and the Nissan Maxima—some tough competition. The Galant was redesigned in 1994, adding a V6

1993 Mitsubishi Galant

midway through the 1995 model year and was then completely redesigned again in 1999. With the 1994 redesign came dual airbags and a conventional seat belt and the 1999 redesign added front side airbags standard ABS.

	1993	1994	1995	1996	1997
Size Class	Compact	Compact	Compact	Compact	Compact
Drive	Front	Front	Front	Front	Front
Crash Test	Poor	Good	Good	Good	Good
Airbags	None	Dual	Dual	Dual	Dual
ABS	4-Whl*	4-Whl*	4-Whl*	4-Whl*	4-Whl*
Parts Cost	Very High	Very High	High	High	Low
Complaints	Very Good	Very Poor	Very Poor	Poor	Average
Insurance	Regular	Regular	Regular	Surcharge	Surcharge
Fuel Econ.	21	22	22	23	23
Theft Rating	Very Low	Average	Very High	Low	High
Bumpers	Strong	Weak	Weak	Weak	Weak
Recalls	0	2	2	1	1
Trn. Cir. (ft.)	34.8	34.8	34.8	34.8	34.8
Weight (lbs.)	2712	2755	2866	2755	2777
Whlbase (in.)	102.4	103.7	103.7	103.7	103.7
Price	$2-4,000	$4-6,000	$5-7,000	$6-8,000	$8-10,000
OVERALL■	Poor	Very Poor	Very Poor	Poor	Average

■Cars without crash tests do not receive an overall rating.*Optional **Estimate

2002 Mitsubishi Galant

The 2.4 4-cylinder and 3.0-liter V6 are more powerful and economical than the older and 2.4-liter 4-cylinder engines. The older Galant Sigma's V6 and later V6 models also consume a lot more gas. The Galant's ride tends to be firm. The handling is decent, typical of mid-size Japanese sedans; the new GS's sport tuned suspension should be better. The roominess in the rear seat shrinks on the 1994 and later models and is tight for adults.

	1998	1999	2000	2001	2002
Size Class	Compact	Compact	Compact	Compact	Compact
Drive	Front	Front	Front	Front	Front
Crash Test	Good	Good	Good	Good	Good
Airbags	Dual	Dual	Dual	Dual	Dl./Sd.(F)
ABS	4-Whl*	4-Whl	4-Whl	4-Whl	4-Whl
Parts Cost	Low	Very Low	Very Low	Low	Low
Complaints	Good	Very Poor	Very Good	Very Good	Poor
Insurance	Surcharge	Surcharge	Surcharge	Surcharge	Surcharge
Fuel Econ.	23	23	23	23	24
Theft Rating	High	Very High	Average	Average**	Average**
Bumpers	Weak		Strong	Strong	Strong
Recalls	1	2	7	3	0
Trn. Cir. (ft.)	34.8	34.8	34.8	34.8	36.1
Weight (lbs.)	2778	2835	2835	2835	3031
Whlbase (in.)	103.7	103.7	103.7	103.7	103.7
Price	$9-11,000	$11-13,000	$12-14,000	$14-16,000	$18-21,000
OVERALL■	Average	Poor	Very Good	Good	Good

Mitsubishi Mirage 1993-2002

The Mirage was restyled for 1993, and finally, in 1997, the Mirage received yet another facelift. From 1989 until 1993, Mirages have motorized shoulder belts with separate lap belts.

1993 Mitsubishi Mirage

In 1994, the Mirage got a driver airbag and regular seat belt, but the right front seat kept a motorized belt and separate lap belt until 1995 when a passenger airbag was added. ABS became available in 1993, but only on top sedans. For the 1995 and 1996 models, ABS is not offered, since sedans were relegated to

	1993	1994	1995	1996	1997
Size Class	Subcomp.	Subcomp.	Subcomp.	Subcomp.	Subcomp.
Drive	Front	Front	Front	Front	Front
Crash Test	Good[1]	Good[1]	Good[1]	Good[1]	N/A
Airbags	None	Driver	Dual	Dual	Dual
ABS	4-Whl*	4-Whl*	None	None	4-Whl*
Parts Cost	Average	Average	High	Very High	High
Complaints	Very Poor	Poor	Poor	Good	Very Poor
Insurance	Regular	Surcharge	Surcharge	Surcharge	Surcharge
Fuel Econ.	27	28	28	32	33
Theft Rating	Very Low	Very Low	Very Low	Very Low	Very Low
Bumpers					Weak
Recalls	4	0	0	0	1
Trn. Cir. (ft.)	32.8	32.8	32.8	32.8	32.8
Weight (lbs.)	2085	2085	2085	2085	2127
Whlbase (in.)	96.1	96.1	96.1	96.1	96.1
Price	<$3,000	<$3,000	$3-5,000	$4-6,000	$5-7,000
OVERALL■	Poor	Average	Poor	Average	

■Cars without crash tests do not receive an overall rating.[1]Data given for sedan. Crash test for coupe is Average. *Optional **Estimate

2002 Mitsubishi Mirage

fleet status at the end of 1994, but it now comes standard. The Mirage's performance with the standard 4-cylinder (1.5 or 1.6-liter) is fine, but all models do better with the 1.8-liter 4-cylinder engine. Gas mileage is good. The 5-speed is a better match than the 3-speed automatic for these engines. Handling is good especially on turbo models; however, it tends to be imprecise but still safe on newer base models. The interior is comfortable for four and the instrument panel layout is good.

	1998	1999	2000	2001	2002
Size Class	Subcomp.	Subcomp.	Subcomp.	Subcomp.	Subcomp.
Drive	Front	Front	Front	Front	Front
Crash Test	N/A	N/A	N/A	N/A	N/A
Airbags	Dual	Dual	Dual	Dual	Dual
ABS	4-Whl*	4-Whl*	4-Whl*	4-Whl*	4-Whl
Parts Cost	Average	Average	Average	Low	Low
Complaints	Good	Good	Very Good	Very Good	Average
Insurance	Surcharge	Surcharge	Surcharge	Surcharge	Surcharge
Fuel Econ.	33	33	33	33	31
Theft Rating	High	High	High**	High**	Average**
Bumpers	Weak	Strong	Strong	Strong	Weak
Recalls	3	0	1	1	0
Trn. Cir. (ft.)	32.8	32.8	32.8	32.8	32.8
Weight (lbs.)	2125	2125	2125	2125	2183
Whlbase (in.)	95.1	95.1	95.1	95.1	95.1
Price	$6-8,000	$7-9,000	$8-10,000	$10-12,000	$12-14,000
OVERALL■					

Mitsubishi Montero 1993-2002

The Montero, designed to be a mid-sized sport utility vehicle that attracts a wealthy customer, has been holding its own in this growing market. Its first redesign since its inception

1993 Mitsubishi Montero

in 1984 occurred in 1992 going from a square look to a more rounded model and it has received a couple of facelifts since then. In terms of safety, airbags were not available until 1994, when a driver airbag became standard; dual airbags became standard in 1996. With its last facelift in 2001, standard side front airbags were added to the

	1993	1994	1995	1996	1997
Size Class	Sp. Util.	Sp. Util.	Sp. Util.	Sp. Util.	Sp. Util.
Drive	2WD/4WD	2WD/4WD	2WD/4WD	2WD/4WD	2WD/4WD
Crash Test	Good	Very Good	Very Good	Average	Average
Airbags	None	Driver	Driver	Dual	Dual
ABS	4-Whl*	4-Whl*	4-Whl*	4-Whl*	4-Whl*
Parts Cost	Average	Average	Average	High	Very High
Complaints	Good	Poor	Very Poor	Poor	Very Poor
Insurance	Surcharge	Surcharge	Surcharge	Surcharge	Surcharge
Fuel Econ.	15	15	15	15	16
Theft Rating	Very High	Very High	Very High	Very High	Very High
Bumpers					
Recalls	3	3	1	1	2
Trn. Cir. (ft.)	38.7	38.7	38.7	38.7	38.7
Weight (lbs.)	4130	4175	4265	4290	4385
Whlbase (in.)	107.3	107.3	107.3	107.3	107.3
Price	$8-10,000	$9-11,000	$10-12,000	$11-13,000	$12-14,000
OVERALL"	Very Poor	Very Poor	Very Poor	Very Poor	Very Poor

"Cars without crash tests do not receive an overall rating.*Optional **Estimate

2002 Nissan Frontier

the Pathfinder: a 3.3-liter V6. The 1998-99 models only have a 2.4-liter, however. The Frontier did well on front crash tests and very well on side crash tests. It also offers the largest bed of all the compact pickups and a regular and king cab are available.

	1998	1999	2000	2001	2002
Size Class	Cmpct. Truck	Cmpct. Truck	Cmpct. Truck	Cmpct. Truck	Cmpct. Truck
Drive	Rear/4	Rear/4	Rear/4	Rear/4	Rear/4
Crash Test	Good	Good	Good	Good	Good
Airbags	Dual	Dual	Dual	Dual	Dual
ABS	4-Whl*	4-Whl*	4-Whl*	4-Whl*	4-Whl*
Parts Cost	Very Low	Very Low	Very Low	Very Low	Low**
Complaints	Average	Very Good	Good	Very Good	Good
Insurance	Regular	Regular	Regular	Regular	Surcharge
Fuel Econ.	21	21	21	21	21
Theft Rating	Average	Low	Low	Low**	Low**
Bumpers					
Recalls	2	1	2	0	0
Trn. Cir. (ft.)	35.5	35.5	35.5	35.5	35.5
Weight (lbs.)	3433	3433	3433	3433	3433
Whlbase (in.)	104.3	104.3	104.3	104.3	104.3
Price	$9-11,000	$10-12,000	$13-15,000	$14-16,000	$19-21,000
OVERALL■	Very Good	**BEST BET**	Very Good	**BEST BET**	Average

Nissan Maxima 1993-2002

The Maxima is the most expensive sedan model sold under the Nissan name. A redesign in 1995 and another in 2002 brought more interior room and a more powerful engine.

9 Nissan Maxima

The 1989-94 Maximas have motorized shoulder belts and separate lap belts; 1992-94 models supplement these belts with a driver's airbag, though it is only standard from 1993 on. For 1995, dual airbags and conventional belts were added and in 2002, an optional side airbag is offered. ABS is a common option on 1989-97 models,

	1993	1994	1995	1996	1997
Size Class	Intermd.	Intermd.	Intermd.	Intermd.	Intermd.
Drive	Front	Front	Front	Front	Front
Crash Test	Average	Average	Average	Average	Average
Airbags	Driver	Driver	Dual	Dual	Dual
ABS	4-Whl*	4-Whl*	4-Whl*	4-Whl*	4-Whl*
Parts Cost	High	High	Average	Average	Very High
Complaints	Average	Good	Average	Good	Very Good
Insurance	Discount	Regular	Regular	Surcharge	Regular
Fuel Econ.	19	19	21	21	22
Theft Rating	Very High	Very High	Very High	Very High	Very High
Bumpers			Weak	Weak	Weak
Recalls	3	2	0	0	0
Trn. Cir. (ft.)	36.7	36.7	34.8	34.8	34.8
Weight (lbs.)	3139	3165	3010	3001	3001
Whlbase (in.)	104.3	104.3	106.3	106.3	106.3
Price	$4-6,000	$6-8,000	$8-10,000	$10-12,000	$12-14,000
OVERALL■	Poor	Poor	Average	Poor	Average

■Cars without crash tests do not receive an overall rating.*Optional **Estimate

2002 Nissan Maxima

but now come standard.

The Maxima uses a 3.5-liter 250 hp engine, which provides ample performance. Maxima's handling is good, particularly on the later models, and the ride is on the firm side. The rear seat has enough room for two adults, and the trunk can accommodate luggage for four and the new 2002 model has even more space. The Maxima is a good mid-size car, marred by the unavoidable automatic belt system on earlier models.

	1998	1999	2000	2001	2002
Size Class	Intermd.	Intermd.	Intermd.	Intermd.	Intermd.
Drive	Front	Front	Front	Front	Front
Crash Test	Good	Good	Very Good	Very Good	Very Good
Airbags	Dual/Side*	Dual/Side*	Dual/Side*	Dual/Side*	Dual/Side*
ABS	4-Whl*	4-Whl*	4-Whl*	4-Whl*	4-Whl
Parts Cost	Very High	Very High	Very High	Very High	Very High
Complaints	Good	Very Good	Very Good	Very Good	Very Good
Insurance	Regular	Surcharge	Surcharge	Surcharge	Surcharge
Fuel Econ.	22	22	22	22	24
Theft Rating	Very High	High	Average	High**	Very High**
Bumpers	Weak	Strong	Weak	Weak	Strong
Recalls	0	0	0	0	2
Trn. Cir. (ft.)	34.8	34.8	34.8	34.8	34.8
Weight (lbs.)	3012	3012	3012	3012	3261
Whlbase (in.)	106.3	106.3	106.3	106.3	108.3
Price	$14-16,000	$16-18,000	$19-21,000	$20-22,000	$25-27,000
OVERALL■	Average	Good	Good	Good	Good

Nissan Pathfinder 1993-2002

The Pathfinder comes in three trim levels: the XE, the SE and the LE. All-new in 1996, the Pathfinder is complete with dual airbags, unlike any previous model year. Since 1991, ABS has been standard on rear wheels only but moved to all four wheels in 1997. A 3-liter V6 is the only engine choice on the Pathfinder between '89 and '95; a larger V6 is optional in 1996 and 1997. Both engines could be ordered with 5-speed manual or automatic overdrive. Handling, like the Jeep Cherokee's, is about as

1993 Nissan Pathfinder

	1993	1994	1995	1996	1997
Size Class	Sp. Util.	Sp. Util.	Sp. Util.	Sp. Util.	Sp. Util.
Drive	Rear/4	Rear/4	Rear/4	Rear/4	Rear/4
Crash Test	Poor	Poor	Poor	Poor	Poor
Airbags	None	None	None	Dual	Dual
ABS	2-Whl	2-Whl	2-Whl	2-Whl	4-Whl
Parts Cost	Low	Low	Low	Low	High
Complaints	Average	Poor	Average	Average	Average
Insurance	Surcharge	Surcharge	Surcharge	Discount	Surcharge
Fuel Econ.	17	15	15	17	16
Theft Rating	Very High	Very High	Very High	Very High	Very High
Bumpers					
Recalls	0	1	0	2	0
Trn. Cir. (ft.)	35.5	35.4	35.5	35.4	37.4
Weight (lbs.)	3520	3885	4090	3815	3675
Whlbase (in.)	104.3	104.3	104.3	104.3	106.3
Price	$5-7,000	$7-9,000	$9-11,000	$11-13,000	$13-15,000
OVERALL■	Very Poor	Very Poor	Very Poor	Average	Very Poor

■Cars without crash tests do not receive an overall rating.*Optional **Estimate

268

2002 Nissan Pathfinder

good as it gets for a sport utility vehicle, but it's still short of the mark set by better cars. The ride is forgiving, better than most utility vehicles. Interior room in 1989-95 models is a bit tight and not too comfortable in back; the new 1996 has a larger wheelbase which provides more room. As in the pickup, major controls and gauges are good. Cargo area is on the small side. With the addition of airbags and other safety features, the Pathfinder has moved up near the top of this class.

	1998	1999	2000	2001	2002
Size Class	Sp. Util.	Sp. Util.	Sp. Util.	Sp. Util.	Sp. Util.
Drive	Rear/4	Rear/4	Rear/4	Rear/4	Rear/4
Crash Test	Poor	Poor	Very Good	Very Good	Very Good
Airbags	Dual	Dual	Dual	Dual	Dual/Side[*]
ABS	4-Whl	4-Whl	4-Whl	4-Whl	4-Whl
Parts Cost	Very High	Very High	High	High	Average
Complaints	Good	Very Good	Very Good	Average	Very Good
Insurance	Surcharge	Regular	Regular	Regular	Discount
Fuel Econ.	16	16	15	15	16
Theft Rating	Very High	High	High	Very High[**]	Very High[**]
Bumpers					
Recalls	0	0	0	1	0
Trn. Cir. (ft.)	37.4	37.4	37.4	37.4	37.4
Weight (lbs.)	3675	3675	3675	3675	3975
Whlbase (in.)	106.3	106.3	106.3	106.3	106.3
Price	$15-17,000	$18-20,000	$21-23,000	$23-26,000	$28-30,000
OVERALL[■]	Very Poor	Average	Very Good	Average	**BEST BET**

Nissan Sentra 1993-2002

The Sentra has been transformed many times since its birth in 1982. The 1991-94 Sentra looks like its predecessor with rounder edges. The 1995 Sentra comes only as a 4-door (2-door

1993 Nissan Sentra

version is renamed the 200SX) with even rounder edges to compete with the Toyota Tercel, Saturn SL and Neon sedans. The 2000 model got a facelift with new headlights and grille. Driver airbags became available in 1993, but automatic belts remained; the late 1995 models have standard dual airbags. The 2000 model also

	1993	1994	1995	1996	1997
Size Class	Subcomp.	Subcomp.	Subcomp.	Subcomp.	Subcomp.
Drive	Front	Front	Front	Front	Front
Crash Test	Good	Good	Good	Good	Good
Airbags	Driver*	Driver*	Driver*	Dual	Dual
ABS	4-Whl*	4-Whl*	4-Whl*	4-Whl*	4-Whl*
Parts Cost	Average	Average	Average	Low	Average
Complaints	Good	Good	Good	Average	Good
Insurance	Surcharge	Surcharge	Surcharge	Surcharge	Surcharge
Fuel Econ.	27	26	26	30	29
Theft Rating	Average	Very Low	Very Low	Very Low	Very Low
Bumpers	Weak	Weak			
Recalls	0	0	2	3	4
Trn. Cir. (ft.)	30.2	30.2	30.2	34.1	34.1
Weight (lbs.)	2346	2324	2324	2315	2315
Whlbase (in.)	95.7	95.7	95.7	99.8	99.8
Price	<$3,000	$3-5,000	$4-6,000	$5-7,000	$6-8,000
OVERALL■	Good	Good	Good	Good	Average

■Cars without crash tests do not receive an overall rating.*Optional **Estimate

2002 Nissan Sentra

comes with optional front side airbags. ABS was available beginning in 1991 and still remains optional.

The base engine is peppy with either a 5-speed or an automatic transmission with overdrive. The SE-R comes with a hotter engine and a 5-speed. The Sentra is fun to drive in SE-R form, but other models don't handle as well. The ride is fairly good on lesser models. The front seat is adequate, but the rear seat is cramped.

	1998	1999	2000	2001	2002
Size Class	Subcomp.	Subcomp.	Subcomp.	Subcomp.	Subcomp.
Drive	Front	Front	Front	Front	Front
Crash Test	Average	Average	Very Good	Very Good	Very Good
Airbags	Dual	Dual	Dual	Dual	Dl./Sd.(F)*
ABS	4-Whl*	4-Whl*	4-Whl*	4-Whl*	4-Whl.*
Parts Cost	Average	Average	Average	Average	High
Complaints	Very Good	Very Good	Very Good	Very Good	Very Good
Insurance	Surcharge	Surcharge	Surcharge	Regular	Regular
Fuel Econ.	30	29	29	27	30
Theft Rating	Average	Average	Average	Average**	Average**
Bumpers	Weak	Strong	Weak	Weak	Strong
Recalls	1	0	3	4	2
Trn. Cir. (ft.)	34.1	34.1	34.1	34.1	34.1
Weight (lbs.)	2315	2617	2617	2617	2581
Whlbase (in.)	99.8	99.8	99.8	99.8	99.8
Price	$7-9,000	$9-11,000	$11-13,000	$12-14,000	$13-15,000
OVERALL■	Good	Good	Good	Very Good	BEST BET

Oldsmobile 88 1993-1999

Like the Buick LeSabre and the Pontiac Bonneville, the 88 has undergone many changes in the past 10 years. In 1992, the 88 received a new body but kept the same chassis. In

1993 Oldsmobile 88

'96, Oldsmobile dropped the highest trim level, renamed it the LSS, and marketed it as a different car; but don't be fooled—it's still based on the 88. In 1992, all 88s received a driver's airbag and conventional belts; the 1994 models added a passenger airbag. ABS is standard on all 1993 and later models. For the past 10 years,

	1993	1994	1995	1996	1997
Size Class	Large	Large	Large	Large	Large
Drive	Front	Front	Front	Front	Front
Crash Test	Good	Good	Good	Good	Good
Airbags	Driver	Dual	Dual	Dual	Dual
ABS	4-Whl	4-Whl	4-Whl	4-Whl	4-Whl
Parts Cost	Average	Low	Average	Average	Average
Complaints	Average	Average	Poor	Good	Average
Insurance	Discount	Discount	Discount	Discount	Discount
Fuel Econ.	19	19	19	18	19
Theft Rating	Very Low	Very Low	Very Low	Very Low	Very Low
Bumpers					
Recalls	2	1	1	2	0
Trn. Cir. (ft.)	39.4	40.7	40.7	40.7	40.7
Weight (lbs.)	3404	3439	3400	3455	3465
Whlbase (in.)	110.8	110.8	110.8	110.8	110.8
Price	$5-7,000	$6-8,000	$7-9,000	$8-10,000	$9-10,000
OVERALL"	Good	BEST BET	Very Good	Very Good	Very Good

"Cars without crash tests do not receive an overall rating.**Estimate

272

1999 Oldsmobile 88

Oldsmobile has offered only one engine choice, a 3.8-liter 6-cylinder, which should provide plenty of power. The 88 with standard suspension gives a mushy ride at the expense of good handling. There's room for five and trunk space is generous. If you like the car but are turned off by the gauges and controls, consider a Bonneville.

	1998	1999	2000	2001	2002
Size Class	Large	Large			
Drive	Front	Front			
Crash Test	Good	Good			
Airbags	Dual	Dual			
ABS	4-Whl	4-Whl			
Parts Cost	Low	Low			
Complaints	Good	Good			
Insurance	Discount	Discount			
Fuel Econ.	19	19			
Theft Rating	Very Low**	Very Low**			
Bumpers					
Recalls	0	0	NO MODEL PRODUCED		
Trn. Cir. (ft.)	40.7	40.7			
Weight (lbs.)	3455	3455			
Whlbase (in.)	110.8	110.8			
Price	$10-12,000	$12-14,000			
OVERALL■	BEST BET	BEST BET			

Oldsmobile Aurora 1995-2002

Olds stepped into the 21st century in 1995 by introducing the Aurora—called the Aurora by Oldsmobile, not Oldsmobile Aurora, which represents Oldsmobile's effort to

1995 Oldsmobile Aurora

distance themselves from the past. Instead of big, heavy, and boxy cars, the Aurora introduces Oldsmobile's new line of big, heavy, and curved cars. The powerfully built Aurora comes with dual airbags, ABS, traction control, speed variable power steering, and a host of other items, which are all standard. Oldsmobile tried to add as many

	1993	1994	1995	1996	1997
Size Class			Large	Large	Large
Drive			Front	Front	Front
Crash Test			Average	Average	Average
Airbags			Dual	Dual	Dual
ABS			4-Whl	4-Whl	4-Whl
Parts Cost			Low	Low	High
Complaints			Very Poor	Poor	Poor
Insurance			Discount	Discount	Discount
Fuel Econ.			17	17	17
Theft Rating			Very Low	Very Low	Very Low
Bumpers					
Recalls			0	1	0
Trn. Cir. (ft.)			41	41	41.9
Weight (lbs.)			3967	3967	3967
Whlbase (in.)			113.8	113.8	113.8
Price			$8-10,000	$10-12,000	$13-15,000
OVERALL■			Good	Good	Average

NO MODEL PRODUCED

■Cars without crash tests do not receive an overall rating.**Estimate

2002 Oldsmobile Aurora

bells and whistles as they could. It performed only average in government crash testing during its early years but in later years did very well. Its safety features also make it a good buy. The Aurora benefits greatly from a very rigid structure and rides well for a car its size. However, like many large cars, the Aurora wallows in turns. The 4-liter V8, Aurora's large engine, is more powerful than any competitor's, and its fuel economy, though not notable by any means, holds its own against the competition.

	1998	1999	2000	2001	2002
Size Class	Large	Large	Large	Large	Large
Drive	Front	Front	Front	Front	Front
Crash Test	Average	Average	Average	Good	Good
Airbags	Dual	Dual	Dual	Dual	Dl./Sd.(F)
ABS	4-Whl	4-Whl	4-Whl	4-Whl	4-Whl
Parts Cost	High	Average	Average	Average	Average
Complaints	Average	Good	Very Good	Poor	Average
Insurance	Discount	Discount	Discount	Discount	Discount
Fuel Econ.	17	17	17	17	21
Theft Rating	Low	Average	Average	Average**	Average**
Bumpers				Strong	Strong
Recalls	0	0	0	0	0
Trn. Cir. (ft.)	41.9	41	41	39.5	39.5
Weight (lbs.)	3967	3967	3967	3627	3627
Whlbase (in.)	113.8	113.8	113.8	112.2	112.2
Price	$15-17,000	$17-19,000	$20-22,000	$22-25,000	$32-34,000
OVERALL■	Good	Very Good	Very Good	Good	**BEST BET**

Oldsmobile Cutlass Ciera 1993-96, Cutlass 1997-2000

A very dramatic change took place at Oldsmobile, as the Ciera was finally replaced in 1997 with the all-new Cutlass. The 1997 Cutlass is now the twin of the all-new Chevrolet Malibu.

1993 Oldsmobile Cutlass Ciera

Over the years, Cieras have come in several trim levels including some sport packages. Prior to 1997, all models got GM's horrible, door-mounted seat belts. For 1993, models offered an optional airbag and ABS, which both became standard in 1994, though the Ciera kept the door-mounted belts in front. For 1997 on, dual

	1993	1994	1995	1996	1997
Size Class	Intermd.	Intermd.	Intermd.	Intermd.	Intermd.
Drive	Front	Front	Front	Front	Front
Crash Test	Good	Good	Good	Good	Good
Airbags	Driver*	Driver	Driver	Driver	Dual
ABS	4-Whl*	4-Whl	4-Whl	4-Whl	4-Whl*
Parts Cost	Very Low	Low	Very Low	Very Low	Low
Complaints	Very Good	Very Good	Very Good	Very Good	Poor
Insurance	Discount	Discount	Discount	Regular	Regular
Fuel Econ.	20	19	25	24	20
Theft Rating	Low	Low	Very Low	Average	Very Low
Bumpers	Weak	Weak	Weak	Weak	
Recalls	2	4	1	1	0
Trn. Cir. (ft.)	38.1	38.1	38.1	38.1	36.1
Weight (lbs.)	2886	2833	2931	2924	2982
Whlbase (in.)	104.9	104.9	104.9	104.9	107
Price	<$3,000	$2-4,000	$4-6,000	$6-8,000	$8-10,000
OVERALL■	BEST BET	Very Good	BEST BET	BEST BET	Good

■Cars without crash tests do not receive an overall rating.*Optional **Estimate

1999 Oldsmobile Cutlass

airbags are standard; ABS is optional. Like the Century, the Ciera offers a good ride on smooth roads, but look elsewhere for responsive handling. The Cutlass provides a better ride. Skip the 4-cylinder engine in the Ciera wagon—it's a slug. Get the base V6 with automatic overdrive for both the Ciera and the new Cutlass. Some earlier models offer the big 3.8-liter V6 that comes in GM's full-size models; it's plenty powerful, but gas mileage is second rate for a mid-sized car.

	1998	1999	2000	2001	2002
Size Class	Intermd.	Intermd.	Intermd.		
Drive	Front	Front	Front		
Crash Test	Good	Good	Good		
Airbags	Dual	Dual	Dual		
ABS	4-Whl	4-Whl	4-Whl		
Parts Cost	Low	Low	Low		
Complaints	Poor	Very Poor	Very Good		
Insurance	Regular	Regular	Regular		
Fuel Econ.	20	22	22		
Theft Rating	Very Low	Very Low**	Very Low**		
Bumpers					
Recalls	0	0	0		
Trn. Cir. (ft.)	36.1	36.3	36.3		
Weight (lbs.)	3102	3102	3102		
Whlbase (in.)	107	107	107		
Price	$9-11,000	$10-12,000	$12-14,000		
OVERALL■	Good	Good	BEST BET		

(columns 2001 and 2002: NO MODEL PRODUCED)

Pontiac Bonneville 1993-2002

Although the Bonneville was redesigned several times in the 80's, its styling remained basically the same throughout the 90's until its redesign in 2000. The 2000

1993 Pontiac Bonneville

redesign added interior space and safety features, such as daytime running lamps, driver and front side airbags and a tire pressure monitor. Older Bonnevilles only have driver or dual airbags (dual standard on SSEi and all 1994-97 models, optional on 1993 SSE; driver's only on 1993 SE). ABS is standard. The base 3.8-liter V6

	1993	1994	1995	1996	1997
Size Class	Large	Large	Large	Large	Large
Drive	Front	Front	Front	Front	Front
Crash Test	Good	Good	Good	Good	Good
Airbags	Driver#	Dual	Dual	Dual	Dual
ABS	4-Whl	4-Whl	4-Whl	4-Whl	4-Whl
Parts Cost	Average	Low	Average	Average	Average
Complaints	Poor	Good	Poor	Good	Average
Insurance	Discount	Discount	Discount	Discount	Discount
Fuel Econ.	16	19	19	19	19
Theft Rating	Very Low	Very Low	Very Low	Very Low	Very Low
Bumpers					
Recalls	1	0	1	2	1
Trn. Cir. (ft.)	39.4	39.4	40.5	40.5	40.5
Weight (lbs.)	3362	3446	3587	3446	3446
Whlbase (in.)	110.8	110.8	110.8	110.8	110.8
Price	$3-5,000	$5-7,000	$7-9,000	$8-10,000	$9-11,000
OVERALL"	Good	BEST BET	Very Good	Very Good	Very Good

"Cars without crash tests do not receive an overall rating.#Passenger Side Optional. **Estimate

2002 Pontiac Bonneville

engine found on most models is powerful enough; the optional supercharged V6 only adds a little more power and more repair complexity. The SSE is a pleasure to drive, but its ride is firm. Room for four is ample, as is trunk space. Look for optional gauges but avoid the silly heads-up speedometer. The early dashboard ('93-'94) is thoughtfully designed. The 1993-2002 Bonneville is GM's best product and a very competent automobile.

	1998	1999	2000	2001	2002
Size Class	Large	Large	Large	Large	Large
Drive	Front	Front	Front	Front	Front
Crash Test	Good	Good	Very Good	Very Good	Very Good
Airbags	Dual	Dual	Dual/Side	Dual/Side	Dl./Sd.(F)
ABS	4-Whl	4-Whl	4-Whl	4-Whl	4-Whl
Parts Cost	Low	Very Low	Very Low	Low	Average
Complaints	Average	Average	Very Good	Very Good	Good
Insurance	Discount	Discount	Discount	Discount	Discount
Fuel Econ.	19	19	19	19	23
Theft Rating	Low	Very Low	Very Low	Very Low**	Very Low**
Bumpers		Strong	Strong	Strong	
Recalls	0	2	1	0	0
Trn. Cir. (ft.)	40.5	40.5	40.5	40.5	40.5
Weight (lbs.)	3446	3446	3590	3590	3590
Whlbase (in.)	110.8	110.8	112.2	112.2	112.2
Price	$11-13,000	$14-16,000	$17-19,000	$19-21,000	$26-28,000
OVERALL*	BEST BET	BEST BET	BEST BET	BEST BET	BEST BET

Pontiac Firebird 1993-2002

The Pontiac Firebird, similar to the Chevrolet Camaro, is a vestige of the American pony cars (Mustang clones) of the late 1960s. Firebirds have undergone two major changes

1993 Pontiac Firebird

since 1970, the latest being in 1993 with a new body featuring many plastic body panels and a revised chassis. A convertible is available in 1994-97. Firebirds since 1993 come with standard dual airbags. All 1993-2002 Firebirds have ABS and remain excellent crash test performers.

	1993	1994	1995	1996	1997
Size Class	Intermd.	Intermd.	Intermd.	Intermd.	Intermd.
Drive	Rear	Rear	Rear	Rear	Rear
Crash Test	Very Good	Very Good	Very Good	Very Good	Very Good
Airbags	Dual	Dual	Dual	Dual	Dual
ABS	4-Whl	4-Whl	4-Whl	4-Whl	4-Whl
Parts Cost	Low	Average	Average	Average	High
Complaints	Poor	Poor	Poor	Average	Poor
Insurance	Surcharge	Surcharge	Surcharge	Surcharge	Surcharge
Fuel Econ.	19	19	19	19	19
Theft Rating	Very High	Low	Average	Average	Average
Bumpers					
Recalls	0	1	1	0	1
Trn. Cir. (ft.)	37.9	37.9	37.9	37.9	37.9
Weight (lbs.)	3241	3232	3230	3311	3311
Whlbase (in.)	101.1	101.1	101.1	101.1	101.1
Price	$4-6,000	$6-8,000	$8-10,000	$10-12,000	$13-15,000
OVERALL■	Average	Average	Average	Average	Poor

■Cars without crash tests do not receive an overall rating.**Estimate

2002 Pontiac Firebird

The 2.8-, 3.1-, or 3.4-liter V6 engines are found on older Fire-birds, but new Firebirds come with a 3.8-liter V6 or the Z28's 5.7-liter V8. For 1993, chassis and suspension changes made the Firebird feel more solid than previous models. Ride is typical of large sporty cars, and handling is responsive. The Firebird is mid-sized outside but really fits only two inside because the back seat is a real squeeze, even for kids.

	1998	1999	2000	2001	2002
Size Class	Intermd.	Intermd.	Intermd.	Intermd.	Intermd.
Drive	Rear	Rear	Rear	Rear	Rear
Crash Test	Very Good	Very Good	Very Good	Very Good	Very Good
Airbags	Dual	Dual	Dual	Dual	Dual
ABS	4-Whl	4-Whl	4-Whl	4-Whl	4-Whl
Parts Cost	High	Average	Average	Average	Average
Complaints	Poor	Good	Very Good	Very Good	Poor
Insurance	Surcharge	Surcharge	Surcharge	Surcharge	Surcharge
Fuel Econ.	19	19	19	19	23
Theft Rating	Average	Average	Average	Average**	Average**
Bumpers					
Recalls	0	1	0	0	1
Trn. Cir. (ft.)	37.9	37.9	37.9	37.9	37.9
Weight (lbs.)	3477	3341	3341	3341	3341
Whlbase (in.)	101.1	101.1	101.1	101.1	101.1
Price	$16-18,000	$18-20,000	$19-21,000	$21-23,000	$23-25,000
OVERALL■	Poor	Good	Very Good	Very Good	Average

Pontiac Grand Am 1993-2002

The Grand Am got a new body and grew nearly ten inches in length in 1992 but kept the old chassis. In '96, Pontiac redesigned the interior and exterior slightly, giving the Grand Am

1993 Pontiac Grand Am

a new hood, new fenders, and a new instrument panel. In 1999, the Grand Am was completely overhauled again, giving it even more interior room, a new cockpit design, redesigned bucket seats, four-wheel independent suspension, enhanced traction system, and fog lamps. Until 1995, they have GM's notorious door-mounted belts as

	1993	1994	1995	1996	1997
Size Class	Compact	Compact	Compact	Compact	Compact
Drive	Front	Front	Front	Front	Front
Crash Test	Very Poor[1]	Poor[1]	Poor[1]	Good[1]	Good[1]
Airbags	None	Driver	Driver	Dual	Dual
ABS	4-Whl	4-Whl	4-Whl	4-Whl	4-Whl
Parts Cost	Low	Low	Low	Low	Average
Complaints	Average	Poor	Poor	Average	Average
Insurance	Regular	Surcharge	Surcharge	Regular	Regular
Fuel Econ.	22	22	22	23	23
Theft Rating	Very Low	Very Low	Very Low	Very Low	Very Low
Bumpers	Weak	Weak	Weak	Weak	Weak
Recalls	1	2	1	4	2
Trn. Cir. (ft.)	34.1	36.4	35.3	35.3	35.3
Weight (lbs.)	2728	2793	2888	2881	2835
Whlbase (in.)	103.4	103.4	103.4	103.4	103.4
Price	$3-5,000	$4-6,000	$5-7,000	$6-8,000	$7-9,000
OVERALL■	Poor	Very Poor	Very Poor	Good	Good

■Cars without crash tests do not receive an overall rating.[1]Data given for sedan. Crash test for coupe for 1993-95 is Average, 1996-97 is Very Good. **Estimate

2002 Pontiac Grand Am

standard equipment, though the 1994 adds a standard driver's airbag. For 1996, Grand Ams come with standard dual airbags and conventional belts. Now the Grand Ams come standard with a front side airbag. The basic 4 performs adequately; the Quad 4 is quick, but rough and possibly unreliable. The V6 is smoother but uses more fuel. Automatics on all Grand Ams through 1993 have only 3 speeds, and performance and economy suffer. It improves with sport suspension, but the ride suffers.

	1998	1999	2000	2001	2002
Size Class	Compact	Compact	Compact	Compact	Compact
Drive	Front	Front	Front	Front	Front
Crash Test	Very Good[1]	Very Good	Very Good	Very Good	Very Good
Airbags	Dual	Dual	Dual	Dual	Dl./Sd.(F)
ABS	4-Whl	4-Whl	4-Whl	4-Whl	4-Whl
Parts Cost	High	Average	High	Average	Low
Complaints	Good	Poor	Good	Very Good	Average
Insurance	Regular	Regular	Regular	Surcharge	Surcharge
Fuel Econ.	23	22	22	21	27
Theft Rating	Average	Average	High	High**	Average**
Bumpers	Weak		Strong	Strong	Strong
Recalls	0	2	3	1	0
Trn. Cir. (ft.)	35.3	37.7	37.7	37.7	35.1
Weight (lbs.)	2877	3066	3066	3066	3066
Whlbase (in.)	103.4	107	107	107	107.2
Price	$8-10,000	$10-12,000	$12-14,000	$13-15,000	$18-20,000
OVERALL■	Good	Good	Good	Very Good	BEST BET

Pontiac Grand Prix 1993-2002

A 4-door Grand Prix sedan joined the line in 1990, available as an all-wheel drive STE model that had previously been part of the Pontiac 6000 series. Changes for 1997 include a

1994 Pontiac Grand Prix

wider stance and a lower roofline, which give a sportier look. Every '93 has GM's awful door-mounted front belts; in 1994-96, only the coupes have them and they were finally eliminated in the 1997 version. For 1994-97, models have standard dual airbags and the 2002 model comes with standard front side airbags. ABS first became

	1993	1994	1995	1996	1997
Size Class	Intermd.	Intermd.	Intermd.	Intermd.	Intermd.
Drive	Front	Front	Front	Front	Front
Crash Test	Good	Average	Average	Average	Good
Airbags	None	Dual	Dual	Dual	Dual
ABS	4-Whl*	4-Whl*	4-Whl*	4-Whl*	4-Whl
Parts Cost	Low	Low	Average	Average	High
Complaints	Average	Poor	Average	Good	Very Poor
Insurance	Discount	Discount	Discount	Discount	Discount
Fuel Econ.	19	19	19	20	20
Theft Rating	Very Low	Very Low	Very Low	Very Low	Very Low
Bumpers					Weak
Recalls	1	1	2	0	1
Trn. Cir. (ft.)	36.7	39	36.7	36.7	36.9
Weight (lbs.)	3312	3370	3318	3243	3396
Whlbase (in.)	107.5	107.5	107.5	107.5	110.5
Price	$3-5,000	$4-6,000	$5-7,000	$6-8,000	$9-11,000
OVERALL■	Good	Good	Good	Very Good	Average

■Cars without crash tests do not receive an overall rating.*Optional **Estimate

2002 Pontiac Grand Prix

optional in 1989 and became standard in 1997. A theft deterrent system and Onstar communications are some of the options now offered. Earlier models have a 2.8-liter V6, which provides adequate power in this heavy car. Later V6 models have more power, and the GTP's 3.4 V6 is as quick as a V8. The early Grand Prix focuses on ride, not agility. Room inside is reasonable, but comfort is average. Trunk space is generous. From 1993 on, Grand Prix models have improved each consecutive year.

	1998	1999	2000	2001	2002
Size Class	Intermd.	Intermd.	Intermd.	Intermd.	Intermd.
Drive	Front	Front	Front	Front	Front
Crash Test	Good	Good	Good	Good	Good
Airbags	Dual	Dual	Dual	Dual	Dl./Sd.(F)
ABS	4-Whl	4-Whl	4-Whl	4-Whl	4-Whl
Parts Cost	Low	Low	Low	Very Low	Very Low
Complaints	Very Poor	Average	Very Good	Very Good	Average
Insurance	Discount	Discount	Discount	Discount	Discount
Fuel Econ.	20	20	20	20	23
Theft Rating	Average	Average	Average	Average**	Average**
Bumpers		Strong	Strong	Strong	Strong
Recalls	0	1	2	2	0
Trn. Cir. (ft.)	36.9	36.9	36.9	36.9	36.9
Weight (lbs.)	3396	3414	3414	3414	3384
Whlbase (in.)	110.5	110.5	110.5	110.5	110.5
Price	$10-12,000	$12-14,000	$14-16,000	$15-17,000	$24-26,000
OVERALL■	Very Good	BEST BET	BEST BET	BEST BET	BEST BET

Pontiac Sunbird 1993-94, Sunfire 1995-2002

The Sunbird, like its twin the Cavalier, goes back a long way. Over the years, Sunbirds have come in a wide range of body styles. By 1994, these were reduced to a con-

1993 Pontiac Sunbird

vertible, 2-door coupe, and 4-door sedan. The Sunbird was replaced in 1995 by the Sunfire. For 1990-94, Sunbirds have door-mounted front belts. ABS is standard on all models starting in 1992, but airbags were not offered until the 1995 redesign, which brought dual airbags. The Sunbird's 4-cylinder engines perform adequately at

	1993	1994	1995	1996	1997
Size Class	Compact	Compact	Compact	Compact	Compact
Drive	Front	Front	Front	Front	Front
Crash Test	Good	Good	Good	Good	Good
Airbags	None	None	Dual	Dual	Dual
ABS	4-Whl	4-Whl	4-Whl	4-Whl	4-Whl
Parts Cost	Low	Low	Low	Low	High
Complaints	Good	Good	Average	Poor	Average
Insurance	Regular	Surcharge	Regular	Surcharge	Surcharge
Fuel Econ.	20	23	24	25	25
Theft Rating	Very Low	Very Low	Very Low	Very Low	Very Low
Bumpers	Weak	Weak	Weak	Weak	Weak
Recalls	2	0	5	6	5
Trn. Cir. (ft.)	34.3	35.3	37.2	37.2	37.2
Weight (lbs.)	2537	2502	2679	2679	2627
Whlbase (in.)	101.3	101.3	104.1	104.1	104.1
Price	$2-4,000	$3-5,000	$4-6,000	$5-7,000	$6-8,000
OVERALL■	Average	Average	Good	Poor	Poor

■Cars without crash tests do not receive an overall rating.**Estimate

2002 Pontiac Sunfire

best. A V6 option first became available in 1985, but it's almost too powerful. The GT has a turbocharged 4. If you want an automatic, you're stuck with a 3-speed, which means inferior gas mileage. A 4-speed automatic is available starting in 1996. The 5-speed transmission isn't too smooth or precise, but later ones are better. The ride isn't up to the standard for compacts, but handling is responsive, especially on the GT. Controls improved dramatically on the Sunfire.

	1998	1999	2000	2001	2002
Size Class	Compact	Compact	Compact	Compact	Compact
Drive	Front	Front	Front	Front	Front
Crash Test	Good	Good	Good	Good	Good
Airbags	Dual	Dual	Dual	Dual	Dual
ABS	4-Whl	4-Whl	4-Whl	4-Whl	4-Whl
Parts Cost	Average	Low	Low	Low	Low
Complaints	Very Good	Very Good	Good	Very Good	Good
Insurance	Surcharge	Surcharge	Surcharge	Surcharge	Surcharge
Fuel Econ.	25	24	24	24	27
Theft Rating	Low	Average	Average	Average**	Average**
Bumpers	Weak	Strong	Strong	Strong	Strong
Recalls	1	1	0	0	0
Trn. Cir. (ft.)	37.2	35.6	35.6	35.6	35.6
Weight (lbs.)	2670	2630	2630	2630	2606
Whlbase (in.)	104.1	104.1	104.1	104.1	104.1
Price	$7-9,000	$8-10,000	$9-11,000	$10-12,000	$15-17,000
OVERALL■	Good	Very Good	Very Good	Very Good	Very Good

Saab 900 1993-98, 9-3 1999-2002

The Saab 9-3 is a close relative of the 1979 Saab 900, which ran until 1999. The 9-3 comes as a coupe, a 5-door sedan or a con-vertible. Older 900 models included the plain

1993 Saab 900

900, the fancier 900S, the 900 Turbo, and the SPG (Special Perfor-mance Group). The 1994 900 got a complete redesign, resembling the old 900, but it's a bit more conventional. Since 1990, all models have ABS, regular belts, and a driver's airbag. The 1994 900 (except convertible) and later models have dual airbags. A standard child

	1993	1994	1995	1996	1997
Size Class	Compact	Intermd.	Intermd.	Intermd.	Intermd.
Drive	Front	Front	Front	Front	Front
Crash Test	N/A	Good	Good	Good	Good
Airbags	Driver	Dual	Dual	Dual	Dual
ABS	4-Whl	4-Whl	4-Whl	4-Whl	4-Whl
Parts Cost	Average	High	Very High	Average	Very High
Complaints	Poor	Very Poor	Very Poor	Poor	Very Good
Insurance	Surcharge	Surcharge	Regular	Discount	Discount
Fuel Econ.	19	19	19	19	21
Theft Rating	High	High	High	High	Very Low
Bumpers	Weak	Strong	Strong	Strong	Strong
Recalls	0	8	6	3	3
Trn. Cir. (ft.)	33.8	35.4	35.4	34.4	34.3
Weight (lbs.)	2770	2950	3120	2990	2940
Whlbase (in.)	99.1	102.4	102.4	102.4	102.4
Price	$6-8,000	$8-10,000	$10-12,000	$11-13,000	$13-15,000
OVERALL■		Very Poor	Very Poor	Good	Very Good

■Cars without crash tests do not receive an overall rating.**Estimate

288

2002 Saab 9-3

booster seat was added in 1994. In 1999, the Saab 9-3 added safety features such as front side and head airbags, and other niceties such as more trunk room and wider seats.

All pre-1994 900 engines have 4 cylinders: single-cam, twin-cam, or twin-cam turbo. A 2.5-liter V6 is optional for 1994. Avoid older, used turbos—they're likely to require expensive repairs. The 9-3 comes with a 2.0-liter turbo engine, which is more than adequate.

	1998	1999	2000	2001	2002
Size Class	Intermd.	Intermd.	Intermd.	Intermd.	Intermd.
Drive	Front	Front	Front	Front	Front
Crash Test	Good	N/A	N/A	N/A	N/A
Airbags	Dual	Dual	Dual	Dual	Dl./Sd.(F)/Hd.
ABS	4-Whl	4-Whl	4-Whl	4-Whl	4-Whl
Parts Cost	Very High	Very High	Average	Average	Average
Complaints	Average	Average	Very Good	Very Good	Very Good
Insurance	Discount	Regular	Discount	Regular	Discount
Fuel Econ.	22	20	20	20	24
Theft Rating	Very Low	Very Low**	Very Low**	Very Low**	Very Low**
Bumpers	Strong		Strong	Strong	Strong
Recalls	3	2	1	1	1
Trn. Cir. (ft.)	34.3	34.4	34.4	34.4	34.4
Weight (lbs.)	2990	2990	2990	2990	3220
Whlbase (in.)	102.4	111.3	111.3	111.3	102.6
Price	$14-16,000	$19-21,000	$20-22,000	$22-24,000	$28-30,000
OVERALL■	Good				

Saab 9000 1993-98, 9-5 1999-2002

The 9000 had not changed much since 1986 until its complete redesign and new name in 1999. Before the recent return on the hatchback in 2002, Saab was one of the last

1993 Saab 9000

automakers to offer a hatchback car; most automakers and consumers went to traditional sedans. The 9000 CD and CDE are notchback sedans with separate trunks, and the CS and CSE are hatchbacks. For 1996, Saab dropped the sedan models and concentrated solely on the hatchback. Most of the changes to the 9000 have

	1993	1994	1995	1996	1997
Size Class	Intermd.	Intermd.	Intermd.	Intermd.	Intermd.
Drive	Front	Front	Front	Front	Front
Crash Test	Good	Good	Good	Good	Good
Airbags	Driver	Dual	Dual	Dual	Dual
ABS	4-Whl	4-Whl	4-Whl	4-Whl	4-Whl
Parts Cost	Average	Very High	High	High	Very High
Complaints	Very Poor	Poor	Average	Good	Very Good
Insurance	Discount	Discount	Discount	Discount	Regular
Fuel Econ.	18	18	20	20	20
Theft Rating	Very Low	Average	Average	Average	Very Low
Bumpers					
Recalls	5	4	0	0	1
Trn. Cir. (ft.)	35.8	35.8	35.8	35.8	35.8
Weight (lbs.)	3110	3210	3260	3110	3130
Whlbase (in.)	105.2	105.2	105.2	105.2	105.2
Price	$6-8,000	$8-10,000	$10-12,000	$12-14,000	$14-16,000
OVERALL"	Average	Average	Very Good	Very Good	Good

"Cars without crash tests do not receive an overall rating.**Estimate

2002 Saab 9-5

been minor in nature or additions to standard safety equipment. For 1994, Saab added a standard passenger airbag to the already standard driver's. The 9-5 comes with standard front side airbags as well as head airbags. ABS is standard from 1990 on. Saab's standard 2.3-liter 4-cylinder turbocharged engine provides enough power. The optional 3.0-liter V6 delivers even more, but you don't need it. All of these models provide plenty of space for five and generous room for luggage.

	1998	1999	2000	2001	2002
Size Class	Intermd.	Intermd.	Intermd.	Intermd.	Intermd.
Drive	Front	Front	Front	Front	Front
Crash Test	Good	N/A	N/A	N/A	N/A
Airbags	Dual	Dual	Dual	Dual	Dl./Sd.(F)/Hd.
ABS	4-Whl	4-Whl	4-Whl	4-Whl	4-Whl
Parts Cost	Very High	Very High	Low	High	Very Low
Complaints	Average	Very Good	Good	Good	Very Good
Insurance	Regular	Regular	Regular	Discount	Discount
Fuel Econ.	21	21	21	21	23
Theft Rating	Very Low	Very Low[**]	Very Low[**]	Very Low[**]	Very Low[**]
Bumpers			Strong	Strong	Strong
Recalls	1	1	1	1	1
Trn. Cir. (ft.)	35.7	35.4	35.4	35.4	35.4
Weight (lbs.)	3250	3280	3280	3280	3280
Whlbase (in.)	105.2	106.4	106.4	106.4	106.4
Price	$17-19,000	$22-24,000	$28-30,000	$32-34,000	$34-36,000
OVERALL[■]	Average				

Saturn SC/SL 1993-2002, SW 1993-2001

The first SC coupes were equivalent in trim to the fancy SL2 sedans, and when sales didn't meet expectations, Saturn introduced a base model SC1 for 1993. The SW wagon joined the line in 1993.

1993 Saturn SL

The SL and SW models were all-new for '96 and the SC was all-new in '97. Watch out for models prior to '95; all Saturns through 1994 have motorized front shoulder belts with separate lap belts. Standard driver's airbag became standard in 1993; dual airbags and manual belts became standard in 1995 and head airbags

	1993	1994	1995	1996	1997
Size Class	Subcomp.	Subcomp.	Subcomp.	Subcomp.	Subcomp.
Drive	Front	Front	Front	Front	Front
Crash Test	Average	Average	Very Good	Very Good[1]	Very Good[1]
Airbags	Driver	Driver	Dual	Dual	Dual
ABS	4-Whl*	4-Whl*	4-Whl*	4-Whl*	4-Whl*
Parts Cost	Very Low	Very Low	Very Low	Very Low	Very Low
Complaints	Poor	Poor	Poor	Good	Average
Insurance	Regular	Regular	Regular	Regular	Discount
Fuel Econ.	23	25	28	25	28
Theft Rating	Low	Low	Very Low	Very Low	Very Low
Bumpers	Weak	Weak	Weak	Weak	Weak
Recalls	2	0	2	1	3
Trn. Cir. (ft.)	37.1	37.1	37.1	37.1	37.1
Weight (lbs.)	2320	2314	2325	2282	2321
Whlbase (in.)	102.4[2]	102.4[2]	102.4[2]	102.4[2]	102.4[2]
Price	$2-4,000	$3-5,000	$4-6,000	$5-7,000	$6-8,000
OVERALL■	Average	Good	Very Good	**BEST BET**	**BEST BET**

■Cars without crash tests do not receive an overall rating.[1]Data given for SL/SW. SC has not been tested. [2]Data given for SL/SW. Wheelbase for SC is 99.2. *Optional **Estimate

2002 Saturn SC

are now optional. ABS is optional beginning in 1992. The twin-cam engine on the SC, SC1, SL2, and SW2 is quicker than the base models' standard 4-cylinder, yet almost as economical. Both engines can be noisy. The 5-speed is more pleasant than the automatic and a better choice with the base engine. Handling is very good. Ride is decent, but you'll feel the bumps. Front seat comfort is fairly good, but in back it's cramped and uncomfortable for adults. The sedan and wagon have excellent crash tests.

	1998	1999	2000	2001	2002
Size Class	Subcomp.	Subcomp.	Subcomp.	Subcomp.	Subcomp.
Drive	Front	Front	Front	Front	Front
Crash Test	Very Good[1]	Very Good[1]	Very Good[1]	Very Good[1]	Very Good[1]
Airbags	Dual	Dual	Dual	Dual	Dual/Head*
ABS	4-Whl*	4-Whl*	4-Whl*	4-Whl*	4-Whl
Parts Cost	Very Low	Very Low	Very Low	Very Low	Very Low
Complaints	Good	Average	Very Good	Very Good	Very Good
Insurance	Discount	Discount	Regular	Regular	Regular
Fuel Econ.	28	29	29	29	29
Theft Rating	Very Low	Very Low	Very Low	Very Low**	Very Low**
Bumpers	Weak	Strong	Strong	Strong	Strong
Recalls	0	0	7	2	1
Trn. Cir. (ft.)	37.1	37.1	37.1	37.1	37.1
Weight (lbs.)	2326	2320	2320	2320	2368
Whlbase (in.)	102.4[2]	102.4[2]	102.4[2]	102.4[2]	102.4
Price	$7-9,000	$8-10,000	$9-11,000	$10-12,000	$12-14,000
OVERALL■	BEST BET	BEST BET	BEST BET	BEST BET	BEST BET

Subaru Forester 1998-2002

Following the success of the Outback series, but based on the Impreza, the Subaru Forester is a mix of station wagon and sport utility. As with all Subarus, height adjustable seat

1998 Subaru Forester

belts, pretensioners and all-wheel drive come standard. Four-wheel ABS is optional, however. Dual and front side airbags are standard.

A 2.5-liter 4-cylinder engine powers the Forester, which is adequate because of the Forester's size. Compared to other sport utili-

	1993	1994	1995	1996	1997
Size Class					
Drive					
Crash Test					
Airbags					
ABS					
Parts Cost					
Complaints					
Insurance					
Fuel Econ.			NO MODEL PRODUCED		
Theft Rating					
Bumpers					
Recalls					
Trn. Cir. (ft.)					
Weight (lbs.)					
Whlbase (in.)					
Price					
OVERALL■					

■Cars without crash tests do not receive an overall rating.**Estimate

2002 Subaru Forester

ties, the Forester has a lower stance, which increases stability and makes getting in and out easier. The Forester also continues to do well in crash tests, scoring a good on the frontal crash test and a very good on the side crash test.

	1998	1999	2000	2001	2002
Size Class	Sp. Util.	Sp. Util.	Sp. Util.	Sp. Util.	Sp. Util.
Drive	All	All	All	All	All
Crash Test	Good	Good	Good	Good	Good
Airbags	Dual	Dual	Dual	Dual	Dl./Sd.(F)
ABS	4-Whl	4-Whl	4-Whl	4-Whl	4-Whl
Parts Cost	Average	High	Average	Average	Average
Complaints	Poor	Poor	Good	Average	Average
Insurance	Surcharge	Surcharge	Surcharge	Surcharge	Surcharge
Fuel Econ.	24	24	24	24	24
Theft Rating	Very Low	Very Low	Very Low	Very Low**	Very Low**
Bumpers	Weak	Strong	Strong	Strong	Strong
Recalls	1	1	0	0	0
Trn. Cir. (ft.)	34.7	34.7	34.7	34.7	34.7
Weight (lbs.)	3125	3125	3125	3125	3125
Whlbase (in.)	99.4	99.4	99.4	99.4	99.4
Price	$13-15,000	$15-17,000	$17-19,000	$19-21,000	$22-24,000
OVERALL■	Average	Average	Very Good	Good	Very Good

Subaru Impreza 1993-2002

The Impreza is Subaru's entrance in the crowded subcompact market. Its base price is slightly higher than most subcompacts, and it comes with a dizzying array of options, so expect

1993 Subaru Impreza

to pay more. A driver's airbag was standard in 1993, a passenger's airbag was optional in 1994, and dual airbags became standard in 1995. Standard front airbags were added in the redesigned 2002 model. ABS was optional with its introduction, but it became standard in 1998. The older Impreza's base model's engine is a 1.8-liter

	1993	1994	1995	1996	1997
Size Class	Subcomp.	Subcomp.	Subcomp.	Subcomp.	Subcomp.
Drive	Front/All	Front/All	Front/All	Front/All	Front/All
Crash Test	Good	Good	Good	Good	Good
Airbags	Driver#	Driver#	Dual	Dual	Dual
ABS	4-Whl*	4-Whl*	4-Whl*	4-Whl*	4-Whl*
Parts Cost	Average	Average	Average	Average	Average
Complaints	Average	Average	Poor	Good	Average
Insurance	Regular	Regular	Regular	Surcharge	Surcharge
Fuel Econ.	24	24	24	25	23
Theft Rating	Very Low	Very Low	Very Low	Very Low	Very Low
Bumpers					
Recalls	1	0	0	0	0
Trn. Cir. (ft.)	33.5	33.5	33.5	33.5	33.5
Weight (lbs.)	2325	2325	2400	2565	2720
Whlbase (in.)	99.2	99.2	99.2	99.2	99.2
Price	<$3,000	$3-5,000	$5-7,000	$7-9,000	$8-10,000
OVERALL■	Good	Good	Good	Good	Average

■Cars without crash tests do not receive an overall rating. #Passenger Side Optional. *Optional **Estimate

2002 Subaru Impreza

4-cylinder that is adequate, though a more powerful 2.2-liter 4-cylinder is standard on the LX and optional on the L and Outback models. The 2002 Impreza comes with a more powerful 2.5-liter engine. Fuel economy falls below other subcompacts. The 2002 models are all-wheel drive, but older base models are only front-wheel drive. Handling and ride are typical of subcompacts. Front seats are comfortable; the back seat is the typical subcompact squeeze, and trunk space is small.

	1998	1999	2000	2001	2002
Size Class	Subcomp.	Subcomp.	Subcomp.	Subcomp.	Subcomp.
Drive	Front/All	Front/All	Front/All	Front/All	Front/All
Crash Test	Good	Good	Good	Good	N/A
Airbags	Dual	Dual	Dual	Dual	Dl./Sd.(F)
ABS	4-Whl	4-Whl	4-Whl	4-Whl	4-Whl
Parts Cost	Average	Average	Average	Average	Very Low
Complaints	Average	Good	Average	Very Good	Average
Insurance	Surcharge	Surcharge	Surcharge	Surcharge	Regular
Fuel Econ.	23	22	22	22	24
Theft Rating	Very Low	Very Low	Very Low	Very Low**	Very Low**
Bumpers			Strong	Strong	Strong
Recalls	0	0	0	0	0
Trn. Cir. (ft.)	33.5	33.5	33.5	33.5	35.4
Weight (lbs.)	2720	2730	2730	2730	3140
Whlbase (in.)	99.2	99.2	99.2	99.2	99.4
Price	$10-12,000	$12-14,000	$15-17,000	$17-19,000	$20-22,000
OVERALL■	Average	Good	Good	Very Good	Good

Subaru Legacy 1993-2002

For many years, the Legacy has been Subaru's best selling vehicle, although it was not a truly good vehicle until 1993. The Legacy first came out in mid-1989 and received a significant

1993 Subaru Legacy

redesign with more interior room for 1995 and again in 2000. An airbag for the driver became standard in 1993, and a second airbag was added in 1995. The 2000 redesign brought in front side airbags. Getting ABS is tricky—it's more likely found on the more expensive models, such as the LSi and Touring; however, it's stan-

	1993	1994	1995	1996	1997
Size Class	Compact	Compact	Compact	Compact	Compact
Drive	Front/All	Front/All	Front/All	Front/All	Front/All
Crash Test	Good	Good	Very Good	Very Good	Very Good
Airbags	Driver	Driver	Dual	Dual	Dual
ABS	4-Whl*	4-Whl*	4-Whl*	4-Whl	4-Whl
Parts Cost	High	High	High	Average	Average
Complaints	Average	Poor	Poor	Average	Very Poor
Insurance	Regular	Regular	Regular	Discount	Regular
Fuel Econ.	22	21	24	24	23
Theft Rating	Very Low	Very Low	Very Low	Very Low	Very Low
Bumpers	Weak	Weak	Weak	Weak	Weak
Recalls	1	0	1	2	5
Trn. Cir. (ft.)	33.6	33.5	34.8	36.7	34.8
Weight (lbs.)	2800	2825	2655	3080	2885
Whlbase (in.)	101.6	101.6	103.5	103.5	103.5
Price	$3-5,000	$4-6,000	$6-8,000	$9-11,000	$10-12,000
OVERALL■	Average	Poor	Average	Very Good	Average

■Cars without crash tests do not receive an overall rating.*Optional **Estimate

2002 Subaru Legacy

dard on 1996-2002 models. The older 2.2-liter 4-cylinder engine is average for compacts in power and mileage. Starting in 1996, models come with an optional 2.5-liter 4-cylinder engine that offers more power with only a slight loss in gas mileage. In 2000, the 2.5-liter became standard. A turbo was standard on Sport and Touring models, and full-time 4-wheel drive is a Subaru exclusive on low-priced cars.

	1998	1999	2000	2001	2002
Size Class	Compact	Compact	Compact	Compact	Compact
Drive	Front/All	Front/All	Front/All	Front/All	Front/All
Crash Test	Good	Good	Good	Good	Good
Airbags	Dual	Dual	Dual	Dual	Dl./Sd.(F)
ABS	4-Whl	4-Whl	4-Whl	4-Whl	4-Whl
Parts Cost	Average	Average	Average	Average	Very Low
Complaints	Good	Good	Good	Very Good	Good
Insurance	Regular	Regular	Regular	Regular	Surcharge
Fuel Econ.	23	22	22	22	23
Theft Rating	Very Low	Very Low**	Low	Very Low**	
Bumpers	Weak	Strong	Strong	Strong	Strong
Recalls	3	2	1	0	1
Trn. Cir. (ft.)	34.8	34.8	35.4	35.4	35.4
Weight (lbs.)	2885	2885	3320	3320	3320
Whlbase (in.)	103.5	103.5	104.3	104.3	104.3
Price	$12-14,000	$13-15,000	$15-17,000	$19-21,000	$21-23,000
OVERALL■	Good	Very Good	Very Good	BEST BET	Very Good

Suzuki Esteem 1996-2002

The Esteem, the larger of Suzuki's two models, is their first entry into the compact sedan market, a competitive and crowded market. The base model comes with dual airbags and

1996 Suzuki Esteem

optional ABS; the upgraded GLX has added features. It was revamped in 1999 and received new sheet metal work, grille, fenders, and headlights.

In 1997, the standard 1.6-liter 4-cylinder engine offered poor

	1993	1994	1995	1996	1997
Size Class				Subcomp.	Subcomp.
Drive				Front	Front
Crash Test				N/A	N/A
Airbags				Dual	Dual
ABS				4-Whl*	4-Whl*
Parts Cost				Very High	Very High
Complaints		NO MODEL PRODUCED		Good	Good
Insurance				Surcharge	Surcharge
Fuel Econ.				30	30
Theft Rating				Average**	Average**
Bumpers					
Recalls				0	0
Trn. Cir. (ft.)				32.2	32.2
Weight (lbs.)				2227	2227
Whlbase (in.)				97.6	97.6
Price				$3-5,000	$4-6,000
OVERALL■					

■Cars without crash tests do not receive an overall rating.*Optional **Estimate

2002 Suzuki Esteem

power and little excitement, but in 1999, it was improved. The larger 1.8-liter engine provides more power and doesn't sacrifice much in fuel economy. The interior is small, if not tight, and trunk space is likewise. Pack lightly. Noise levels are minimal. Though the price is as small as the car, your money would be well spent elsewhere.

	1998	1999	2000	2001	2002
Size Class	Subcomp.	Subcomp.	Subcomp.	Subcomp.	Subcomp.
Drive	Front	Front	Front	Front	Front
Crash Test	N/A	N/A	N/A	N/A	N/A
Airbags	Dual	Dual	Dual	Dual	Dual
ABS	4-Whl*	4-Whl*	4-Whl*	4-Whl*	4-Whl*
Parts Cost	Very High	Very High	Very High	Very High	Very High
Complaints	Average	Good	Average	Good	Good
Insurance	Surcharge	Surcharge	Surcharge	Surcharge	Surcharge
Fuel Econ.	30	30	30	30	30
Theft Rating	Average**	Average**	Average**	Average**	Average**
Bumpers		Weak			
Recalls	0	0	0	0	0
Trn. Cir. (ft.)	32.2	32.2	32.2	32.2	32.2
Weight (lbs.)	2227	2227	2227	2227	2271
Whlbase (in.)	97.6	97.6	97.6	97.6	97.6
Price	$6-8,000	$7-9,000	$8-10,000	$10-12,000	$15-17,000
OVERALL■					

Suzuki Grand Vitara 1999-2002

Suzuki came out with the all-new Grand Vitara in 1999, going along with the small SUV concept. The Grand Vitara is based on its twin, the Chevy Tracker. The safety features are marginal, with only dual airbags and optional 4-wheel ABS, but it has scored well on the frontal crash test.

1999 Suzuki Grand Vitara

While smaller Vitaras come with a 2.0-liter 4-cylinder engine, a 2.5-liter V6 engine powers the Grand Vitara. You can choose

	1993	1994	1995	1996	1997
Size Class					
Drive					
Crash Test					
Airbags					
ABS					
Parts Cost					
Complaints					
Insurance					
Fuel Econ.					
Theft Rating					
Bumpers					
Recalls					
Trn. Cir. (ft.)					
Weight (lbs.)					
Whlbase (in.)					
Price					
OVERALL■					

NO MODEL PRODUCED

■Cars without crash tests do not receive an overall rating.#Standard on Limited Edition. *Optional **Estimate

2002 Suzuki Grand Vitara

between 2-wheel drive and 4-wheel drive, but the 2-wheel tends to be more popular, since drivers of small SUV's tend to stay on the road. In 2000, the Grand Vitara came in a 2- or 4-door version, but 4-door models were the only option in 1999. High maintenance costs, a bad warranty and below average safety features make this vehicle mediocre.

	1998	1999	2000	2001	2002
Size Class		Sm. Sp. Util.	Sm. Sp. Util.	Sm. Sp. Util.	Sm. Sp. Util.
Drive		Rear/4/All	Rear/4/All	Rear/4/All	Rear/4/All
Crash Test		Good	Good	Good	Good
Airbags		Dual	Dual	Dual	Dual
ABS		4-Whl*	4-Whl*	4-Whl*	4-Whl*#
Parts Cost		Very High	Very High	Very High	Very High
Complaints		Very Poor	Very Poor	Average	Poor
Insurance		Regular	Regular	Regular	Regular
Fuel Econ.		20	20	20	20
Theft Rating		Average	Average	Average**	Average**
Bumpers	NO MODEL PRODUCED				
Recalls		5	1	2	0
Trn. Cir. (ft.)		34.8	34.8	34.8	34.8
Weight (lbs.)		3197	3197	3197	3197
Whlbase (in.)		97.6	97.6	97.6	97.6
Price		$11-13,000	$13-15,000	$14-16,000	$21-23,000
OVERALL■		Very Poor	Poor	Poor	Poor

Toyota 4Runner 1993-2002

The 4Runner, a thinly disguised Toyota compact pickup, is now a major SUV player. Before 1996, the 4Runner trailed the pack with respect to safety; this sport utility never

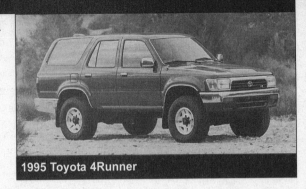
1995 Toyota 4Runner

offered its occupants an airbag, and ABS was only offered on rear wheels. All this changed in '96 as the 4Runner got a standard driver airbag and optional 4-wheel ABS. Dual airbags were standard in 1997. The later model crash tests have improved vastly from those on the early 90's 4Runner. 4Runners used to have a standard 2.4-

	1993	1994	1995	1996	1997
Size Class	Sp. Util.	Sp. Util.	Sp. Util.	Sp. Util.	Sp. Util.
Drive	Rear/4	Rear/4	Rear/4	Rear/4	Rear/4
Crash Test	Poor	Poor	Poor	Average	Very Good
Airbags	None	None	None	Driver	Dual
ABS	2-Whl*	2-Whl*	2-Whl	4-Whl*	4-Whl*
Parts Cost	Average	Average	Average	Average	High
Complaints	Good	Good	Good	Good	Good
Insurance	Surcharge	Surcharge	Surcharge	Surcharge	Surcharge
Fuel Econ.	18	17	19	19	16
Theft Rating	High	Very High	Very High	Very High	Very High
Bumpers				Weak	Weak
Recalls	0	0	0	2	1
Trn. Cir. (ft.)	37.4	37.4	37.4	37.4	37.4
Weight (lbs.)	3800	3820	3825	3825	3440
Whlbase (in.)	103.3	103.3	103.3	103.3	105.3
Price	$6-8,000	$8-10,000	$10-12,000	$12-14,000	$14-16,000
OVERALL■	Very Poor	Very Poor	Very Poor	Very Poor	Poor

■Cars without crash tests do not receive an overall rating. *Optional **Estimate

2002 Toyota 4Runner

liter 4-cylinder engine, which resulted in a barely adequate 116 hp. Optional was a 3-liter V6, which boosts output to a more satisfying 150 hp. They now have a 4- or 6-liter engine, which provide more power. The 4Runner comes in a 2-door model as well as a 4-door, and 4-wheel drive was dropped as an option on the 2-door model. Ride, handling, rear seat room and comfort have all improved over the years. Head and legroom are still cramped, although for 1996 these improve slightly.

	1998	1999	2000	2001	2002
Size Class	Sp. Util.	Sp. Util.	Sp. Util.	Sp. Util.	Sp. Util.
Drive	Rear/4	Rear/4	Rear/4	Rear/4	Rear/4
Crash Test	Very Good	Very Good	Very Good	Very Good	Very Good
Airbags	Dual	Dual	Dual	Dual	Dual
ABS	4-Whl*	4-Whl*	4-Whl*	4-Whl*	4-Whl
Parts Cost	Very High	High	High	Average	High
Complaints	Good	Good	Good	Very Good	Good
Insurance	Surcharge	Surcharge	Surcharge	Surcharge	Regular
Fuel Econ.	17	17	17	17	17
Theft Rating	Very High	High	High	High**	Very High**
Bumpers	Weak				Weak
Recalls	1	0	0	0	0
Trn. Cir. (ft.)	37.4	37.4	37.4	37.4	38.1
Weight (lbs.)	3440	3440	3440	3440	4070
Whlbase (in.)	105.3	105.3	105.3	105.3	105.3
Price	$16-18,000	$18-20,000	$21-23,000	$25-28,000	$27-29,000
OVERALL■	Poor	Average	Average	Good	Good

Toyota Avalon 1995-2002

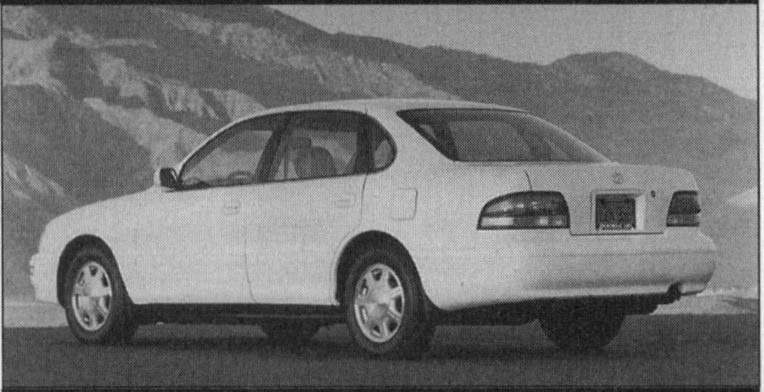

1995 Toyota Avalon

In 1995, Toyota brought the long running Cressida back—this time as the Avalon. The 1981 Cressida was the first car sold in the U.S. with motorized shoulder belts and manual lap belts, a design later used by dozens of manufacturers. The Avalon comes standard with dual airbags and optional 4-wheel ABS until 1999, when it became standard. In 1998, front side airbags also became standard.

	1993	1994	1995	1996	1997
Size Class	NO MODEL PRODUCED		Intermd.	Intermd.	Intermd.
Drive			Front	Front	Front
Crash Test			Very Good	Very Good	Very Good
Airbags			Dual	Dual	Dual
ABS			4-Whl*	4-Whl*	4-Whl*
Parts Cost			High	High	High
Complaints			Average	Average	Average
Insurance			Regular	Discount	Discount
Fuel Econ.			20	20	21
Theft Rating			Very Low	Very Low	Very Low
Bumpers			Weak	Weak	Weak
Recalls			0	0	1
Trn. Cir. (ft.)			37.6	37.6	37.6
Weight (lbs.)			3263	3263	3263
Whlbase (in.)			107.1	107.1	107.1
Price			$9-11,000	$10-12,000	$12-14,000
OVERALL■			Good	Very Good	Very Good

■Cars without crash tests do not receive an overall rating. *Optional **Estimate

2002 Toyota Avalon

The Avalon offers only one engine choice, a revamped 3.0-liter V6 similar to the one found in the Cressida. Both are spirited but consume quite a bit of fuel. The balance between ride and handling slightly favors the ride. The interior is comfortable, and the trunk is nicely shaped.

	1998	1999	2000	2001	2002
Size Class	Intermd.	Intermd.	Intermd.	Intermd.	Intermd.
Drive	Front	Front	Front	Front	Front
Crash Test	Very Good	Very Good	Good	Good	Good
Airbags	Dual/Side	Dual/Side	Dual/Side	Dual/Side	Dl./Sd.(F)
ABS	4-Whl*	4-Whl	4-Whl	4-Whl	4-Whl
Parts Cost	High	High	High	High	High
Complaints	Poor	Good	Good	Good	Good
Insurance	Discount	Discount	Discount	Discount	Discount
Fuel Econ.	21	21	21	21	24
Theft Rating	Average	Average	Low	Low**	Low**
Bumpers	Weak	Strong	Strong	Strong	Weak
Recalls	1	1	1	1	0
Trn. Cir. (ft.)	37.6	37.6	37.6	37.6	37.6
Weight (lbs.)	3340	3340	3340	3340	3417
Whlbase (in.)	107.1	107.1	107.1	107.1	107.1
Price	$15-17,000	$18-20,000	$22-24,000	$25-27,000	$26-28,000
OVERALL■	Very Good	BEST BET	BEST BET	BEST BET	BEST BET

Toyota Camry 1993-2002

In 1994, a coupe joined the line of these mid-sized cars. Finally, an all-new version was available for 1997 with a new, conservative look. In 2002, the look was improved with yet

1995 Toyota Camry

another redesign. The 1993 Camry has a driver's airbag and regular belts; 1994 models add a passenger airbag. The 1997 redesign offered optional front side airbags and in 2002 optional head airbags were added to the list. ABS becomes standard only this year. The 1993-97 Camry 4-cylinder engine has a lively twin cam. You can

	1993	1994	1995	1996	1997
Size Class	Intermd.	Intermd.	Intermd.	Intermd.	Intermd.
Drive	Front	Front	Front	Front	Front
Crash Test	Very Good	Good	Good	Good	Good
Airbags	Driver	Dual	Dual	Dual	Dual
ABS	4-Whl*	4-Whl*	4-Whl*	4-Whl*	4-Whl*
Parts Cost	Very High	High	High	High	High
Complaints	Average	Average	Good	Good	Average
Insurance	Discount	Discount	Discount	Regular	Regular
Fuel Econ.	21	21	21	23	23
Theft Rating	Average	High	Very High	Average	High
Bumpers	Weak	Weak	Weak	Weak	Weak
Recalls	0	1	0	2	2
Trn. Cir. (ft.)	35.4	35.4	35.4	35.4	35.4
Weight (lbs.)	2943	2932	3086	2932	2976
Whlbase (in.)	103.1	103.1	103.1	103.1	105.1
Price	$4-6,000	$5-7,000	$7-9,000	$8-10,000	$10-12,000
OVERALL■	Good	Good	Very Good	Average	Poor

■Cars without crash tests do not receive an overall rating.*Optional **Estimate

2002 Toyota Camry

choose an optional V6 engine, which is quite powerful. You can choose between power and better ride with the V6 and economy and better handling with the 4. The 2002 Camry comes with a powerful 2.4-liter 4-cylinder engine, which produces 157 hp. A 3.0-liter V6 is optional. The bumper system on 1993-97 models was incredibly weak, but improved in 1997 and weakened again in 2002. The interior is comfortable for four. It has a history of good crash tests as well, although the 2002 has yet to be tested.

	1998	1999	2000	2001	2002
Size Class	Intermd.	Intermd.	Intermd.	Intermd.	Intermd.
Drive	Front	Front	Front	Front	Front
Crash Test	Very Good	Very Good	Very Good	Very Good	
Airbags	Dual/Side*	Dual/Side*	Dual/Side*	Dual/Side*	Dl./Sd.(F)*/Hd.*
ABS	4-Whl*	4-Whl*	4-Whl*	4-Whl*	4-Whl
Parts Cost	Very High	Very High	High	Average	Average
Complaints	Average	Good	Good	Very Good	Average
Insurance	Regular	Regular	Regular	Regular	Regular
Fuel Econ.	23	23	23	24	27
Theft Rating	Average	Average	Average	Average**	Average**
Bumpers		Strong	Strong	Strong	Weak
Recalls	2	2	2	1	2
Trn. Cir. (ft.)	35.4	35.4	35.4	35.4	34.8
Weight (lbs.)	2998	2998	2998	2998	3086
Whlbase (in.)	105.1	105.1	105.1	105.1	107.1
Price	$11-13,000	$13-15,000	$15-17,000	$16-19,000	$20-22,000
OVERALL■	Average	Good	Very Good	BEST BET	

Toyota Celica 1993-2002

The Celica is a cheaper and smaller Corolla. A 4-wheel drive All-Trac model was offered in 1989-93. The Celica received new styling for 1994, and the ST and All-Trac disap-

1995 Toyota Celica

peared. The 1993 model has a driver's airbag and regular belts; 1994 models have dual airbags. The Celica was reinvented for 2000 with a shorter length, longer wheelbase, and some serious new styling. Front side airbags also became optional with this model. The base engine is fairly powerful; on the highway, it's reasonably

	1993	1994	1995	1996	1997
Size Class	Compact	Compact	Compact	Compact	Compact
Drive	Front/All	Front	Front	Front	Front
Crash Test	Good	N/A	N/A	N/A	N/A
Airbags	Driver	Dual	Dual	Dual	Dual
ABS	4-Whl*	4-Whl*	4-Whl*	4-Whl*	4-Whl*
Parts Cost	Very High	High	Very High	Very Low	High
Complaints	Good	Very Good	Good	Good	
Insurance	Surcharge	Regular	Surcharge	Surcharge	Surcharge
Fuel Econ.	21	26	22	29	29
Theft Rating	Average	Average	Low	Very Low	Average
Bumpers	Weak				
Recalls	0	0	0	1	0
Trn. Cir. (ft.)	36.1	34.2	34.1	34.1	34.2
Weight (lbs.)	2646	2415	2560	2415	2415
Whlbase (in.)	99.4	99.9	99.9	99.9	99.9
Price	$5-7,000	$7-9,000	$8-10,000	$11-13,000	$12-14,000
OVERALL■	Poor				

■Cars without crash tests do not receive an overall rating.*Optional **Estimate

2002 Toyota Celica

economical. Buyers can get a turbocharged 4-cylinder engine on the older GTS, which will provide more power with only a slight loss in fuel economy. New Celicas come with a 1.8-liter 140 hp engine, but the GTS adds 40 more hp to the engine. The 5-speed and automatic are good performers. The standard suspension handles capably, but the GTS is even better. On all models, the ride is decent and, at times, noisy. The dashboard is typically functional and intelligently laid out.

	1998	1999	2000	2001	2002
Size Class	Compact	Compact	Compact	Compact	Compact
Drive	Front	Front	Front	Front	Front
Crash Test	N/A	N/A	Very Good	Very Good	Very Good
Airbags	Dual	Dual	Dual/Side*	Dual/Side*	Dl./Sd.(F)*
ABS	4-Whl*	4-Whl*	4-Whl*	4-Whl*	4-Whl*
Parts Cost	High	High	High	Average	Average
Complaints	Very Good	Very Good	Average	Very Good	Average
Insurance	Surcharge	Surcharge	Surcharge	Surcharge	Surcharge
Fuel Econ.	29	22	28	28	31
Theft Rating	Average	Average	Average**	Average**	Average**
Bumpers		Strong	Strong	Strong	Weak
Recalls	0	0	0	0	0
Trn. Cir. (ft.)	34.2	34.2	36.1	36.1	36.1
Weight (lbs.)	2415	2580	2425	2425	2425
Whlbase (in.)	99.9	99.9	102.4	102.4	102.4
Price	$15-17,000	$16-18,000	$18-20,000	$19-21,000	$19-22,000
OVERALL■			Good	BEST BET	Good

Toyota Corolla 1993-2002

Toyota's major entry in the compact market, the Corolla has performed very well over the past 15 years and is still one of Toyota's best selling models. In 1993, the Corolla had driv-

1995 Toyota Corolla

er's airbag and regular belts. In 1994, Toyota added dual airbags. ABS was optional in 1993. Side airbags became an option in 1998.

In older models, the single-cam 1.6-liter engine provides adequate power but is noisy with the 3-speed automatic. The twin-cam 1.6-liter or 1.8-liter 4-cylinder is quicker, and fuel economy remains

	1993	1994	1995	1996	1997
Size Class	Subcomp.	Subcomp.	Subcomp.	Compact	Compact
Drive	Front	Front	Front	Front	Front
Crash Test	Average	Good	Good	Good	Good
Airbags	Driver	Dual	Dual	Dual	Dual
ABS	4-Whl*	4-Whl*	4-Whl*	4-Whl*	4-Whl*
Parts Cost	High	High	Very High	Average	High
Complaints	Average	Good	Good	Very Good	Very Good
Insurance	Regular	Regular	Regular	Surcharge	Surcharge
Fuel Econ.	26	26	28	31	31
Theft Rating	Low	Average	Average	Average	Average
Bumpers					
Recalls	2	4	3	1	2
Trn. Cir. (ft.)	32.2	32.2	32.2	32.2	32.2
Weight (lbs.)	2304	2315	2381	2315	2337
Whlbase (in.)	97	97	97	97	97
Price	$2-4,000	$4-6,000	$5-7,000	$6-8,000	$7-8,000
OVERALL▪	Poor	Average	Average	Very Good	Good

▪Cars without crash tests do not receive an overall rating.*Optional **Estimate

2002 Toyota Corolla

good. For 2001, the 1.8-liter became the standard and with 125 horses, this engine shows a lot of pep. The handling is good, but tricky at higher speeds. The Corolla can transport four people in modest comfort with room for luggage. Typical of Toyotas, controls are logical and easy to use. The Corolla is an outstanding compact, but be wary of models with average to poor crash test scores. In the past, the Prizm could save you money, but now you can get a base Corolla for less.

	1998	1999	2000	2001	2002
Size Class	Compact	Compact	Compact	Compact	Compact
Drive	Front	Front	Front	Front	Front
Crash Test	Good	Good	Good	Good	Good
Airbags	Dual/Side*	Dual/Side*	Dual/Side*	Dual/Side*	Dl./Sd.(F)*
ABS	4-Whl*	4-Whl*	4-Whl*	4-Whl*	4-Whl*
Parts Cost	High	High	High	High	
Complaints	Good	Very Good	Very Good	Very Good	Very Good
Insurance	Surcharge	Surcharge	Surcharge	Surcharge	Surcharge
Fuel Econ.	31	31	31	21	34
Theft Rating	Average	Average	Average	Average**	Average**
Bumpers	Weak	Strong	Strong	Strong	Weak
Recalls	0	0	0	0	0
Trn. Cir. (ft.)	32.2	32.2	32.2	32.2	32.2
Weight (lbs.)	2414	2414	2414	2414	2410
Whlbase (in.)	97	97	97	97	97
Price	$8-10,000	$9-11,000	$11-13,000	$13-15,000	$14-16,000
OVERALL■	Average	Very Good	Very Good	Good	Good

Toyota Land Cruiser 1993-2002

The Land Cruiser has been around in various forms since the 1960's, the current series running 12 long years. This SUV allows drivers to get off-road easily with lots of power.

1993 Toyota Land Cruiser

From 1993 to 1997 it had a 4.5-liter V6 engine, in 1998, a 4.7-liter, V6 engine, and in 2000 a 4.7 V8. It can tow up to 6500 pounds and has a huge cargo space of 908 square feet. Dual airbags, ABS, day running lamps, and pretensioners are all standard.

	1993	1994	1995	1996	1997
Size Class	Sp. Util.	Sp.Util.	Sp. Util.	Sp. Util.	Sp. Util.
Drive	All/4	All/4	All/4	All/4	All/4
Crash Test	N/A	N/A	N/A	N/A	N/A
Airbags	None	None	None	Dual	Dual
ABS	4-Whl*	4-Whl*	4-Whl*	4-Whl	4-Whl
Parts Cost	Average	Average	Average	Low	Very High
Complaints	Poor	Average	Very Good	Good	Good
Insurance	Regular	Regular	Surcharge	Surcharge	Surcharge
Fuel Econ.	13	13	14	14	14
Theft Rating	Very High	Very High	Very High	Very High	Very High
Bumpers					
Recalls	1	0	0	0	0
Trn. Cir. (ft.)	40.4	40.4	40.4	40.4	40.4
Weight (lbs.)	4933	4933	4933	4933	4933
Whlbase (in.)	112.2	112.2	112.2	112.2	112.2
Price	$15-17,000	$17-19,000	$20-22,000	$22-24,000	$25-27,000
OVERALL■					

■Cars without crash tests do not receive an overall rating.*Optional **Estimate

2002 Toyota Land Cruiser

The Land Cruiser does not change much year to year and only comes in one model, the base. Because of its cumbersome build and hefty weight, the acceleration is slow and its huge engine guzzles gas.

	1998	1999	2000	2001	2002
Size Class	Sp. Util.	Sp. Util.	Sp. Util.	Sp. Util.	Sp. Util.
Drive	All/4	All/4	All/4	All/4	All/4
Crash Test	N/A	N/A	N/A	N/A	N/A
Airbags	Dual	Dual	Dual	Dual	Dual
ABS	4-Whl	4-Whl	4-Whl	4-Whl	4-Whl
Parts Cost	Very High	Very High	High	Very Low	High
Complaints	Very Good	Very Good	Very Good	Very Good	Average
Insurance	Regular	Regular	Regular	Discount	Discount
Fuel Econ.	15	15	15	14	14
Theft Rating	Very High	Very High	Very High	Very High**	Very High**
Bumpers					
Recalls	0	0	0	0	0
Trn. Cir. (ft.)	40.4	40.4	40.4	40.4	40.4
Weight (lbs.)	4933	4933	4933	4933	4933
Whlbase (in.)	112.2	112.2	112.2	112.2	112.2
Price	$33-35,000	$37-39,000	$41-43,000	$45-47,000	$52-54,000
OVERALL■					

Toyota RAV4 1996-2002

The Toyota RAV4 (Recreational Active Vehicle with 4WD) is designed to be a light, off-road vehicle that seats five. Toyota has equipped this new vehicle well, with standard dual airbags and optional 4-wheel ABS. All the power options are available on the base model and standard on the L version.

1996 Toyota RAV4

The RAV4 is powered by an average 2-liter 4-cylinder engine, which can beat out many sporty coupes and sedans but is unable to

	1993	1994	1995	1996	1997
Size Class				Sp. Util.	Sp. Util.
Drive				2WD/4WD	2WD/4WD
Crash Test				Average	Very Good
Airbags				Dual	Dual
ABS				4-Whl*	4-Whl*
Parts Cost				High	High
Complaints				Good	Very Good
Insurance				Regular	Regular
Fuel Econ.				22	22
Theft Rating				Average	Average
Bumpers		NO MODEL PRODUCED			
Recalls				0	0
Trn. Cir. (ft.)				33.5	36.1
Weight (lbs.)				2789	2789
Whlbase (in.)				86.6	94.9
Price				$8-10,000	$10-12,000
OVERALL■				Average	Very Good

■Cars without crash tests do not receive an overall rating.*Optional **Estimate

2002 Toyota RAV4

compete with some of the other small sport utilities. It has a wide stance, which gives it decent room inside for four. You have your choice between a 2- and 4-door model, and from many different appearance packages. The RAV4 was redesigned in 2001, and you'll find a bit more cargo space in the first generation model as well as adjustable front cup holders and a footrest for the passenger.

	1998	1999	2000	2001	2002
Size Class	Sp. Util.	Sp. Util.	Sp. Util.	Sp. Util.	Sp. Util
Drive	2WD/4WD	2WD/4WD	2WD/4WD	2WD/4WD	2WD/4WD
Crash Test	Very Good	Very Good	Very Good	Good	Good
Airbags	Dual	Dual	Dual	Dual	Dual
ABS	4-Whl*	4-Whl*	4-Whl*	4-Whl*	4-Whl*
Parts Cost	High	High	Very High	Average	Very High
Complaints	Good	Very Good	Very Good	Good	Average
Insurance	Regular	Regular	Regular	Surcharge	Surcharge
Fuel Econ.	24	24	24	25	26
Theft Rating	Average	Average	Average	Average**	Average**
Bumpers					Weak
Recalls	2	2	0	0	0
Trn. Cir. (ft.)	36.1	36.1	33.5	35.4	35.4
Weight (lbs.)	2701	2701	2701	2711	2711
Whlbase (in.)	94.9	94.9	94.9	98	98
Price	$12-14,000	$13-15,000	$16-18,000	$18-20,000	$19-21,000
OVERALL▪	Good	Very Good	Very Good	Good	Poor

Toyota Sienna 1998-2002

This 3-liter, V6 minivan is worth a look. Beginning in 1998, Toyota produced the Sienna to match the Chrysler mini-vans, with the mindset, if you can't beat 'em, copy 'em! It per-

1998 Toyota Sienna

forms very well in the crash tests, due to dual airbags, height adjustable seat belts (a huge plus for shorter drivers), pretensioners, and 4-wheel ABS, all coming standard since 1998. Watch out, though, because it could do some damage to your wallet if it needs

	1993	1994	1995	1996	1997
Size Class					
Drive					
Crash Test					
Airbags					
ABS					
Parts Cost					
Complaints			NO MODEL PRODUCED		
Insurance					
Fuel Econ.					
Theft Rating					
Bumpers					
Recalls					
Trn. Cir. (ft.)					
Weight (lbs.)					
Whlbase (in.)					
Price					
OVERALL■					

■Cars without crash tests do not receive an overall rating.*Optional **Estimate

318

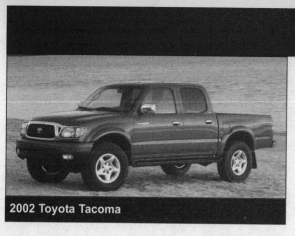
2002 Toyota Tacoma

sions. A 4-door double cab and S Runner sport truck are availab and you can choose between 2WD or 4WD model. You can also choose regular or extended cab models. Crea ture comforts and interior design give this truck a passenger car feeling.

	1998	1999	2000	2001	2002
Size Class	Cmpt. Pkup	Cmpt. Pkup	Cmpt. Pkup	Cmpt. Pkup	Cmpt. Pkup
Drive	Rear/4	Rear/4	Rear/4	Rear/4	Rear/4
Crash Test	Good	Good	Good	Good	Good
Airbags	Dual	Dual	Dual	Dual	Dual
ABS	4-Whl*	4-Whl*	4-Whl*	4-Whl*	4-Whl*
Parts Cost	Average	Average	High	Average	Average
Complaints	Average	Good	Very Good	Very Good	Average
Insurance	Surcharge	Surcharge	Surcharge	Surcharge	Surcharg
Fuel Econ.	21	20	20	20	20
Theft Rating	High	High	Average	Average**	Average*
Bumpers					
Recalls	1	0	0	0	0
Trn. Cir. (ft.)	34.4	34.4	34.4	34.4	34.4
Weight (lbs.)	3215	3215	3215	3215	3215
Whlbase (in.)	103.3	103.3	103.3	103.3	103.3
Price	$11-13,000	$12-14,000	$13-15,000	$14-16,000	$15-17,00
OVERALL■	Average	Average	Average	Good	Average

Toyota Tercel 1993-98

Toyota's cheapest car, the Tercel, offers more than most competitive subcompacts. The 1987 Tercel got new styling, and a notchback coupe joined the line. The old Tercel wagons carried

1995 Toyota Tercel

over into 1987, and the 4-wheel drive wagon was replaced by the Corolla AllTrac wagon in 1988. The redesigned 1991 models kept the original Tercel's chassis, but rounded the edges. The all-new 1995 model did not look much different from the previous generation. In 1990-92, and on the passenger side of the 1993-94 Tercels,

	1993	1994	1995	1996	1997
Size Class	Subcomp.	Subcomp.	Subcomp.	Subcomp.	Subcomp.
Drive	Front	Front	Front	Front	Front
Crash Test	Good	Good	Average	Average	Average[1]
Airbags	Driver	Driver	Dual	Dual	Dual
ABS	4-Whl*	4-Whl*	4-Whl*	4-Whl*	4-Whl*
Parts Cost	High	High	High	High	High
Complaints	Good	Very Good	Good	Good	Very Good
Insurance	Surcharge	Surcharge	Surcharge	Surcharge	Surcharge
Fuel Econ.	28	28	31	30	32
Theft Rating	Very Low	Very Low	Very Low	Very Low	Very Low
Bumpers	Weak	Weak			
Recalls	0	0	0	0	0
Trn. Cir. (ft.)	31.5	31.5	31.5	31.5	31.5
Weight (lbs.)	2005	1950	2005	1950	2001
Whlbase (in.)	93.7	93.7	93.7	93.7	93.7
Price	<$3,000	$2-4,000	$3-5,000	$4-6,000	$6-8,000
OVERALL■	Average	Good	Average	Average	Good

■Cars without crash tests do not receive an overall rating. [1]Data given for Sedan. Crash test for the coupe is Good. *Optional.

1997 Toyota Tercel

occupants have an automatic shoulder belt and a separate manual lap belt. Starting in 1993, Tercels were equipped with a standard driver's airbag and optional ABS; dual airbags became standard with the 1995 redesign. Tercels are certainly not sports cars. Early Tercels have a 4-speed manual transmission, minimal sound insulation, and few options. Find one with a 5-speed for best performance and gas mileage. The room inside is typical of subcompacts. You'll find the controls and gauges are easy to use.

	1998	1999	2000	2001	2002
Size Class	Subcomp.				
Drive	Front				
Crash Test	Average[1]				
Airbags	Dual				
ABS	4-Whl*				
Parts Cost	High				
Complaints	Very Poor				
Insurance	Surcharge				
Fuel Econ.	32				
Theft Rating	Very Low				
Bumpers					
Recalls	0				
Trn. Cir. (ft.)	31.5				
Weight (lbs.)	2001				
Whlbase (in.)	93.7				
Price	$7-9,000				
OVERALL■	Poor				

NO MODEL PRODUCED

Volkswagen Golf/Jetta 1993-2002

The Golf, introduced in 1985, was more rounded and aerodynamic than the long running Rabbit series it replaced; the Jetta is essentially a Golf with a separate trunk. The Jetta comes in base, GL and sporty GLI trim; the top model Golf is the high performance GTI. After a complete revision late in 1993, they were called Golf or Jetta III, but the new models look much like the old ones. For 1994, a driver's airbag was standard and a passenger airbag was optional. Starting in 1995, dual airbags are standard and since the

1993 Volkswagen Jetta

	1993	1994	1995	1996	1997
Size Class	Subcomp.	Compact	Compact	Compact	Compact
Drive	Front	Front	Front	Front	Front
Crash Test	Average	Average	Average	Average	Average
Airbags	None	Driver#	Dual	Dual	Dual
ABS	4-Whl*	4-Whl*	4-Whl*	4-Whl*	4-Whl*
Parts Cost	Average	Average	Average	Average	High
Complaints	Poor	Very Poor	Poor	Poor	Good
Insurance	Surcharge	Regular	Surcharge	Surcharge	Surcharge
Fuel Econ.	24	21	24	22	22
Theft Rating	Low	Low	Low	Very Low	Very Low
Bumpers	Weak	Weak	Weak	Weak	Weak
Recalls	5	6	5	1	1
Trn. Cir. (ft.)	32.6	32.6	32.6	32.6	32.8
Weight (lbs.)	2320	2577	2577	2577	2661
Whlbase (in.)2	97.3	97.4	97.4	97.4	97.4
Price	$3-5,000	$4-6,000	$5-7,000	$7-9,000	$8-10,000
OVERALL■	Very Poor	Very Poor	Very Poor	Poor	Poor

■Cars without crash tests do not receive an overall rating. #Passenger Side Optional. [1]Data given for Jetta. Golf Complaints Poor in 2001.
[2]Wheelbase given for Golf. Wheelbase for Jetta is 98.9. *Optional **Estimate

2002 Volkswagen Golf

1999 redesign, both side and head airbags are standard. ABS is optional beginning in 1991. Golfs and Jettas share a 1.6-liter diesel engine and a gasoline-fueled 1.8- or 2-liter 4-cylinder; newer Jettas offer a 2.8-liter V6 engine. The diesels are slow but economical. A high number of complaints and high insurance costs bring the Golf and Jetta down. However, the recent crash tests have been excellent. The 2000-2002 Golfs and Jettas are a "Best Bet."

	1998	1999	2000	2001	2002
Size Class	Compact	Compact	Compact	Compact	Compact
Drive	Front	Front	Front	Front	Front
Crash Test	Average	Very Good	Very Good	Very Good	Very Good
Airbags	Dual/Side*	Dual/Side*	Dual/Side*	Dual/Side*	Dl./Sd.(F)/Hd.
ABS	4-Whl*	4-Whl*	4-Whl*	4-Whl*	4-Whl
Parts Cost	Average	Average	Average	High	High
Complaints	Poor	Poor	Average	Good[1]	Good
Insurance	Surcharge	Surcharge	Surcharge	Surcharge	Surcharge
Fuel Econ.	24	24	24	25	27
Theft Rating	Average	Average	Average	Average**	Average**
Bumpers	Weak	Weak	Strong	Strong	Strong
Recalls	1	1	0	1	1
Trn. Cir. (ft.)	32.8	32.8	32.8	32.8	35.8
Weight (lbs.)	2729	2729	2729	2729	2826
Whlbase (in.)[1]	97.4	97.4	97.4	97.4	97.4
Price	$10-12,000	$11-13,000	$14-16,000	$15-17,000	$16-18,000
OVERALL■	Poor	Average	Good	Good	Very Good

Volkswagen New Beetle 1999-2002

Based on the popular Volkswagen Bugs from the 60's, the New Beetles are safer (the engine is now in the front) and more powerful than before. Both dual and front side airbags are standard and the New Beetle comes with standard 4-wheel ABS and pretensioners.

The Beetle reemerges in 1999 with a 2-liter, 4-cylinder gas engine or a 1.9-liter 4-cylinder diesel engine. Known in the commercials

1999 Volkswagen New Beetle

	1993	1994	1995	1996	1997
Size Class					
Drive					
Crash Test					
Airbags					
ABS					
Parts Cost					
Complaints					
Insurance					
Fuel Econ.					
Theft Rating		NO MODEL PRODUCED			
Bumpers					
Recalls					
Trn. Cir. (ft.)					
Weight (lbs.)					
Whlbase (in.)					
Price					
OVERALL■					

■Cars without crash tests do not receive an overall rating.**Estimate

2002 Volkswagen New Beetle

depicting how round spaces are a marvel, riders will appreciate the 87 cubic feet of passenger room (85 ft. starting in 2000) and 12 cubic feet of luggage room. The New Beetle has also performed very well in front and side crash tests.

	1998	1999	2000	2001	2002
Size Class		Subcomp.	Subcomp.	Subcomp.	Subcomp.
Drive		Front	Front	Front	Front
Crash Test		Very Good	Very Good	Very Good	Very Good
Airbags		Dual/Side	Dual/Side	Dual/Side	Dl./Sd.(F)
ABS		4-Whl	4-Whl	4-Whl	4-Whl
Parts Cost		High	High	Average	Very High
Complaints		Average	Average	Very Good	Very Good
Insurance		Regular	Regular	Regular	Regular
Fuel Econ.	NO MODEL PRODUCED	24	24	25	25
Theft Rating		Low	Low	Low**	Low**
Bumpers		Strong	Strong	Strong	Strong
Recalls		0	0	0	1
Trn. Cir. (ft.)		32.8	32.8	32.8	32.8
Weight (lbs.)		2886	2886	2886	2886
Whlbase (in.)		98.9	98.9	98.9	98.9
Price		$13-15,000	$15-17,000	$16-18,000	$17-19,000
OVERALL■		Very Good	Very Good	**BEST BET**	**BEST BET**

Volkswagen Passat 1993-2002

First introduced in 1990 as the replacement for the Dasher, the front-wheel drive Passat is marketed as a European luxury sedan/wagon without the luxury price tag. This model led a

1993 Volkswagen Passat

relatively quiet existence until the 1995 model year, when it was redesigned and VW finally paid some advertising attention to it. In 1999, the Jetta was restyled again, which propelled its popularity to new heights. Airbags were not available until the 1995 redesign gave it two; before that, you were stuck with motorized shoulder

	1993	1994	1995	1996	1997
Size Class	Intermd.	Intermd.	Intermd.	Intermd.	Intermd.
Drive	Front	Front	Front	Front	Front
Crash Test	Poor	Poor	Good	Good	Good
Airbags	None	None	Dual	Dual	Dual
ABS	4-Whl	4-Whl	4-Whl	4-Whl	4-Whl
Parts Cost	High	Average	High	High	Very High
Complaints	Very Poor	Poor	Very Poor	Very Poor	Poor
Insurance	Surcharge	Surcharge	Surcharge	Surcharge	Surcharge
Fuel Econ.	21	18	18	20	38
Theft Rating	Very High	High	High	Very High	Very High
Bumpers			Weak	Weak	Weak
Recalls	3	1	1	0	0
Trn. Cir. (ft.)	35.1	38.4	38.4	38.4	38.4
Weight (lbs.)	2985	3152	3140	3140	3175
Whlbase (in.)	103.3	103.3	103.3	103.3	103.3
Price	$4-6,000	$5-7,000	$6-8,000	$9-11,000	$12-14,000
OVERALL■	Very Poor	Very Poor	Very Poor	Very Poor	Poor

■Cars without crash tests do not receive an overall rating.**Estimate

2002 Volkswagen Passat

belts and separate lap belts in the front seats. Since 1999, the Jetta has come with standard front side and head airbags. Four-wheel ABS became standard in 1993.

The 2.8-liter V6 is available on 1993-2002 GLX sedans as well as wagons. The Passat has a spacious, comfortable interior, but the ride can actually be a little too firm. Cargo space is generous, and passengers will be comfortable on long trips. The latest Passats are a good choice for their excellent crash tests.

	1998	1999	2000	2001	2002
Size Class	Intermd.	Intermd.	Intermd.	Intermd.	Intermd.
Drive	Front	Front	Front	Front	Front
Crash Test	Very Good	Very Good	Very Good	Very Good	Very Good
Airbags	Dual/Side	Dual/Side	Dual/Side	Dual/Side	Dl./Sd.(F)/Hd.
ABS	4-Whl	4-Whl	4-Whl	4-Whl	4-Whl
Parts Cost	Average	High	High	High	High
Complaints	Very Poor	Very Poor	Good	Good	Poor
Insurance	Surcharge	Surcharge	Regular	Regular	Regular
Fuel Econ.	23	23	23	23	25
Theft Rating	Low	Average	Average	Average**	Average**
Bumpers		Strong	Strong	Strong	Strong
Recalls	2	1	3	1	0
Trn. Cir. (ft.)	37.4	37.4	37.4	37.4	37.4
Weight (lbs.)	3120	3120	3120	3120	3411
Whlbase (in.)	106.4	106.4	106.4	106.4	106.4
Price	$15-17,000	$17-19,000	$20-22,000	$22-24,000	$23-25,000
OVERALL▪	Average	Average	Very Good	Very Good	Very Good

Volvo 850 1993-97, C70/S70/V70 1998-2000, C70/V70 2001-2002

In 1993, Volvo introduced a new, smoother model, the 850. The Volvo 850 maintained Volvo's reputation for safety, performing well in government crash tests and coming standard with dual airbags and 4-wheel ABS. New for 1996, Volvo once again led the industry by offering side impact airbags. The new driver and passenger side airbags can be found in the front doors. They are standard on the Turbo sedans, optional on the base and GLT sedans and wagons. The 850 became the 70 Series line in

1993 Volvo 850

	1993	1994	1995	1996	1997
Size Class	Intermd.	Intermd.	Intermd.	Intermd.	Intermd.
Drive	Front	Front	Front	Front	Front
Crash Test	Good	Good	Good	Good	Good
Airbags	Dual	Dual	Dual	Dual	Dual
ABS	4-Whl	4-Whl	4-Whl	4-Whl	4-Whl
Parts Cost	Average	Average	Average	Average	High
Complaints	Very Poor	Poor	Poor	Poor	Poor
Insurance	Discount	Discount	Discount	Discount	Discount
Fuel Econ.	20	20	20	20	20
Theft Rating	Very Low	Very Low	Very Low	Very Low	Very Low
Bumpers	Weak	Weak	Weak	Weak	Weak
Recalls	1	2	2	1	1
Trn. Cir. (ft.)	33.5	33.5	33.5	33.5	33.5
Weight (lbs.)	3232	3232	3232	3232	3232
Whlbase (in.)	104.9	104.9	104.9	104.9	104.9
Price	$8-10,000	$9-11,000	$11-13,000	$13-15,000	$15-17,000
OVERALL"	Good	Good	Good	Good	Good

"Cars without crash tests do not receive an overall rating.**Estimate

332

2002 Volvo C70

1998, offering a sedan, a coupe or a wagon, but the sedan was dropped after 2000. This is the first front-wheel drive vehicle Volvo has sold in the U.S. There is a turbo option, but it is probably unnecessary. In 1998, Volvo began the transition to the 70 series with a restyled, more aerodynamic exterior. Inside, accommodations for four people are good; five may be a squeeze. A fold out booster seat for children is standard on wagons and optional on sedans—an excellent feature.

	1998	1999	2000	2001	2002
Size Class	Intermd.	Intermd.	Intermd.	Intermd.	Intermd.
Drive	Front	Front	Front	Front	Front
Crash Test	N/A	N/A	N/A	N/A	N/A
Airbags	Dual/Side	Dual/Side	Dual/Side	Dual/Side	Dl./Sd./Hd.
ABS	4-Whl	4-Whl	4-Whl	4-Whl	4-Whl
Parts Cost	Average	Average	Average	Average	Average
Complaints	Poor	Good	Very Good	Very Good	Very Good
Insurance	Discount	Discount	Regular	Regular	Regular
Fuel Econ.	20	20	20	20	24
Theft Rating	Low	Very Low**	Very Low**	Very Low**	Very Low**
Bumpers			Strong	Weak	Weak
Recalls	1	1	0	0	0
Trn. Cir. (ft.)	33.5	38.4	38.4	38.4	38.4
Weight (lbs.)	3152	3601	3601	3601	3300
Whlbase (in.)	104.9	104.9	104.9	104.9	104.9
Price	$18-20,000	$21-23,000	$23-25,000	$27-29,000	$35-37,000
OVERALL■					

Volvo 900 Series 1993-97, S90/V90 1998, S80 1999-2002

The S90/V90 line was created in 1998 to replace the 900 Series, but the sedan was the only model to make it to 1999, when it was renamed the S80. During the 1990's, the 960

1993 Volvo 940

was Volvo's top-level model, with a six-cylinder engine, leather upholstery, and many options. All 900 Series cars have a driver's airbag. The 1993 960 got a standard passenger airbag, and Volvo added this to the 940 for 1994. In 1996, side-impact airbags came as standard equipment—a first in the industry. With the name change

	1993	1994	1995	1996	1997
Size Class	Intermd.	Intermd.	Intermd.	Intermd.	Intermd.
Drive	Rear	Rear	Rear	Rear	Rear
Crash Test	Good	Good	Good	Good	Good
Airbags	Driver	Dual	Dual	Dual	Dual
ABS	4-Whl	4-Whl	4-Whl	4-Whl	4-Whl
Parts Cost	Very High	Average	Average	Average	Average
Complaints	Poor	Poor	Poor	Very Poor	Very Good
Insurance	Discount	Discount	Discount	Discount	Regular
Fuel Econ.	19	19	19	18	18
Theft Rating	Average	Average	Average	Low	Low
Bumpers					
Recalls	0	0	2	1	1
Trn. Cir. (ft.)	32.2	32.2	32.2	31.8	31.8
Weight (lbs.)	3067	3205	3208	3461	3461
Whlbase (in.)	109.1	109.1	109.1	109.1	109.1
Price	$6-8,000	$8-10,000	$10-12,000	$12-14,000	$14-16,000
OVERALL■	Average	Average	Average	Good	Very Good

■Cars without crash tests do not receive an overall rating. **Estimate

2002 Volvo S80

in 1998 came standard head airbags. All models have ABS. The new S90/V90 and S80's come with a 2.9-liter V6 while the 940 comes with a twin-cam 4, regular or turbocharged; the 960 gets a Porsche-designed 6-cylinder engine. The base 940 will be slower, especially in wagon form, but more economical. The interior comfort and room for four are exceptional. There's a clever, foldaway child booster in the rear center seat. The wagon's cargo area is large, and the sedan's trunk is roomy.

	1998	1999	2000	2001	2002
Size Class	Intermd.	Intermd.	Intermd.	Intermd.	Intermd.
Drive	Rear	Front	Front	Front	Front
Crash Test	Good	Very Good	Very Good	Very Good	Very Good
Airbags	Dual/Side	Dual/Side	Dual/Side	Dual/Side	Dl./Sd./Hd.
ABS	4-Whl	4-Whl	4-Whl	4-Whl	4-Whl
Parts Cost	Average	Average	High	High	High
Complaints	Very Poor	Average	Average	Good	Average
Insurance	Regular	Regular	Discount	Discount	Discount
Fuel Econ.	18	18	18	19	22
Theft Rating	Low	Average	Average**	Average**	Average**
Bumpers			Weak	Weak	Weak
Recalls	0	1	0	0	0
Trn. Cir. (ft.)	31.8	35.8	37	37	39
Weight (lbs.)	3461	3300	3602	3602	3583
Whlbase (in.)	109.1	109.9	109.9	109.9	109.9
Price	$17-19,000	$24-26,000	$26-28,000	$28-30,000	$38-40,000
OVERALL■	Average	Very Good	Very Good	BEST BET	Very Good

Index

Blue book, *see* Price
Brakes
  inspection, 26
  rear light, 28
Buying
  auctions, 7
  classified ads, 8
  new car dealers, 5
  private sales, 6-7
  rental car companies, 6
  superstores, 7
  used car dealers, 5-6
Checking out a used car, 9-30
  air conditioning, 12, 23
  Consumer groups
    Center for Auto Safety,
      46
Engine
  inspection, 18-19
Fair Credit Reporting Act, *see*
    Repairs—payment by
    credit card

Insurance, 41-43
Odometer fraud, 24-25
Price
  "blue book," 34
  Kelley Blue Book, 34
  negotiating, 31-33
Ratings
  Best Bets, 48-49
  cars to stay away from, 50
  explanation, 51-52
Repairs
  dealing with a mechanic,
    43-44
  payment by credit card, 44
Safety checklist, 27-28
Selling your used car, 36-40
Warranty, 34-36
  expressed, 35
  known defects disclosure,
    36
  secret, 45-46